THE PROFESSIONALIZATION OF WOMEN WRITERS IN EIGHTEENTH-CENTURY BRITAIN

The Professionalization of Women Writers in Eighteenth-Century Britain is the first full study of a group of women who, though they have been dismissed as mere domestic, conservative, and imitative novelists, were actively and ambitiously engaged in a wide range of innovative publications, as well as in creating the formal and informal institutions of the republic of letters. Working at the height of the century and contributing to its proliferation of print materials from the 1740s onwards, these women – Frances Sheridan, Frances Brooke, Sarah Scott, Sarah Fielding, and Charlotte Lennox – were welcomed as participants in the literary and even political public spheres. Using personal correspondence, records of contemporary reception, research into contemporary print culture, and sociological models of professionalization, Betty A. Schellenberg challenges oversimplified assumptions of women's cultural role in the period, focusing on those women who have been most obscured by subsequent literary history, whether traditional or feminist.

BETTY A. SCHELLENBERG is Associate Professor of English at Simon Fraser University. She is the author of *The Conversational Circle: Rereading the English Novel, 1740–1775* (1996), co-editor of *Reconsidering the Bluestockings* (2003), and co-editor of a volume in the forthcoming *Cambridge Edition of the Correspondence of Samuel Richardson*.

THE PROFESSIONALIZATION OF WOMEN WRITERS IN EIGHTEENTH-CENTURY BRITAIN

BETTY A. SCHELLENBERG

CAMBRIDGE
UNIVERSITY PRESS

CAMBRIDGE UNIVERSITY PRESS

Cambridge, New York, Melbourne, Madrid, Cape Town, Singapore, São Paulo

Cambridge University Press
The Edinburgh Building, Cambridge CB2 2RU, UK

Published in the United States of America by Cambridge University Press, New York

www.cambridge.org
Information on this title: www.cambridge.org/9780521850605

First published 2005

Printed in the United Kingdom at the University Press, Cambridge

A catalogue record for this book is available from the British Library

ISBN-13 978-0-521-85060-5 hardback
ISBN-10 0-521-85060-6 hardback

For Anne,
Ruth, Linda, and Kathie

It is not the bringing known Characters again upon the Stage that is, or can be decried, if it is done with equal Humour and Spirit, as in their first Appearance; but it is building so much on Public Approbation as to endeavour to put off a second-rate insipid Piece, void of the Spirit of the first, that ought to meet with universal Censure.

(Preface to *Volume the Last*, by Sarah Fielding, 1753)

Contents

Acknowledgments

Like the work of the women writers who are the subjects of this study, my book is embedded in a culture of letters and arises out of the oral and print exchanges which embody that culture. While the attachment of one author's name to the title page obscures those exchanges, I am grateful for the opportunity to acknowledge my debts here.

Susan Staves, Isobel Grundy, and Katherine Binhammer, though they would not know this, made what proved to be direction-altering comments at key moments in the conception of this project. Leith Davis, Paul Delany, Gordon Fulton, Mary Ann Gillies, Paul Keen, Margaret Linley, Mark Phillips, and June Sturrock offered valuable research leads. Members of the C-18 electronic discussion list untangled factual knots on several occasions, and Nicole Pohl cheerfully helped tie up loose research ends. Kevin Berland, Linda Bree, Frans DeBruyn, Mary Ann Gillies, Isobel Grundy, Betty Rizzo, and Tom Lockwood read portions of the book in progress. I thank them, the anonymous readers of *Eighteenth-Century Fiction* and *Studies in Eighteenth-Century Culture*, and George Justice and Thomas Keymer, the Cambridge University Press readers, for generously sharing their expertise with me. April London, as well as my departmental colleagues Leith, Mary Ann, and Margaret, have offered years of steady encouragement and sound advice; my debt to them is strongly felt.

A very early statement of this book's problematic was presented at the Orlando Project's Women and Literary History Conference; parts of the resulting essay are scattered throughout my study, reprinted from *Women and Literary History: 'For There She Was,'* edited by Katherine Binhammer and Jeanne Wood (Delaware, 2003). I also thank the editors of *Eighteenth-Century Fiction* for permission to use revised versions of "Frances Sheridan Reads John Home: Placing *Sidney Bidulph* in the Republic of Letters," *Eighteenth-Century Fiction* 13:4 (July 2001), 561–77, and of "From Propensity to Profession: Female Authorship and the Early

Career of Frances Burney," *Eighteenth-Century Fiction* 14:3–4 (April–July 2002), 345–70. Chapter 3 originally appeared in *Studies in Eighteenth-Century Culture* 32 (2003), edited by Ourida Mostefai and Catherine Ingrassia. I wish also to acknowledge the financial support of the Social Sciences and Humanities Research Council of Canada, Simon Fraser University Vice-President of Research Bruce Clayman, and the SFU Publications Grant Fund, and I thank my colleague Carole Gerson for her willing and expert guidance in the pursuit of such funding. Megan Fairbanks, Anna Miegon, and Jef Clarke have been outstanding research assistants in the care and commitment with which they have carried out their tasks. It has been a great pleasure to work with Linda Bree, Maartje Scheltens, Elizabeth Davey, and Libby Willis of Cambridge University Press as this book has taken its final shape.

Christian, Samuel, and Luc Couture, in the small but significant accommodations of each day, make it possible for me to pursue my own professional goals; my loving thanks, as always, go to them. Finally, this book is dedicated to my mother and sisters, whose various career narratives – their negotiations of domestic responsibilities, personal aspirations, and professional expectations – I follow with continuing interest and admiration.

A note on citations

Quotations from the *Monthly Review* and the *Critical Review* are cited throughout using the abbreviations *MR* and *CR*. Because the publishers of the original editions of works by the principal writers in this study are germane to the argument, their names are provided in citations of these editions. In other cases of eighteenth- and nineteenth-century texts, city and date only are provided.

Introduction: "building on public approbation"

> I am much more hurt on your account than my own at your losing by this book; I hope it may yet sell: but if not, I have no judgment or St. Forlaix will make you amends; if I tho't it woud not I should be very unhappy.
>
> I am much obligd to your delicacy in not telling me this sooner, but you need never make any ceremony with me; for I am one who can hear truth tho' it makes against me.
>
> In any future publication I will take care you shall not lose; I will share the profit or loss of the history; & if, in any other, you disapprove that mode, we will not fix the price till what I write has been six months publish'd. I have thots of writing for the theatre, after the hist. is finishd; but it is difficult to get things done: if I succeed that way, I shall give up all others, as I like it best; in that case you know the price is always fix'd.[1]
>
> (Frances Brooke to James Dodsley, 17??)

BEYOND FEMINIST LITERARY HISTORY?

Eschewing ceremony, able to hear the truth, negotiating future terms, liking the playwright's chances for success best – the writer of this 1769 letter to James Dodsley is clearly a competent literary professional, an economic agent confidently offering authorial expertise and flexibility as the basis for a durable and productive collaboration with this prominent bookseller. Yet this writer is also a woman, Frances Brooke, whom Janet Todd included in her 1989 *The Sign of Angellica: Women, Writing and Fiction, 1660–1800* in a group of "ladies approved by the Doctor [Samuel Johnson]" because, unlike the contemporaries he describes with "horror" as a "'generation of Amazons of the pen,'" these ladies "will never openly handle a weapon or in any way defy 'masculine tyranny.'"[2] The Frances Brooke designated by Todd and other feminist literary historians as a "Modest Muse" cannot readily be aligned with this letter-writer.[3] It is this gap between the eighteenth-century evidence and the late twentieth-century perspective that this book will address.

My inquiry took root in graduate student days in the late 1980s, when my discovery of eighteenth-century studies coincided with a re-invigoration of the field through exciting new historicist, materialist, print culture, and above all, feminist approaches. The novelty of the attention paid to noncanonical women writers in such overviews of the period as Jane Spencer's *The Rise of the Woman Novelist: From Aphra Behn to Jane Austen* (1986), Kathryn Shevelow's *Women and Print Culture: The Construction of Femininity in the Early Periodical* (1989), and Janet Todd's *The Sign of Angellica* (1989) was captured by Patricia Meyer Spacks, who in 1990 reviewed *The Sign of Angellica* as responding to "a great recent shift in literary assumptions" with what "only a few years [before], would have seemed inconceivable to write, or to read, a literary history of the Restoration and eighteenth century focused entirely on women."[4]

The influence of these studies was equally felt in the form of an interpretive frame they had adopted – the model of a separate-spheres gender economy, established with the rise of a bourgeois class in the eighteenth century, which relegated women to the private (domestic) sphere, and to rigid codes of sexual chastity, propriety, and silence.[5] From this starting point, women writers' interventions in the public realm of print were by definition transgressive. As Shevelow put it, women writers were permitted to enter the public sphere of letters only to reinforce the figure of "the domestic woman, constructed in a relation of difference to men, a difference of kind rather than degree." Forays into print had therefore to present a legitimizing face to the public, whether that of an authorizing male literary figure or that of the author herself in an apologetic preamble about "domestic distress, financial necessity, and the urge to instruct other women."[6] The actual matter of such publications, it followed, would either be genuinely orthodox, and in that case produced by the appropriated voice of a submissive woman, or itself in masquerade, its subversion peeping slyly out from beneath a surface orthodoxy, in the case of a writer of genuine feminist convictions. Thus this account of eighteenth-century women writers, using gender as fundamental binary cause, produced layers of oppositional and inevitably value-laden categories of masculine and feminine, cultural gatekeeper and supplicant, surface and depth, orthodox and subversive, appropriated and feminist.

I must emphasize that in Spencer, Shevelow, and Todd the model I have just described is more nuanced than its influence on subsequent literary criticism would suggest.[7] Nevertheless, the interpretive frame had a tendency to become increasingly schematic with each application, especially in the area that concerns me here, the height of the eighteenth century. For the binary synchronic structure of this model was given narrative momentum by a diachronic explanation of the long eighteenth century which might be called, if somewhat disrespectfully, the "sandwich model." Restoration and early eighteenth-century writers such as Aphra Behn and Delarivier Manley engaged in a brief flowering of feminism characterized by what Todd described as "sophisticated insights and techniques," displayed in productions which were "erotic and worldly." A century later, fiction "seem[ed] to gain a new strength from an assumption of the moralist's authority" with Frances Burney, Ann Radcliffe, and Mary Wollstonecraft. Between these endpoints, writers such as Frances Brooke, along with Sarah Fielding, Frances Sheridan, and Sarah Scott, on the other hand, represented an eclipse of feminism by the so-called "modest muse," constrained and appropriated by patriarchal figures like Samuel Richardson, and characterized by "a moralistic . . . colluding with the growing ideology of femininity, preaching and greatly rewarding self-sacrifice and restraint."[8] Spencer argued, similarly, that eighteenth-century women writers increasingly succeeded in the public sphere through skillful reinforcement of the ideology locating women's lives in the domestic realm. In other words, they learned to meet "the Terms of Acceptance" for their writing in order to gain acknowledgment of their talents.[9]

As Spacks noted in her review, "Todd's sympathy appears fully engaged" with Restoration and early eighteenth-century writers, but she "has more difficulty" with mid-century writers of sentiment, making their works "sound unappealing indeed," only to have "her interest intensif[y] as she considers the century's final decade."[10] Not surprisingly, such treatments led to much further work on those early and later writers where evidence of feminist convictions, or at least subversion, was relatively easy to find, especially when it took the form of representations of female sexual desire. The Restoration and early eighteenth-century writers Behn, Manley, and Eliza Haywood, for example, have been reexamined in their significantly different political and professional contexts, not only by Todd and Spencer, but also by Ros Ballaster, Catherine Ingrassia, and others.[11] Ultimately, one effect of such work has been to put pressure on a rigid separate-sphere thesis, resulting in a more nuanced approach to all women writers of this time. Recent work has increasingly represented the relation between gender ideology and the individual writer's experience and works as contested and variable. Exploiting the potential for a much-broadened perspective of eighteenth-century publication enabled by the ongoing *English Short Title Catalogue (ESTC)* project, Paula McDowell, in her exemplary 1998 study *The Women of Grub Street: Press, Politics and Gender in the London Literary Marketplace 1678–1730*, employs the methods of book history to challenge the public–private gender dichotomy in the sphere of print publication. One effect of McDowell's discovery of women's extensive engagement in a wide range of publishing activities is to challenge notions of their lack of agency in the political public sphere.[12] With respect to an individual writer, the late Restoration royalist Jane Barker, Kathryn King has in turn pointed out that reading Barker "*within* a narrative of the emerging bourgeois femininity and *against* the more flamboyant literary practices of the sex-and-scandal school of female popular fiction" is at best unhelpful for this writer marginalized in multiple senses as a Catholic, a Jacobite, an intellectual woman, and a spinster. King's study demonstrates that "gender-driven, oppositional accounts of early modern women writers, so hugely productive over the last couple of decades, have reached a point of diminishing returns and will need to be supplemented by more inclusive pictures of women's involvement in early modern culture if feminist literary history is to move forward."[13]

Indeed, feminist historians of the pre-twentieth century have for some time been raising concerns about the value of this broad-brush model as an analytical tool, in part because of its seeming applicability to any number of historical moments and because of its reliance on suspect combinations of prescriptive and descriptive sources. In her 1993 article "Golden Age to Separate Spheres? A Review of the Categories and Chronology of English Women's History," Amanda Vickery helpfully reviewed theoretical and methodological critiques from the late 1980s, while noting the continued reliance of historians of British women's experience on the assumption that a gendered public–private dichotomy developed in England from the late seventeenth to the early nineteenth centuries. Vickery concluded that

> the notion of separate spheres . . . has done modern women's history a great service. With this conceptual framework women's history moved beyond a Whiggish celebration of the rise of feminism, or a virtuous rediscovery of those previously hidden from history. In asserting the instrumental role of the ideology of separate spheres in modern class formation, historians asserted the wider

historical significance of gender. Thereby the interpretation offered powerful justification for the study of women when the field was embattled. Yet strategic concerns do not in themselves justify the deployment of an artificial and unwieldy conceptual vocabulary. In the attempt to map the breadth and boundaries of female experience, new categories and concepts must be generated, and this must be done with more sensitivity to women's own manuscripts.[14]

In a similar vein, but dealing more directly with historiography of the eighteenth century, Lawrence E. Klein, in a 1995 article on "Gender and the Public/Private Distinction in the Eighteenth Century," has questioned the "domestic thesis" for superimposing the two binary oppositions of male/female and public/private to argue for "the persistent exclusion of women from public roles, power and citizenship." Klein notes that this model fails to take into account evidence that "even when theory was against them, women in the eighteenth century had [conscious] public dimensions to their lives."[15] Such work revisits Jürgen Habermas's influential discussion of the rise of the bourgeois public sphere in eighteenth-century England, in order to pry open the fissure between Habermas's scheme of a public sphere of letters which is broadly inclusive and a public political sphere which grows out of the former, but is made up of private individuals who are male, middle-class heads of households.[16]

For some time, then, the call for a new theory and methodology of eighteenth-century women's literary history has been sounded, and it has been taken up in some of the studies of early eighteenth-century writers noted above. More pertinently here, however, the more nuanced and particularized approach has done little to alter one aspect of the original model: its representation of the "filling" in the sandwich. Turning again and again to generalizations about female writers cowering behind their anonymity before censorious or condescending male contemporaries, studies of works by women novelists, in particular, have remained firmly grounded in variations on a view of the 1740s to 1770s as the Age of Johnson, Richardson, and Fielding. It has seemed that there is nothing new to say about writers of whom it has been said that "each fulfills [Richardson's] demand and indeed writes in his shadow."[17] McDowell's book is a case in point: it relies once again on 1980s histories of women's writings to claim that, unlike the "unprecedented" and "heterogeneous" involvement of women in print in the early eighteenth century, the period she has examined closely, the remainder of the century was characterized by an increasing "depoliticization" of women.[18]

Thus the generalization that Frank Donoghue, in his 1996 *The Fame Machine: Book Reviewing and Eighteenth-Century Literary Careers*, uses to describe the 1750s and 1760s, might in fact unwittingly describe our own critical habits in approaching those decades; he speaks of "the particular difficulty women experienced not only in writing professionally, but in having a professional life story analogous to those of successful male writers."[19] It is troubling to encounter this deeply entrenched way of seeing in Donoghue's own otherwise valuable study of eighteenth-century literary careers. He begins with a warning against a focus on Samuel Johnson as "lead[ing] one to forget how unique a figure he was, . . . thereby skew[ing] a literary history of his time." If uniqueness skews history, the corrective Donoghue supplies in the case of women writers goes to the opposite extreme. His fine chapter-length examinations of Laurence Sterne, Oliver Goldsmith, and Tobias Smollett in turn are followed by a single, sixteen-page chapter subtitled "Female Literary Careers," featuring three paragraphs on Charlotte Smith, Charlotte Lennox, and Sarah Fielding combined, less than six pages on Elizabeth Griffith and Frances Sheridan, and a final five pages on Frances Burney.

The message is that none of these women's careers could be unique, while collectively they represent something definably uniform: the female literary career. Indeed, this is made explicit in the chapter's opening, where we are told categorically, with a supporting reference only to Elaine Showalter's work on nineteenth-century women writers, that "Just as women could only produce literature under marginalizing conditions, so too was the reception of their writing uniformly compromised." Given such a starting point, it is not surprising that when Donoghue sets out "to explore some of the strategies that women writers employed to try to circumvent the institutional handicaps under which they labored," his findings bring him to the bleak conclusion "that all their efforts were destined to fail. In the early stages, described here, the literary career was an exclusively male form of social practice."[20] In short, for most accounts of women writing at the height of the century, it has remained beyond question that gender is the essential explanatory fact, that a female author's achievement in the sphere of print letters, in its modes and its degree, is predicated upon the conditions governing her life as a woman. Todd's words resonate still: "What women created in the mid-eighteenth century was not simply writing but *feminine* writing."[21]

This study therefore arises out of an ongoing dissatisfaction with the standard frameworks used for discussion of these women writers, and out of an attempt to find new ways of seeing. For I have come to believe that the problem now lies, not so much in a lack of evidence about these women's professional lives, but rather in our continued attempt to fit the evidence into habitual frames of reference; we need, to shift my metaphor, new wineskins in which to store our new wine. In two 1993 analyses that have been influential in my own thinking, Margaret J. M. Ezell and Paula McDowell identified the last half of the eighteenth century as a crux of lasting importance in telling the story of women as authors. In *Writing Women's Literary History*, Ezell argued that the historiographical models, and accompanying biases, of eighteenth- and nineteenth-century literary biographers were set in the 1750s by collectors of female worthies such as George Ballard, whose ideal of the "modest, middle-class, well-read, pious, and charitable" woman who "does not challenge her society in any direct way except to urge further educational activities," discreetly hidden under the antiquarian's objective stance, was instrumental in "marginalizing or even erasing women writers who did not fit within his criteria."[22] McDowell simultaneously identified this historical moment as the point of origin of "a distinct literary history of women," which in its "mass marketing of the 'literary lady' in anthologies, miscellanies, and collections, functioned to contain and control what was by the eighteenth century recognized as a genuine threat to the existing social order: the unprecedented opportunities inherent in the new literary marketplace for women's public political and social critique."[23] Most importantly for my purposes, Ezell claimed that Ballard's categories, together with the ensuing gradual restriction of the "literary" to imaginative writing, have reached centuries forward, impairing the ability of much more recent feminist literary historiographers to see the writerly activity and influence of women who were in their own time active, successful, and respected publishing authors in a wide range of genres. In short, while rejecting Ballard's values, Ezell notes, we have tended to adopt his dichotomous, essentialist categories of women writers and what they were writing.[24]

While Ezell and McDowell were concerned to identify the effects of this phenomenon on the historiography of earlier women writers, the period wherein they laid the blame, the mid-eighteenth century, is of double importance to me as that on which I am focusing in this study. In the end, both Ezell and McDowell maintained their assumption of the victimization of women writers, of their exclusion, silencing, even "positive erasure,"[25] while they historicized and particularized this erasure as the product of a specific cultural moment, in which the dynamics of print production, gender ideology, and reader tastes were implicated. But where in this crucial moment were the women who were researching, writing, patronizing, or managing, and what were they saying? Was the cultural and discursive system indeed as monolithically oppressive as it has been represented to be, and were women indeed its victims to the extent we have assumed?[26] Furthermore, were reading and writing always construed as essentially gendered, forcing female participants either to engage in "patriarchal discourse" or to subvert it through a defiant choice of "feminine" modes? A binary of oppressor and victim does not tell us enough, indeed, misleads us.

Recently, there have been indications that historians are prepared to challenge the assumption that the middle decades of the century represent an eclipse of women's self-assertion and a full retreat into bourgeois domesticity. In her 2000 *Small Change: Women, Learning, Patriotism, 1750–1810*, Harriet Guest challenges the oppositional thesis, arguing that, in fact, "domesticity is always a contested proposition," in part because it "fails to secure to women those forms of personal worth which only participation in the labor market offers." Ultimately, she finds that "domesticity gains in value as a result of its continuity with the social or the public, and not only as a result of its asocial exclusion"; intellectual or bluestocking women who have been read simply as advocates of a rigid separation of spheres are therefore in fact working out subtle but influential definitions of their own gender roles and, thereby, of the nature of the political subject.[27] Rereading a number of the celebrations of "female worthies" which figure so consistently in poetry, painting, journalism, and anthologies of the period, and which are the foundation of Ezell's and McDowell's arguments that the domestic confinement and eventual marginalization of women arose here, both Elizabeth Eger and Charlotte Grant have discovered a culturally central, active, and public place for women as leaders in every aspect of the arts, both in the iconography and in the reality of the day.[28] Eger, in particular, suggests an influence of the period's "phenomenal interest in their growing activity" on women writers themselves, concluding that "Their intervention in literary and artistic tradition was inevitably self-conscious, involving a sense of group identity and a commitment to women's education and in the words of Mary Hays, an interest in 'their advancement in the grand scale of rational and social existence.' The future of critical reason appeared to belong to both sexes."[29]

In a stimulating study bringing together a wide array of women's public "performance" with the theory and representation of women's speech, Patricia Howell Michaelson has arrived at the conclusion that women used stereotypes of their relation to the spoken word strategically, "while insisting implicitly that their gender identity was not always the most salient one."[30] Supporting such arguments is a growing understanding of the crucial civilizing role awarded to women in Enlightenment theories of progress, a role which has been identified by Sylvana Tomaselli and which is exemplified in the essays of Hume, as well as in the works of other Scottish Enlightenment philosophers.[31]

THE FEMALE NOVELIST PROBLEM

My study shares these scholars' dissatisfactions with the state of women's literary history for the eighteenth century, but seeks to move understanding forward, not by looking at the roles of women in clearly public domains such as the performing arts, but through a reexamination of a group of women writers who have most often been viewed as epitomizing women's relegation to the domestic sphere, and as displaying the resulting doubleness this relegation forced upon them as aspiring authors. These five authors are Frances Chamberlaine Sheridan (1724–1766), Frances Moore Brooke (1724–1789), Sarah Robinson Scott (1723–1795), Sarah Fielding (1710–1768), and Charlotte Ramsay Lennox (1729[?]–1804). The sense that the "evidence" is created by its interpretive frame for this group in particular can be illustrated briefly by reference to Charlotte Lennox, the most problematic of these writers for those attempting a dichotomous classification of submissive or subversive. Critical attention has focused on Lennox's 1752 novel *The Female Quixote,* which notoriously resolves the problem of its heroine Arabella (who has been deluded by reading French heroic romances into believing that her social world and lifestory conform to their outlines) by having her "converted," through a dialogue with a "Pious and Learned" clergyman, to a recognition of her place as an heiress in her society's economy of courtship and marriage. The ideal fiction to which she is directed as a guide for her own behavior is Richardson's *Clarissa.*

Given the "immodesty" of Lennox's self-assertion as an author, and the vicissitudes of her own unhappy marriage, this orthodox moral cannot, according to our dominant explanatory model, be Lennox's desired solution; either the apparent conservatism is a cover for a radical critique of eighteenth-century marriage practices and ideals of female propriety or it is simply not Lennox's at all. The former position is represented by such readers as Laurie Langbauer, who begins her influential 1990 discussion with the premise that Arabella "comes to exemplify Lennox's own dilemma as a woman writer: the imperative to leave behind the insubstantial world of romance, the only realm in which the woman (writer) is given a place, however illusory." Langbauer argued that the novel celebrates the pleasures of romance, which govern its own narrative, but she was then led to claim that in its conclusion, Arabella's only "escape from romance is to stop being a woman."[32] The difficulty for Langbauer lay in the fact that Lennox's resolution is indeed based on an explicit identification of legitimate fiction with the authority of the male author. The conversion chapter is heavily encrusted with praise of Samuel Johnson, both as "the greatest Genius in the present Age" and as the model in sentiments and style for the "Pious and Learned" clergyman who effects Arabella's cure. Richardson is explicitly authorized here, in contrast to the writers of heroic romances, as "an admirable Writer of our own Time," while his novel *Clarissa* offers its reader "the most solid Instructions, the noblest Sentiments, and the most exalted Piety, in the pleasing Dress of a Novel."[33]

Hence the view that this cannot have been what Lennox really wanted to say. It has been almost a critical commonplace to argue that Lennox was forced by "the censorship of critics" to the "necessity" of disguising her presumed feminism, toeing an orthodox line in order to achieve publication.[34] This position makes feminist literary history ironically continuous with the unsubstantiated claim of traditional criticism that Lennox indeed did *not* write the conversion chapter – Johnson wrote it for her.[35] Not only do both of these explanations of the novel's conclusion – Lennox as subversive-in-hiding and Lennox as author forced to abdicate – require that Lennox be stripped of agency at the most significant moment in her narrative, they are also simply unconvincing when this conclusion is placed against the work of some of her female contemporaries who did find it possible to problematize marriage endings and stories of female reading within the supposedly rigid constraints of the novel of courtship. Lennox chose to write an ending, in short, which does nothing to dismantle the hierarchies of gender and reading upon which her plot is constructed. At best, as Elizabeth Kraft has concluded, while Lennox "discovers . . . the need for a narrative alternative," she does not discover "the form it should take."[36]

I began this project, then, simply by focusing on those women who have repeatedly been identified as the modest novelists of the mid-century. Four of them, indeed, are grouped together by Todd when she notes in passing, while discussing Frances Brooke as novelist of clichéd sensibility, that she, together "with Charlotte Lennox, Sarah Fielding and Frances Sheridan, was much appreciated by Johnson and Richardson." Spencer in turn classifies Fielding with Sheridan and Sarah Scott as typical "women novelists of the mid-century" who were "Delighted to find [in *Clarissa*] an argument that made intellectual study acceptable in them, and a champion of their sex like Richardson to promote it," and therefore "sought to keep masculine approval by disclaiming any intention to overturn the sexual hierarchy."[37] Thus a second, related characteristic of the group is their shared links with Johnson and Richardson, two male mentors whose very approval has been seen as evidence of these women's subservience. A third basis for the grouping is their prominence as novelists in the period: beginning with Fielding's *Adventures of David Simple* in 1744 and continuing until the end of the 1760s, these women are easily among the ten most prolific British producers of new fiction titles (with the exception of Sheridan, whose premature death at the age of forty-two cut short a very promising career).[38] Not only did they publish regularly, but their work was well received and they attained considerable stature in their own period: their fiction was frequently reprinted, prominently featured by circulating libraries, and named in accounts of important novels.

As this final criterion suggests, these women earned a place in literary history; however, our narratives, both traditional and feminist, have to a significant extent obscured their story. The category of "modest," for example, does a disservice to the professional self-assertion and ambition exhibited by these women throughout their careers. And the related model of male mentorship, while containing important truths, also tends to imply a hierarchical, unidirectional relationship of professional and artistic influence, whereas I contend that the relational dynamics in question were much more collegial and multifaceted than has often been understood to be the case. These women and men moved within overlapping groups, so that Johnson could write to Lennox in 1756, for example, "I have seen Mrs. Brookes, and Miss Reid, since I saw you, and I heard of you at bothe houses, yet, what much surprised me I heard no evil";[39] Alicia Lefanu writes that her grandmother Frances Sheridan and Fielding and Scott were visiting acquaintances at Bath;[40] Richardson writes at various points to Lennox of Fielding and to Fielding of Sheridan;[41] and the history-writer Walter Harte sends his greetings to "Mrs. Scot" via Charlotte Lennox in about 1760.[42] The pattern is that of a complex network, whereby sourcebooks are exchanged, subscriptions promoted, and publishing opportunities watched for, in a spirit of facilitation that was fostered, rather than doled out toward subordinates, by Johnson and Richardson with their valuable trade connections.[43] Similarly, we hesitate to imagine a Sarah Fielding or a Charlotte Lennox or a Frances Sheridan at the center rather than on the margins, as the sought-after literary figure rather than at the periphery of someone else's circle, but in fact, we have contemporary descriptions of each of these three authors using precisely such images. Alicia Lefanu, again, describes both Sheridan and her colleague Sarah Fielding as having been sought-after literary personalities, attracting to themselves not only women writers but also Richardson, Johnson, Ralph Allen, Edward Young, and the like.[44]

A career-distorting critical emphasis on these writers' novels, arising out of a longstanding association of women with the genre that has been reinforced by the domestic-sphere thesis,[45] has created further problems of perception that I will seek to dispel in this study. As Judith Stanton noted some years ago, using early *ESTC* records, there was a steady increase in the second half of the eighteenth century both in the proportion of publishing by women and in the generic range of that publishing. This led her to suggest the existence of a growing body of professionalized women writers – highly literate, versatile, and opportunistic.[46] Guest, noting also the tendency of feminist literary histories to focus on women as writers and characters of novels, examines the writings of a group of intellectual women not primarily remembered for their fiction – Elizabeth Carter, Anna Laetitia Barbauld, Anna Seward, Hannah More, and Mary Wollstonecraft. I attend rather to the fact that all of the women in my study group practiced their craft in a range of forms, embodying within their own oeuvres the principle articulated by Guest, that "eighteenth-century novels themselves participate in debates that cut across genres; they assume readers who are also immersed in periodical literature, in poetry, in histories, readers who discuss plays and parliamentary debates, who perform music, and peer into the windows of print shops."[47]

WOMEN WRITERS AND PRINT CULTURE

My method has been to explore a number of vantage points well established in other areas of critical inquiry, but not often applied to women novelists of the period. A principal perspective has been that of print culture studies. The title of Alvin B. Kernan's 1987 *Printing Technology, Letters, and Samuel Johnson* encapsulates what this approach has to offer a student of eighteenth-century writing by women. Kernan somewhat tendentiously delays the naming of the individual author, whose body of works has been the traditional basis of literary studies, giving pride of place not merely to the larger field of intellectual endeavor, or "letters," but first of all, to the material medium which elicited, shaped, and disseminated that work. The achievement of Johnson according to a model of transcendent literary genius is resituated within a crowded landscape of booksellers protecting their investments, fellow professionals, aspiring writers hoping to trade on his influence, readers of various social stations and capabilities, printers' boys waiting at his door for copy, autobiographers recording his conversation in the style of his written prose, and so on. The motive for this resituation is not to pull Johnson off his pedestal, though it may incidentally disperse, and thereby normalize, many of his achievements, but rather to enrich the ways in which an individual author's agency can be understood, through an understanding of the cross-currents of political, economic, and material forces at the place where he – or more relevantly, she – stood.[48]

In particular, important studies of eighteenth-century print culture have examined the development of interdependent notions of the author as professional, proprietor, and creator. Each of these strands has offered valuable insights for my purposes. The term "professional" is often used in literary histories without explicit definition, but by implication simply to denote writing for financial remuneration, in opposition to the sorts of cultural and material rewards offered by coterie writing for manuscript circulation and publishing as part of a patronage system. However, a fuller sociological model takes into account the structural and institutional aspects of the professions (generally seen to have been in development in the eighteenth century), as well as the professional's claims to offer a specialized set of skills to meet a defined need of society at large, and to be deserving of certain status and economic rewards as a result.[49] While authorship, like other artistic professions, might be described as loosely organized in comparison to the traditional quartet of the military, ecclesiastical, medical, and legal professions,[50] what is most important here is its aspiration in the latter half of the eighteenth century toward these defining characteristics. This movement is evidenced in the development of institutions such as the critical reviews and the Royal Literary Fund, in the increasing typology and hierarchization of forms of authorship, and in the self-consciousness of growing prestige most famously expressed by Samuel Johnson and eagerly responded to, as I will show, by the young Frances Burney.

In addition, the varying modes and combinations of patronage and professionalism represented by pensions, dedications, subscription publication, writing for hire, and sale of single works which Dustin Griffin has shown to be coexistent in the period contributed significantly to the variations on career trajectories that I will be examining in this book.[51] Not to be forgotten among these are opportunities offered by print for a disembodied, physically distanced participation in the republic of letters, a refusal of the "author function" that Michel Foucault has made such a fundamental feature of the organization of modern knowledge.[52] Thus a writer like Sarah Scott, I will show, might be enticed, because of class or gender sensitivities, economic considerations, self-deprecation, or some combination of these, to hide behind an anonymous and fragmented series of publications, while nevertheless exerting herself in the cause of the print-created reading public's improvement and entertainment.

The emphasis of scholars such as Mark Rose and Martha Woodmansee, on the other hand, has been on the relation between developing legal notions of the author as proprietor of his or her work, leading to the emergence of copyright legislation in the period, and of the doctrine of original genius which became increasingly influential in the latter half of the century.[53] Both of these phenomena clearly have implications for those women writers who, unlike Scott, did find attractive the possibility of publicly recognized achievement in the sphere of letters. In the first place, despite the legal limits to a woman's ownership of property, particularly if she were married, in actual practice the production and sale of written works allowed women access to property that, as Cheryl Turner has put it, "was treated by publishers, the public, and by the authors as their own, to dispose of as profitably as they could and to acknowledge if they chose."[54] At the same time, the theory of genius which reinforced arguments for the ontological uniqueness of literary works, and therefore, the rights of proprietary authorship, appears to have worked ultimately, in its longevity as the dominant, "Romantic" model of the author, to subordinate those authors whose work authorized itself by its relation to a tradition, to a contemporary community, or to a social good.[55] Thus much of what the women writers in my study group and their readers articulated as the signs of their success – placement in a male-defined tradition, substantial subscription lists headed by prestigious names, the satisfaction of a loyal group of readers, recognition for their expert craftsmanship or for their modeling of valued social qualities – came to be devalued or deemed irrelevant as measures of literary achievement.

Most broadly, print culture studies offer a start toward a theoretically self-conscious, yet historically nuanced and delimited, understanding of the agency of the woman writer in literary history. Feminist literary histories of the 1980s and early 1990s have left us an invaluable legacy of analyses of texts by women writers – texts, usually fictions, read in terms of their representations of female subjectivity in an overwhelmingly patriarchal system of social, economic, and political institutions. Often, however, these fine textual readings have neglected to read the "fine-print" of the text's, and writer's, paratext and context, relying rather on an extrapolation of the writer's experience from that of the narrative's heroine, combined with the sorts of generalizations about the conditions of female authorship noted above, and supported by prescriptive material like conduct writings. As I have already indicated, such approaches, while they did essential recovery work of women's writing, ironically reinforced many of the assumptions which had necessitated that recovery, in their inability or unwillingness to imagine the woman writer as agent rather than as victim.[56]

This problem of building generalizing abstractions out of readings of isolated texts is of course not unique to feminist literary history. In his poststructuralist study of David Hume's construction of the career of a man of letters as "a symbolic practice . . . that exploited, facilitated, and epitomized the operations of the commercial society which it persuasively represented," Jerome Christensen captures important possibilities created by a developing print economy, in that the "Enlightenment man of letters" can act discursively, "within a theater of representations of his own design," "*form[ing]* by affiliation a class that could reasonably hope to dominate not by virtue of a God-given right or a historically sanctioned prerogative but by means of a refined and refining prose." Thus he "could hope for a success that would surpass that of the king, who sought to be one thing to all men; the courtier, who sought to be all things to one man; and even Garrick, whose protean changes were restricted to the stage at Drury Lane." However, Christensen's premise, that the man of letters lacks "any ascriptive ties that would inhibit his exemplary mobility," begs such questions as gender, even if we are willing to accept its generalized claims based on the career of the Scottish, skeptical, poorly connected, but economically dependent Hume.[57] Did it matter that Hume was a *man* of letters? Since Christensen's fourth chapter elaborates on the dependence of this model on a subordinate female reader, it would seem so.

To what extent, then, did an individual writer's experience of the eighteenth-century print marketplace – including the booksellers' temporary belt-tightening in the 1730s and 1740s and accompanying reluctance to publish new material, followed by a steady, if at first somewhat precarious, increase in print production[58] – depend upon the physical body and its affiliations, and to what extent did the disembodied mechanisms of print replication and distribution offer an opportunity to transcend those particulars? My study is feminist in appropriating for ambitious women writers Christensen's claim that the republic of letters offered the opportunity of maximizing success throughout "a career understood as a calculus which can transform all necessities into opportunities," while at the same time asserting the significance of those various necessities, among them the necessities of gender, in determining the particular career.[59] While it may seem at points that I am attempting, in fact, to deny gender its place in determining an author's agency, it is my aim, more precisely, to ask questions about our assumption that it is the prior explanatory cause overriding all other causal factors.

The question of the degree to which professional literary agency in eighteenth-century England was gendered indeed underlies this entire project and has, to a significant extent, motivated it. My working premise for this study has been a notion of "situated authorial agency" similar to that called for by Seán Burke in *The Death and Return of the Author: Criticism and Subjectivity in Barthes, Foucault and Derrida.* Noting the inability of poststructuralist, New Historicist, and even feminist theory to move beyond a caricature of the author as the vestige of absolutist, transcendental, or impersonal notions of intention and subjectivity, Burke argues that

> Postmodern emphases on locality, on little narratives, on singularity; neo-ethical concerns with respecting the Otherness of the Other; postcolonial specifications of the subaltern, of national and historical contexts – all these drives within contemporary critical discourse pass from the text to its histories without properly acknowledging that an authorial life and its work allow such a passage to be made. The author will be exceeded but never bypassed in the critical movement to the time, the place, the social energies and structures in which the text was constituted.

One implication of working with a situated model of agency, Burke observes, is that "gender would seem to be one form of authorial specificity amongst others." He concludes that "there would seem to be only one tenet that can be stated with any confidence: to wit, that authorship is *the principle of specificity in the world of texts.* So far from consolidating the notion of a universal or unitary subject, the retracing of the work to its author is a working-back to historical, cultural and political embeddedness."[60]

I will therefore approach these writers in a series of case studies that use the tools of particularized historical analysis to gain a sense of their "embeddedness" in a British print culture characterized by increasing structural complexity, multiplying genre and reader categories, and expanding institutional frameworks – all as an effect of increased production. James Raven has demonstrated that the publication of new novels kept pace through the period with this general increase, and that, where authorship is known, women increased in proportion from being responsible for approximately 14 percent of all new novels for the three decades of 1750 to 1779 (as opposed to the almost one-third of new novels identified as authored by men) to a slight majority of known authors at the end of the century.[61] Turner's study of eighteenth-century women novelists concludes that "there was not a significant differential between the sexes as far as copyright payments were concerned," and in fact, that "women novelists were amongst the most commercially successful authors of their day."[62] Simultaneously, the novel's recognition as a distinct genre in the second half of the century could be seen as a coalescence of identifiable, if overlapping narrative types, such as the series of adventures, the private memoir, the oriental tale, and the sentimental-epistolary novel first, followed by the gothic novel and the historical romance. The rise of the reviews contributed to a distribution of publications according to appropriate readerships, including a base identification of much of the novel genre with female writers and readers. Other forms became recognizable as genres in their own right: the historical biography, for example, theorized and practiced by Sarah Scott, or the children's story, pioneered by Sarah Fielding. Meanwhile, translation of foreign-language works helped to feed the presses, new periodical papers were launched (and abandoned) with regularity, and writing for the stage continued a lucrative, if politically fraught option. I am attempting in this study to illuminate the choices my study group of writers faced in this context, and to credit their various strategies for negotiating their way through them.

While tracing the complexity of this world of print might produce a cure for overgeneralization that is worse than the disease, I have attempted to manage the proliferation of variables by means of a combination of detailed individual case studies and relatively controlled comparisons between writers. In the first portion of this book, simplistic male-to-female models of influence are tested by a look at two individual writers' professional affiliations (both synchronic and diachronic), and at a third writer's lack of such professional self-identification. In the first chapter, I look at Frances Sheridan's placement of her 1761 novel *The Memoirs of Miss Sidney Bidulph* with respect not only to her early mentor Richardson, but also to her more recent connection John Home, the playwright whose popular but controversial tragedy *Douglas* offered her, and her theater manager and actor husband, access to current channels of influence. At the same time, Sheridan overwrote Home's alignment of public and private with the masculine and the feminine, insisting that heroic virtue transcends both sphere and sex. Once this participation in issues of heated contemporary debate is made visible, it is possible to turn afresh to the question of the influence of *Clarissa* on Sheridan's novel, seeing Sidney Bidulph as a self-conscious reader and imitator of the Richardsonian exemplary, but also as a reluctant heroine herself, poised between competing and imperfect standards of virtue, and therefore inescapably a moral agent.

In the second chapter, I suggest that Frances Brooke's work throughout her career was driven less by momentary opportunities for profit and influence, as has often been posited in her case, than by a persistent political engagement that crossed boundaries between genre and medium and challenged the powerful in the public spheres of both politics and letters. Consistently responded to by both friends and enemies in political terms, when Brooke and her enemy Garrick do deploy an ideological discourse of gender, it is to disguise their quarrel over theater politics. Like Sheridan, Brooke in fact worked to modify one of the most clichéd vocabularies of the period, that of the Country ideology, claiming in political and social conservatism a freedom from restrictive gender roles.

Chapter 3 focuses more narrowly on a specific authorial choice, on Sarah Scott's deployment of the genre of history-writing as a means of intervening in the discussions that preoccupied Sheridan and Brooke. In Scott's case, however, these interventions are disembodied and fragmentary, preventing the construction of a coherent author function. Thus her professional life and the reception of her work serve to introduce, by negative illustration, the question of the female literary career. Here there is value in reading women writers' texts, as well as women writers' publishing activities, in conjunction with one another. By paying careful attention to the chronological and socioeconomic coherence of the cohort group, the literary historian can more accurately identify the relative significance, or insignificance, of gender constraints for each member of the group. Sarah Fielding, for example, is described by the editors of her correspondence as "seem[ing] to have avoided any kind of contractual business, and happily farm[ing] out such work to her friends," the sort of behavior that has often served as evidence of women's inability to carry out their own business with booksellers,[63] whereas the epigraph to this introduction clearly demonstrates Frances Brooke's lack of hesitation in that regard. Making such differences visible thus serves as a corrective both to oversimplified dichotomies and to a tendency to use single texts or authors as representative of entire generations of publishing history.

The second section of the book, then, is organized around the careers of a number of authors, not with the intention of explaining fully why their experiences and writings took the shape they did, but as a means of isolating the relative importance of a range of factors in determining the various directions of their writing lives. As I have already demonstrated, while the notion of the career is frequently applied to male authors in a manner that assumes its transparency, its use for the woman writer has been contested. This study, though it rejects Donoghue's view that women writers could not have careers, adopts his model of the career as "a product of interpretation . . . a narrative that cannot be authored entirely by its own subject," but is rather constructed in an "uneasy collaboration" between authors and their readers.[64] For Donoghue, these readers are institutional – the writers of the review periodicals which arose in mid-century. While referring frequently to the principal review magazines, I will interpret this collaborative project more broadly, to include fellow writers, particularly women, as contributors to the construction of an authorial career.

My first claim, here, is that we need to pay attention to whole career trajectories, rather than focusing on isolated – usually early and anonymous – publishing events in a woman writer's life. The isolated facts of Sarah Fielding's self-deprecating advertisement to her first novel, *The Adventures of David Simple*, and her brother Henry's condescending preface to its second edition, for example, do not constitute a master key to her career and her own attitude toward it. Rather, the success of this novel provided Sarah Fielding with what Martin Battestin and Clive Probyn have called her "public literary signature" as "the Author of *David Simple*," invoked by one reviewer, for example, with the words, "It were superfluous to compliment the Author of David Simple upon her merits as a Writer."[65] Fielding's last published work, her 1762 translation of Xenophon from the Greek, carried a new authorial name: "Sarah Fielding." Thus a more nuanced understanding of the meaning of anonymity for both female and male writers can allow for less distorted interpretations of career patterns as well.[66] My examination of Fielding's and Lennox's, as well as Edward Kimber's and the Minifie sisters' complex uses of anonymity and "public literary signatures" will attempt to do this for the career launched in mid-century.

Chapter 4 presents a comparative outline of the careers of Sarah Fielding and Charlotte Lennox, weighing the relative importance of opposed factors such as social status versus the developing institutions of the professional, stable provincial social networks versus proximity to the center of the book trade, and the subscription model of publication versus the intertwined market and patronage systems. Examining the influence of such factors on the careers of two women writers allows us to consider whether, for instance, women living at a distance from London needed powerful intermediaries to arrange publication because they were women, or because, as the Irish Reverend Mr. Philip Skelton found in 1754 when he attempted to bring out two volumes of sermons, the oversight of a slow-moving publication process from the geographical periphery posed a daunting challenge to any author.[67] It also allows again for a revisiting of questions of influence – specifically, the influence of Richardson and Johnson as mentors on Fielding and Lennox – in terms more nuanced than those of patriarchal "censorship." Although Lennox is generally viewed as more resistant than Fielding to doctrines of female propriety, I will show that in *The Female Quixote* she offers a less sophisticated engagement of Richardson's model of the feminized reader than does the enthusiastically supportive Fielding in her 1748 pamphlet *Remarks on Clarissa.* This distinction, indeed, is of a piece with the differing publishing choices and modes of affiliation pursued by the two women throughout their careers.

If this chapter illustrates the importance of a range of conditions of mid- and late eighteenth-century authorship to the career trajectories of two women writers who achieved considerable success in both the short and the long term, chapter 5 tests these findings by looking at the experiences of two producers of popular, but more ephemeral, fiction in the same period: Edward Kimber and the collaborative team of Margaret Minifie and Susannah Minifie (later Gunning). This comparison brings to the fore the consolidation of the novel genre in the middle of the century, and its rapid organization, driven and reflected by the reviewers, into subgenres and hierarchies of literary value. I will suggest, in fact, that while our attention to early criticism has often been taken up by the invocation of stereotypes of gender and genre, much of this is "noise" that can be separated from the actual value judgments made by the reviews, and by early historians of imaginative literature such as Clara Reeve. These critics evaluate the newly formulated genre in terms of criteria still recognizable today, suggesting that to reintroduce a discourse of aesthetic value in writing about women writers, one that acknowledges historical situation, yet is in its criteria transhistorical, need not entail writing these women out of the canon.

My final two chapters move toward a retrospective view of the writers discussed in the earlier sections, seeking to shed some light on what happened in the latter decades of the century to relegate them to the margins of literary history. First, I examine the early career of Frances Burney as she self-consciously constructed it in her journals and letters according to her observations of authorship as it was practiced by her predecessors and peers, both women and men. I will argue that Burney was drawn to the professional rather than amateur model of letters, identifying the Streatham circle with Johnson at its literary apex with the former, and Elizabeth Montagu's bluestocking circle with the latter. A gender dichotomy appears to have become an element of this oppositional structure: Burney relegated the "authoress" to the inferior category of amateur and to the embodied relations of patronage in both its traditional and its bluestocking manifestations. Thus both her literary writing – *The Witlings* and *Cecilia* – and her journal records show her steering a course toward identification with authors successful in the marketplace, and thereby choosing to foreground male forebears in the profession. My next chapter will trace more fully her gradual obliteration of even private acknowledgments of her inheritance of a professional space opened up by successful authors such as Sarah Fielding, Frances Brooke, and Charlotte Lennox.

In this concluding chapter, then, I move through the end of the century to return full circle to the problem posed in this introduction, and which has motivated this study – the designation of so many eighteenth-century women writers as mere domestic novelists, and therefore as dispensable footnotes to both mainstream and feminist literary history. Here the premise of women's authorial agency, fundamental to the study as a whole, comes to the fore in a potentially more contentious manner, as I look at the role of mid- and late century women writers in the creation of those literary histories, through their acts of classification, acknowledgment, or more problematically, obliteration, of their immediate forebears or contemporaries. As I have indicated, Burney is a key figure here, along with Catherine Talbot and Elizabeth Carter, Scott, Brooke, and Reeve. At the risk of simply pushing the assumptions of the domestic thesis forward to a later date, this study looks at some evidence for the view that it was in the 1780s and subsequent decades that a shift occurred away from "a tradition in which women's writing on the public sphere was rooted in a discourse of national civic virtue" toward one where it arose out of a more narrowly conceived "place of women in family and home."[68] At the same time, I will suggest that the ephemerality of print materials in the expanding literary marketplace and the respondent emergence of increasingly unitary narratives of literary and generic traditions as a means of preserving literary memory lent an unintended weight to contingent and pragmatic acts of naming or forgetting. With more certainty, this final chapter's account of a forgetting of the public space once occupied by the women writers of my study group underscores the very existence of that space, diversely but self-consciously and even comfortably inhabited by writers as different from one another as Sarah Fielding, Charlotte Lennox, Frances Sheridan, Sarah Scott, and Frances Brooke.

CHAPTER I

Frances Sheridan, John Home, and public virtue

> I am obliged to break off, as I have been interrupted a dozen times since I sat down to write. Indeed I am so distressed for want of a room to myself, that it discourages me from attempting any thing, though I have this winter made a shift to scribble something that you shall hear of another time.
>
> (Frances Sheridan to Samuel Whyte, 1762)[1]

> In a word, as we entertain the highest opinion of the genius, delicacy, and good sense of Mrs. S ——, we cannot but wish she may continue to exert those talents, so honourable to herself, so useful, so entertaining to society, and particularly so beneficial to the republic of letters.
>
> (*The Critical Review* 11 [March 1761])

As I noted in my introduction, scholars have recently questioned the assumption that as a bourgeois public sphere emerged in eighteenth-century Britain, women, severely restricted in political, legal, and economic power, were aligned entirely with an opposing private sphere. According to Lawrence E. Klein, the problem with the "domestic thesis" is that it does not account for the distinction between theory and practice, whereas the evidence indicates that "women in the eighteenth century had public dimensions to their lives." "Moreover," he concludes, ". . . engaging in those public practices involved a consciousness that they were behaving publicly." Klein goes on to suggest that such public dimensions are made conceptually possible by the multiple sets of distinctions for which no one theory, particularly not one dependent on binary oppositions, could ever account. In an overview of refinements in studies of "consumption, the reading public, and the early eighteenth-century domestic woman," Terry Lovell has noted, similarly, that "we may be mistaken in attempting to make too close a fit between culturally available personas and categories of persons." By means of a "closer examination of both space and *language*," then, Klein believes that a more precise account of gender in relation to publicity and privacy can be achieved. This proposal is especially appropriate for studies of women novelists of the mid-eighteenth century, which, as I have already shown, have tended to begin with Kathryn Shevelow's assumption that these writers were permitted to enter the public sphere of print only to reinforce the figure of "the domestic woman, constructed in a relation of difference to men, a difference of kind rather than degree."[2]

In this chapter I will focus on Frances Sheridan, whose brief publishing career has appeared an easy fit within a "private" and "feminized" tradition of the domestic and sentimental. After all, Sheridan is now known primarily for her 1761 novel *The Memoirs of Miss Sidney Bidulph*, dedicated to Samuel Richardson as "The Author of Clarissa and Sir Charles Grandison," in tribute to "exemplary Goodness and distinguished Genius, . . . found united in One Person."[3] Furthermore, Richardson actively encouraged Sheridan as a writer; correspondence from Dublin with Richardson in London shows her entrusting the arrangements for an earlier, never-published novel, to him as a benevolent patron and experienced practitioner of the genre, and he appears to have played some role in bringing *Sidney Bidulph* into print as well.[4] Thus Janet Todd writes of Sheridan as one of the mid-century's "modest muses," fashioning her literary ambitions according to the constraints of a gendered ideology of public and private spheres, creating "not simply writing but *feminine* writing." Jean Coates Cleary's introduction to the modern edition of *Sidney Bidulph* places the book in the tradition of the "conduct novel – inspired by Richardson, dedicated to him, . . . published as he was dying," and "bear[ing] the Richardsonian legacy into the second half of the eighteenth century." Even Margaret Anne Doody, in her insightful analysis of the novel's treatment of the moral dimensions of action and consequences, describes Sheridan as "a not unworthy follower of Richardson," whose probing of Richardson's fictions produces what "are feminine insights, or at least in the eighteenth century could have been expressed only by a female writer . . . only by a sensibility with a deep knowledge of the meaning of powerlessness, and of lack of control over fate."[5] In short, Sheridan has been represented as the perfect exemplar of the "difference of kind rather than degree" argument, entering the public sphere of letters only in the fully self-enclosed frame of the domestic novel which reinforces the association of the feminine with the private.

In the concluding portion of this chapter, I will turn again to the question of Sheridan's "reading" of *Clarissa* in order to demonstrate the inadequacy of the assumption that she took up the pen only to reinforce Richardson's ideal of the virtuous domestic woman. First, however, following Klein, this chapter will pay closer attention to Sheridan's space – defined as the professional communities within which she moved – and language – the gestures of professional, political, and moral alignment that she makes in her novel and in her correspondence. Through this process, a picture will emerge of a woman whose self-identification as a writer included not only domestic and moral, but also public and political aspirations. By particularizing a number of Sheridan's professional associations, as well as her treatment of a controversial contemporary work in her own first major publication, I hope to model an approach to the mid-eighteenth-century woman writer which allows us to move productively beyond a simplistically gendered public–private dichotomy, while recognizing that such a binary opposition might for some writers in fact serve as a starting point for the construction of a meaningful public identity for the virtuous domestic woman. Thus *Sidney Bidulph* models Harriet Guest's principle that eighteenth-century novels "participate in debates that cut across genres" and "assume readers who are also immersed in periodical literature, in poetry, in histories, readers who discuss plays and parliamentary debates, who perform music, and peer into the windows of print shops."[6]

For the reading of Sheridan as one of Richardson's "daughters," if not inaccurate, does not tell the whole story. Such arguments do not acknowledge the other writer named by Sheridan in "The Editor's Introduction" to her tale of a domestic woman in distress, namely John Home, author of the blank-verse tragedy *Douglas*, first performed in Edinburgh and London in 1756 and 1757, respectively. Sheridan's fictional "Editor" introduces the novel with a private reading, in the old-fashioned English country house of an elderly widow, Cecilia, of Home's very publicly successful play. In the ensuing discussion of the play's moral framework, the unrewarded virtue of the highborn, public-spirited hero Douglas is explicitly paralleled by the hostess to the "unhappy fate of a lady, who was my particular friend" (p. 7), which is about to be narrated in epistles addressed to this same Cecilia as a young woman. This critical blind spot to the invocation of Home, in contrast to the heavy emphasis on Richardson, represents the limitations of many of our current investigations of mid-century women novelists. Rather than employing publication merely to promulgate the essential domesticity of woman, Sheridan is in fact carefully *embedding* the private *within* the public, using Home's nationalistic stage play, which was also enormously popular as a closet drama, to mediate between the novel *Sidney Bidulph* and its readers. Rereading Frances Sheridan through John Home, then, enables us to situate her not only in professional circles of the late 1750s and early 1760s as a writer building a career, but also in the republic of letters as a contributor to the ongoing analysis of the very public, political, and literary issue of virtue.

REREADING FRANCES SHERIDAN'S CAREER: HOME, BUTE, AND THE SHERIDANS

As my example of the "invisible" Home reference has suggested, it is literary historians who have, to some extent, projected Sheridan's modesty and desire for obscurity onto her. Beginning with the biography written by her granddaughter Alicia Lefanu in 1824, Sheridan has been characterized as impeccably domestic, willingly subordinating her own intellectual and professional aspirations to those of her actor-manager-author-lecturer husband Thomas, and focusing her energies on her private duties. Prior to this publication, Frances's correspondence with her cousin Samuel Whyte had appeared in his 1800 *Miscellanea Nova*, revealing a woman whose sphere of activity included mediating the financial obligations of her husband to her cousin and wielding influence of her own to secure personally two successive military places for a friend of Whyte's.[7] From this vantage point, Lefanu can be seen carefully selecting and shaping these materials to present us with a woman who "was acknowledged to excel in every branch of domestic economy," and "never superseded the virtues which are peculiar to her sex, and which rendered her a model, whether considered as a wife, a mother, or a friend."[8] Where Sheridan complains to Whyte that she is "obliged to break off [this letter], as I have been interrupted a dozen times since I sat down to write. Indeed I am so distressed for want of a room to myself, that it discourages me from attempting any thing," Lefanu assures us rather that "while fortune smiled, Mrs. Sheridan . . . felt no inclination to court the favour of the public as a writer, and cheerfully sacrificed the gratification of vanity, which she might have obtained as the possessor of distinguished talents, to the duties and avocations to which, as a wife and a mother, she was more particularly called to attend."[9]

If we read against the grain of Lefanu's text, however, we may still catch glimpses of an ambitious and publicly engaged Frances Sheridan. Lefanu continues, "But on a reverse of circumstances, she could not but have felt pleasure on finding the riches and resources of her mind readily acknowledged and justly appreciated by Mr. Richardson." During the Sheridan family's first residence in London from 1754 to 1756, Frances quickly became the central attraction, according to Lefanu, of "an ingenious and distinguished circle of friends" that included Samuel Richardson, Sarah Fielding, Sarah Scott, Samuel Johnson, and Edward Young. During a second English stay, from 1758 to 1763, Sheridan published *Sidney Bidulph* and wrote two plays, both of which were performed in 1763 at the Drury Lane Theatre, where David Garrick was the manager. In the case of the first play, *The Discovery*, Lefanu quotes a letter from Sheridan to Whyte in which she gleefully boasts that Garrick, that powerful arbiter of the playwright's fate, actually "*solicited*" her to give him the script "as soon as it was seen," unlike "most of *us* poor authors, [who] find a difficulty in getting our pieces on the stage, and perhaps are obliged to dangle after managers a season or two." Sheridan might well have been comparing herself favorably here to John Home, whose first play, *Agis*, was rejected by Garrick in 1749; *Douglas*, his second play, met the same fate in 1755. Tobias Smollett, Robert Dodsley, and, as we shall see, Frances Brooke, were other respectable contemporary authors whose dramatic efforts were rejected. Lefanu, however, apparently embarrassed by her grandmother's lack of modesty, merely notes that Sheridan's phrasing reveals "nothing more than the honest exultation, experienced by even the most modest mind, on its efforts being crowned with *success*."[10]

The dates of Frances Sheridan's second residence in London, and particularly her publication in 1761 of *Sidney Bidulph*, take on further resonance when read in terms of the professional sphere of her husband during this period, especially his connection to the Scottish networks associated with John Home, Lord Bute, and through him, the Prince of Wales (who became George III in 1760). Thomas Sheridan had been a principal actor in Covent Garden, where John Rich was manager, during the family's first London period, when Frances established her initial set of London literary contacts with Richardson, Johnson, and their associates. Relations with Garrick, manager of Drury Lane and rival actor to Thomas, had been cool.[11] By the time of this second trip to London, however, the connections had shifted significantly and, it must have seemed, strategically, toward a more Scottish and Drury Lane circle.[12] As manager of the Smock-Alley Theatre in Dublin in the interim, Thomas Sheridan had mounted the recent London success *Douglas*, calling the play a "Perfect Tragedy" on a gold medal which he had engraved for presentation to Home.[13] This assessment echoed the enthusiastic endorsement of Scottish intellectuals such as David Hume in the wake of the play's triumphant Edinburgh production in December of 1756, but diverged from that of the London reviewers, if not of the audiences, of the tragedy's production at Covent Garden in March 1757. Both the *Monthly Review* and the *Critical Review* were prepared to acknowledge the play's superiority to what they called the "exploded trash" of recent stage productions, but they quarreled explicitly with Hume for ascribing to the playwright "the true theatric genius of *Shakespeare* and *Otway*, refined from the unhappy barbarism of the one, and licentiousness of the other."

Thus this London response to the play was in large part a response to its supporters and their perceived personal and party agendas. The *Monthly*'s article, by Oliver Goldsmith, notes that a play of trifling merit may be overpraised because "party roars in its support" (p. 427), and concludes by chastising Hume for an overcommendation which "perhaps raised too much expectation in some, and excited a spirit of envy and critical prejudice in others" (p. 429).[14] Samuel Johnson, on the one hand, is reported by Boswell to have dismissed the play as not having ten good lines in it, while Garrick, on the other, scrambled to rescind his condemnation of Home's first tragedy *Agis* after seeing the phenomenal success of *Douglas* at the rival house.[15]

Sometime after his return to London in the next year, Sheridan entered into negotiations with Garrick for the position of player on shares at Drury Lane; a contract was finalized in 1760.[16] The importance of Frances's access to what Kevin Berland has called "the charmed circle that could provide friendly recommendations [to play managers]"[17] is revealed in the letter to Whyte partially quoted by Lefanu and referred to above, in which Frances explains, "when I came to town, and shewed it [*The Discovery*] to a few people, what was said to me on the occasion encouraged me to take some pains in the finishing of it. Mr. Garrick was pressing to see it, and accordingly I read it to him myself."[18] In 1763 it was Sheridan and Garrick who played the principal male roles in this successful comedy. Richardson had died in 1761,[19] and though Johnson had praised *Sidney Bidulph*, a permanent breach between Thomas Sheridan and Johnson had occurred in 1762 (to the regret of the young Scot James Boswell, who had hoped to meet Johnson by frequenting the Sheridans' home). The falling-out was associated with the pensions both Johnson and Sheridan had received from the new monarch. Johnson's pension, awarded in 1762, and apparently in part negotiated by Sheridan, was devalued in Johnson's eyes by Sheridan's own reward in 1763 for his work on elocution and pronunciation. In addition to other disparagements, Johnson publicly mocked Sheridan for his gift of the medal to Home.[20]

Meanwhile, Thomas Sheridan's elocutionary lectures and pamphlets had been welcomed and patronized above all by the Scottish literati in Edinburgh and by Scotsmen seeking preferment in England. Tobias Smollett had devoted the lead article in his inaugural issue of *The Critical Review* (1756) to Sheridan's *British Education*, and Sheridan, accompanied by Frances, carried out a very successful lecture tour to Edinburgh in 1761. Boswell speaks of him as very closely associated at this point with Alexander Wedderburne (later Lord Loughbourough), whom he coached in pronunciation, and who had ties with Lord Bute.[21] Sheridan is reported to have "uncommonly" pleased the new king in his lead role in a command performance of *King John* in late 1760,[22] and he dedicated his 1762 *Plan for a Pronouncing Dictionary* to Bute, then George III's prime minister. Thomas's pension of £200 and Frances's profitable play, both coming in the following year, must have appeared to put the Anglo-Irish Sheridans firmly on the path toward future successes that might imitate those of John Home. For the story of Home's London career as playwright, and particularly of Garrick's support of his plays between 1757 and 1760, is inextricable from the larger story of his close association with Bute, who in the late 1750s became the recognized favorite of the Prince of Wales. Bute named Home his private secretary; a pension of £100, later increased to £300, followed, and in 1763, a place of another £300.[23] Expectations of preferment through the Scottish connection were of course disappointed, as Bute's resignation and the eclipse of the perceived Scottish ascendancy in the new king's court followed soon after. But the Sheridans' view of their prospects for the time being may well be preserved in Whyte's retrospective grouping of the Home and Sheridan pensions together "as national compliments and earnests of Sovereign Protection to Genius in the several kingdoms of which those gentlemen were respectively natives." Whyte further describes the granting of Johnson's pension as an elaborate stage play employing "Scotch Actors" and "under the Management of an Irish Prompter" – in other words, Thomas Sheridan.[24]

Historians agree that Johnson's sensitivity to political forms of patronage made him particularly anxious to avoid implications that his own pension represented precisely that; this sensitivity seems also to have determined him to dissociate himself from those whom he saw as compromised flatterers and men of faction – the Scottish circle attached to Bute. While implicitly welcoming the new reign of George III in the terms Bute had helped set for it – that of a "new Augustan age of Learning and the fine arts," presided over by a patriot king encouraging public virtue over private interest[25] – Johnson wanted no part of the Scottish Enlightenment's claim to moral ownership of those terms. His position that their rhetoric of seeking the public good merely masked personal ambition suggests that in his view the two impulses were fundamentally at odds. Yet in discussing literary patronage during Bute's ascendancy, Dustin Griffin has argued convincingly that Johnson's antipatronage rhetoric as it is conveyed to us by Boswell does not present an accurate picture of either Johnson's own authorial activity or that of his contemporaries.[26] More specifically, Richard Sher has shown that Lord Bute, and through him George III, patronized John Home in part because they saw him as a teacher of "patriotic 'virtue'" in his plays, the kind of virtue that would override private interests in favor of the public good.[27]

Thus Home in *Douglas*, for example, shows his heroine Lady Randolph hating war for the losses it brings to wives and mothers, while acknowledging that it is in martial valor that her husband's and son's nobility is manifested, and that it is this quality in them that she loves.[28] Similarly, young Douglas himself is eager to sacrifice in defence of his nation the noble identity he has just recovered; he loses his life at the hands of a villain who, by contrast, uses the national crisis to serve his own greed and desire. From such a point of comparison, the seemingly rigid adherence to principle and to her duty which leads Sheridan's Sidney Bidulph repeatedly to deny her passion for her first lover, the romantically appealing Orlando Falkland, represents more than an extreme version of "the cult of female distress" supposedly fostered by female writers of domestic novels.[29] Rather, this parallel to the characters of *Douglas* lends political and public depth to Sidney's self-denying heroism.

As historians have noted of the Bute circle in general, John Home, teacher of patriotic virtue, does not seem to have believed there was a conflict between his private interests and those of the public. Indeed, the financial security offered by patronage, it was argued, ensured disinterested service to the nation.[30] Since the period of Home's highest favor coincides with Frances Sheridan's publication of *Sidney Bidulph*, containing its praise of *Douglas*'s moral lesson as parallel to that of the upcoming novel, one might posit that the Sheridans, too, felt that their contributions to teaching private virtue furthered the public good and were deserving of reward. Certainly Thomas Sheridan had written, fruitlessly as it turned out, to Richardson in March 1758 to request his intervention, as a "good and public spirited man," with the Speaker of the House of Commons in Sheridan's attempt to prevent the licensing of a rival Dublin theater; in Sheridan's view, it was a clearcut "contest . . . whether virtue or vice, liberty or licentiousness, shall hereafter bear sway in this town."[31] The implication of *Sidney Bidulph*'s foregrounding of *Douglas*, then, is that Frances Sheridan published with an eye on Home, private secretary to the prime minister and pensioner of the King, and that she hoped her public service in the cause of virtue would appeal to Lord Bute as much as to a female readership.

PUBLIC AND PRIVATE: SHERIDAN VS. HOME

That the rift between Johnson and the Sheridans was deep and complexly motivated by such partly unarticulated ideological differences is indicated by Boswell's repeated descriptions of unsuccessful attempts to smooth things over by resolving the more accidental, explicitly identified misunderstandings.[32] In one of these accounts, we are told that Johnson particularly regretted the loss of Frances's conversation as a result of the breach.[33] Johnson is also said to have paid Frances Sheridan's novel the "high compliment" of "I know not, Madam, that you have a right, upon moral principles, to make your readers suffer so much."[34] But the very issues Johnson raises in his supposedly complimentary response to Sheridan's novel are those which bring together the novel and the Home play Johnson so disliked. Indeed, they are the concerns which Sheridan herself makes central in her introductory association of the two works. Read as closet drama, *Douglas* evokes in Cecilia and her female friend "that true testimony of nature to its merit – tears" (p. 5). Pathetic in the extreme, the almost unremitting sufferings of the principal characters in both *Douglas* and *Sidney Bidulph* were central to audience response, as reviewers of both works noted. In the case of *Douglas*, the *Critical Review* quotes in its entirety the dramatic scene in which Lady Randolph hears from the old shepherd Norval of the survival of her long-lost infant son Douglas, a scene which the reviewer calls "the principal, and indeed almost the only interesting scene in the whole play." He also approves the epilogue praising "pity [as] the best / The noblest passion in the human breast: / For when its sacred streams the heart o:erflow, / In gushes pleasure with the tide of woe."[35] The play's epilogue, however, does not stop with the pleasures of pity, going on to argue that "when [pity's] waves retire, like those of *Nile*, / They leave behind them such a golden soil, / That there the virtues without culture grow, / There the sweet blossoms of affection blow" (lines 9–12).

With respect to *Sidney Bidulph*, the *Monthly*'s reviewer charges, in terms similar to, but less jocular than, Johnson's, that "the Author seems to have had no other design than to draw tears from the reader by distressing innocence and virtue, as much as possible." He goes on, in fact, to imply a structural flaw in the moral design, in that an excessively heightened pathetic appeal might work against the public good: "Now, tho' we are not ignorant that this may be a true picture of human life, in some instances, yet, we are of opinion, that such representations are by no means calculated to encourage and promote Virtue."[36] But Sheridan, like Home in his epilogue, claims that there is a rightful continuity between suffering and public virtue as she continues her transition between the play and the upcoming fiction. When the neighboring "sensible" lady who has listened to the play and wept over it goes on to object to the moral disincentive of showing a virtuous, noble, and courageous hero "suddenly cut off by an untimely death, and that at a juncture too, when we might (morally speaking) say his virtues *ought* to have been rewarded," the elderly Cecilia, who has also shed tears, responds by arguing that in a truly Christian moral system, justice can only be sought in "an invisible world where the distributions are just and equal." Stories of unrewarded virtue are thus accurate imitations of life, and the story of the admirable Sidney, like that of the noble hero Douglas, is presented to the public as a confirmation of "that great lesson" of the impermanence and insignificance of "the good things of this life" – for Douglas, presumably, public recognition of his status and his courage; for Sidney, happiness and financial security as the wife of Falkland (pp. 6–7). This moral, of course, brings us full circle to one of Samuel Richardson's principal aims for *Clarissa*.[37] Thus we have Sheridan's dedication and introductory frame combining to disturb that boundary between public and private concerns which a long line of readers have erected around her novel, beginning perhaps with Johnson's admiration in Sheridan of what he rejected in Home.

I have claimed that Home, in his "public" sphere of action as playwright and ministerial favorite, and Sheridan, in her "private" sphere as wife, conversational hostess, and novelist of suffering female virtue, may be seen as pursuing similar aesthetic and political ends. Their representations of woman's role in the encouragement of public virtue diverge, however, and it is in this respect that Sheridan is arguably rewriting Home. Home the playwright has been seen as a "transitional" figure in a continuous public, or masculine, literary tradition stretching from classical tragedy to the "Rise of the Romantic Movement."[38] David Wheeler, for example, has argued that, while retaining "vestiges of heroic tragedy," *Douglas* nevertheless downplays the historical and public significance of the noble characters and their impending battle against the Danes in an effort "simply to bring tears to the eyes of his audience," thereby proving "so much the product of the theoretical milieu in which he was writing" – that is, the theories of sensible response elaborated by Joseph Warton, David Hume, Lord Kames, and others – that the play's "main value now is in exploring the relationship between theory and practice."[39] Some recent work has commented on a closely related feature of *Douglas* of which Sheridan appears to have been acutely aware: the feminization of heroic tragedy which results from the play's focus on Lady Randolph's private story of suffering.[40] Such sentimental feminization, however, reinforces, rather than unsettling or dismantling, a gendered moral system by which masculine virtue is principled, active, and martial, while feminine virtue is passive and affective, longsuffering and loyal, but partial and easily vanquished by the threat of violence. In *Douglas*, therefore, "a woman's . . . [and] a warrior's wish" are constantly at odds (1.107).

Primed by Sheridan's introductory comparison of the young Douglas to her own title character, the eighteenth-century reader familiar with *Douglas* would have experienced a sense of disjunction, for it is Lady Randolph and Sidney whose stories are the more obviously parallel. In keeping with a gendered dichotomy of public and private, each is the helpless observer and deeply feeling victim of male military, dynastic, and sexual competition; each loses a romantically attractive husband just after, or on the eve of, marriage; each reluctantly marries an apparently decent man she does not love; each becomes the innocent target of that husband's suspicions of infidelity; each recognizes that deviations from truth-speaking in the past have returned to mar the present; each is briefly united with either the first lover or with his image in the form of their son, only to experience a second, final loss in death. Sheridan must have noted the powerful effects achieved by Home's telling of his story from Lady Randolph's perspective. She may very well have seen herself as rewriting the Scottish noblewoman's story in the form of the domestic tragedy of a heroic Englishwoman of middling social status: Sidney Bidulph, recounting "the last act of [her] tragic story" (p. 455), tells Cecilia that she has been "set up as a mark" by her "Maker" (p. 459), echoing Lady Randolph, who at the climax of her sufferings describes herself as "the object, now, / On which Omnipotence displays itself, / Making a spectacle, a tale of me" (5.243–45).

Yet Sidney improves upon Lady Randolph by showing her ability to act on principle rather than passion, that quality Home so clearly portrays as making a woman behave counter to the public interest. Sidney's disinterestedness is portrayed as "a perfect resignation to [Omnipotence's] will" (p. 459). In this she is diametrically opposed to Lady Randolph, who commits suicide;[41] indeed, in *Sidney Bidulph* it is the romantic hero Falkland who is suspected of taking his own life, after acknowledging that Sidney's "heroic soul is still unmoved, and above the reach of adversity" (p. 462). Whereas obedience to her mother leads Sidney to conceal her former engagement to Falkland from her husband, Lady Randolph acts as one of "woman's fearful kind" in taking "An oath equivocal, that I ne'er would / Wed one of Douglas' name" when her father holds his sword to her breast soon after her secret marriage (1.191–98). In this she significantly resembles Old Norval's "anxious wife" – both lowborn and female – who, "Foreboding evil," persuades her more honorably inclined husband to hide the truth of the foundling Douglas's birth, thereby contributing to his untimely death (3.140–44).

While in Cecilia's description Sidney's response to her ultimate loss of Falkland mingles "no murmurings . . . , no womanish complainings . . . with the tender, yet noble sentiments of her heart" (p. 460), Lady Randolph, "incapable of change" (1.20), grieves eighteen years for a dead husband, seven of those years while married to the next, and plots with her newly discovered son Douglas "To wrest the lands and lordship from the gripe / Of Randolph and his kinsmen" (4.209–10). *Douglas* surely invokes hereby the threat to orderly inheritance that could be posed by a wife whose affections lay outside her marriage; Randolph's suspicion of an adulterous affair between his lady and the unknown Douglas which leads to the play's catastrophe, though literally false, is grounded in symbolic truth. Granted, this disloyalty to a husband in favor of the son of a previous marriage is a conflict avoided by the structure of Sheridan's plot, but Sidney consciously follows duty rather than desire in a similar circumstance, when as a widow she remains "wedded" to the memory of her lawful husband, rather than returning to her first lover (p. 316). Thus Sheridan asserts the possibility of a truly disinterested female heroism. In doing so, she also justifies her introduction's claim that *Douglas*'s hero and her own heroine display a comparable heroic virtue. This in turn implies a critique of Home's conception of Lady Randolph as a sympathetic female character, when she in fact merely reinforces the traditional separation of the heroic from the feminine. In linking her own story to Home's, Sheridan invokes the gendered public–private distinction upon which the play depends, only to deny that it is a moral distinction.[42]

RICHARDSON'S "DAUGHTER" READS THE EXEMPLARY

The title of this section deliberately echoes numerous critical discussions of women writers who responded to Richardson as his "daughters," or of characters who can be considered "Pamela's Daughters" and "Grandison's Heirs."[43] Such terms have often been used dismissively, extrapolating from the early reviewers' ready identification of novels as "another imitation of Richardson's manner."[44] Ruth Perry has recently summarized the gist of many of these arguments much as I would: "Highly impressionable, lacking invention, naturally imitative, women writers, it is implied, responded to Richardson's genius and eagerly followed his lead."[45] A second limitation of this approach lies in its smoothing out of differences.[46] What should be of interest, after all, is not so much that writers were influenced by Richardson – or Milton, or Pope, for that matter – but rather, *how* they represented and rewrote his work.

Where the latter question has been asked, the tendency has been to look to the later fiction of sensibility for Richardson's most complex legacy. Perry, for example, focuses on fiction of the late 1760s and early 1770s, though she notes in passing "[T]he early admiration of women intellectuals for this book" as represented by Sarah Fielding's 1749 *Remarks on Clarissa.* Isobel Grundy, in arguing that for women writers "Richardson served simultaneously as a teacher to be imitated and a father to be challenged," shifts quickly from his "intimate, chiefly female circle" of readers to a survey of writers of "the following generations," though she sees Richardson's author-contemporaries as taking "a leading role in the contemporary debate swirling round [his] work."[47] In the remainder of this chapter, I will look at how Sheridan publicly "read" the novel *Clarissa*, with its powerful influence not only on the matter and mode of domestic fiction, but also, more hypothetically, on the image of the ideal woman writer and reader of texts.[48] I will do so by contrasting Sheridan's framing of Sidney's story with that of her character's own reading of her mother's example and the ethical principles derived from it. I will argue that Sheridan's novel, framed as it is by explicit allusions to Richardson's *Clarissa* and Home's *Douglas* as culturally prominent discussions of private and public virtue, explicitly and extensively questions the assumption that reading and imitating exemplary virtue can replicate it.

But first, it might be helpful to outline briefly the positions which Sheridan is engaging. Jacqueline Pearson's thorough overview of *Women's Reading in Britain, 1750–1835* illustrates the challenge of such a task, not only by demonstrating the cultural centrality and multivalence of "the sign of the reading woman" in this period, but also by emphasizing the potential for women's resistant reading of any text.[49] Nevertheless, both the anxieties and the possibilities can be sketched out by reference to two mid-century commentators on the issue, Johnson and Richardson. On March 31, 1750, three years after the publication of the first installment of *Clarissa*, Samuel Johnson published an essay in his periodical *The Rambler* on what we now call the novel, though he labeled it "the comedy of romance," a kind of writing in which "life [is exhibited] in its true state, diversified only by accidents that daily happen in the world, and influenced by passions and qualities which are really to be found in conversing with mankind." This famous essay paints a dual portrait of the fiction reader, reflecting the vexed nature of precisely these questions of reading and the exemplary character. Johnson's first image of the reader is that of "a shoemaker who happened to stop in his way at the Venus of Apelles" and "censured" the "slipper ill executed" on the basis of his own experience of "the living world." This "common reader," who actively exercises his judgment, is comically focused on the most mundane elements of realism, but is nevertheless capable of challenging the artist and resisting the desired interpretation. He quickly gives way, however, to a paradoxically more narrowly defined, yet more undifferentiated, readership categorized as "the young, the ignorant, and the idle," "unfurnished with ideas," "not fixed by principles," and "not informed by experience." This latter body of readers are the passive victims of whatever they read, "easily susceptible of impressions," "easily following the current of fancy," and "open to every false suggestion and partial account." Unlike the worldly-wise shoemaker, these readers cannot be trusted with the experiential world in full, but must rather be exposed to "the best examples only," "those parts of nature, which are proper for imitation," so that the text will not be "mischievous or uncertain in its effects."[50]

Most critics have interpreted this essay as endorsing the characterization of a Clarissa as "the most perfect idea of virtue." Johnson does insist, however, that this perfection must produce in the susceptible reader a desire to imitate: this is a "virtue not angelical, nor above probability, for what we cannot credit we shall never imitate, but the highest and purest that humanity can reach, which, exercised in such trials as the various revolutions of things shall bring upon it, may, by conquering some calamities and enduring others, teach us what we may hope, and what we can perform."[51] Following this reasoning, Tom Keymer argues in *Richardson's "Clarissa" and the Eighteenth-Century Reader* that Johnson's theory that such reading teaches the reader "by involving him in instructive 'mock encounters' with difficulties, challenges and dilemmas closely related in kind to those he will encounter in life itself" encapsulates Richardson's goals for the reader of his fiction. Keymer thus asserts that Richardson develops "an aesthetic of difficulty" which "frustrate[s] banal attempts at indoctrination and control," rather initiating the reader into a dynamic and demanding process of interpretation.[52] If this theory of reading, exemplified in *Clarissa's* multiple epistolary perspectives and articulated in Richardson's correspondence inviting reader response, is not always lived up to in the author's practice when faced, as he often was, by a reader whose interpretations diverged significantly from his own, he undeniably points the way to engagement of the reader in a process of dialogue-as-interpretation.

We do not have a similarly extensive record of Sheridan engaging in dialogue-as-interpretation about *Sidney Bidulph*; Boswell does not record her response to Samuel Johnson's complaint that she has made her readers suffer too much. We do have the novel's framing discussion with the elderly Cecilia, and we do have Sheridan's conclusion to the 1767 sequel:

> Mrs. Askham . . . concludes her history with many serious reflections, which, though extremely pious and rational, the Editor chuses to omit, thinking it a compliment due to the judgment of his readers to leave them to make reflections for themselves.[53]

Judging from her presentation of her heroine's exalted virtue, her story's *Clarissa*-like moral that virtue and vice are not dealt "poetic justice" in this life, and her use of Richardsonian plot devices and techniques, I believe Sheridan was sincere in her admiration of Richardson's fiction. Nevertheless, her granddaughter and memoirist, Alicia Lefanu, hints intriguingly that "Although . . . she considered Richardson as her master, she had the good sense and judgment to be conscious of his defects."[54] Lefanu refers this only to the length of the latter's works, but Sheridan's active readership of Richardson in general can be illustrated by her echoes of Richardsonian characters and situations, which act as a commentary on how to read exemplary characters. Although the earliest reviews may seem to imply that such borrowings show a lack of inventiveness on her part – the character of the romantic hero Orlando Falkland, for example, is described as "a composition of features borrowed from Grandison and

Lovelace" (*CR* 11 [March 1761], p. 187) – further reflection makes it clear that the very mix of these two superhuman figures is a comment upon the whole notion of an exemplary hero or larger-than-life villain. Sidney's initial description of Falkland arguably opens an ironic gap between herself and Harriet Byron describing Grandison, as well as between Falkland and the role of Miltonic fallen angel that Lovelace cultivates:

> . . . I'll . . . tell you, that he is neither like an Adonis nor an Apollo – that he has no hyacinthine curls flowing down his back; no eyes like suns, whose brightness and majesty strike the beholders dumb; nor, in short, no rays of divinity about him; yet he is the handsomest mortal man that I ever saw (p. 19).[55]

Unfortunately, Sidney herself misses the import of this assertion of fallible humanity until it is too late.

Because of this ironic gap and its heroine's blindness to it, I believe it can be argued that the novel works against its ostensible illustration of exemplary feminine virtue that meets its reward only in another life. From its use of a frame narrator (the elderly Cecilia who was the addressee and later the editor of Sidney's original letters), to its ironic allusions to Richardson's hero in the character and actions of Orlando Falkland, to its almost complete dependence on Sidney's account of her own experience, the novel seems to go out of its way to undermine its stated moral framework, and, above all, to emphasize the avoidable nature of Sidney's sufferings.[56] If Sheridan adopts Richardson's (and Sarah Fielding's – see chapter 4) model of readerly engagement as the ideal for her audience, she chooses to elaborate upon it by forcing a split between the imitation of virtue and virtue itself. Jane Spencer has noted that the novel "explores and questions female moral authority."[57] In her view, however, this is Sheridan's expression of anxiety about female power *because* it is female, whereas I would argue that Sheridan exposes Sidney's lack of moral authority because she refused to assume moral agency.[58] Like Charlotte Lennox's Arabella of *The Female Quixote*, Sheridan's Sidney is an uncritical reader, but unlike Lennox's heroine, she is so because she consciously and insistently chooses not to interpret for herself. Moreover, while Arabella comes close to innocently instigating murder because her models are morally faulty, Sidney can be seen as enabling a murder, a near-murder, and an actual suicide precisely because she devotes herself to following the exemplary.

Sidney deliberately models her behavior after the example of her self-sacrificing mother, who is in turn a poor reader of the epistolary texts and the character types that determine both her own and her daughter's fate.

Since Sidney fails to read independently, choosing dogmatically to apply precepts established by Clarissa-like exemplars rather than to exert her own will, the female reader can therefore make sense of the novel only by interpreting the conventional moralizing for herself, as the heroine does not. And the reader is thereby forced to question the very viability of the theory that the sign of good reading as imitation of the exemplary, based as it is upon an assumption that one individual's experience can be transferred, in the abstracted form of principle, to another's circumstances, without sacrificing truth and usefulness. Johnson's *Rambler*, as we have seen, makes large claims for the moral utility of the novel genre. But if the virtuous Sidney Bidulph can be such a very faulty reader, the moral waters become muddied.

The first character Sheridan introduces to the reader is Sidney's mother, whose description immediately establishes a disjunction between the exemplary character's authority and her less-than-exemplary interventions in the world: "Lady Bidulph was a woman of plain sense, but *exemplary* piety; the strictness of her notions (highly commendable *in themselves*) now-and-then gave a tincture of severity to her *actions*, though she was ever *esteemed* a truly good woman" (p. 11; my italics). This example, the heroine's primary educational influence, has not merely lost its efficacy in the process of its transfer out of the original context which defined the principles, but has in fact become actively harmful. Lady Bidulph's rigid notions of the justice due to wronged women are her own response to her youthful experience of being abandoned by a guilt-ridden lover as he returned to the woman to whom he had first vowed constancy. As Margaret Anne Doody has put it, Lady Bidulph

> turned rejection into active sacrifice, elaborating a moral motif suggested by her wretched bridegroom into a governing law. The Bidulph women in general, and Sidney most especially, rarely initiate important action; their strength is that of reaction. Refusing to take initiative, they also refuse to be mere passive objects of the percussion of experience. They have a talent for transmuting experience into law.[59]

Thus as Sidney grows into the role of her mother with the passage of time, she in turn becomes remarkable for what Falkland calls her "rigid heart" (p. 313). It is this attraction to inflexible law as the basis for action, which the Bidulphs share with Lennox's Arabella, that becomes the primary instrument of evil in this novel; in its most extreme application, it leads to the death by apparent suicide of Sidney's lover Falkland after she has inexorably insisted that he marry the unworthy woman he was enticed into impregnating.

In several senses, then, Sidney and her mother are insistently portrayed as moral agents, and by inference, as morally implicated in evil outcomes. This moral agency is both unavoidable and ineffectively wielded because, long before the novel's final catastrophe, both women have proven to be very poor readers. Lady Bidulph, as principle personified, is a completely inadequate interpreter of both spoken word and written text. She is described three times in the novel's first few pages as a "literal" woman, taking every word she hears at face value (pp. 14, 21, 25). The implications of this become very serious when, reading Falkland's epistolary explanation of his illicit amour, she refuses to read beyond his introductory statement that he paid a price for the girl because she is "afraid of meeting, at every line, something offensive to decency" (p. 45). Unfortunately, in refusing the contextualization of text, and thereby of the action it describes, she cannot recognize metaphor and irony, and therefore never learns that Falkland was not only seduced, but gulled into paying for an aunt's gambling debts at the same time. Thus literal interpretation is revealed to be, in fact, misinterpretation, and its association with this character who has transformed experience into principle points to the ineffectiveness of all such decontextualizing abstractions.

Paradoxically, this abstraction – the reification of experience into a master text that becomes the type to which all future stories can be reduced – is especially dangerous because it presents itself as the hard-earned fruit of such experience. As the literal embodiment of her story's moral, the living example of victory over the passions, Lady Bidulph is irresistible when instructing her daughter in applying moral law to her own story. When the mother counsels the daughter to reject Falkland, she calls her daughter's experience "a case so parallel" to her own (p. 49), thereby interpreting the pregnant third party as innocent and worthy. At her very worst, Lady Bidulph goes beyond literal interpretation-as-misinterpretation to preinterpretation; her predisposition to a favorable reception of the narrative of Falkland's "victim" invites exploitation, eliciting from the canny Miss Burchell a falsified story that will accord with her auditor's view of Falkland. In this sense, while the plot's most obvious allusions are to *Clarissa* and *Sir Charles Grandison*, the most telling rejoinder may be to Richardson's hopes for the moral effect of his stories, demonstrated first by the latter portions of his *Pamela*, wherein the heroine's "story" becomes a detachable and potent plot agent in itself, applicable across all class barriers and social contexts to the case of any young woman faced with sexual overtures, and later by his collections of instructive sentiments distilled from his novels.[60]

Although it is Sidney herself who conveys to the reader these accounts of her mother's interpretive failures, in accepting the application of her mother's example to her own story she makes it clear that her own decisions are based upon a desire to imitate the exemplary: "my mother is rigid in her notions of virtue; and I was determined to shew her that I would endeavour to imitate her" (pp. 48–49). In another moment of insight, she admits, "My mother praises me, and calls me a heroine. I begin to fancy myself one: our pride sometimes stands in the place of virtue" (p. 54). Still, Sidney refuses to question the moral innocence of her own and her mother's decisions, despite what she calls her mother's "despotic . . . government" of her (p. 50) and despite frequent references to the "partiality," "early prepossessions," and "bias" which determine her mother's views (p. 50). In fact, she appears to believe that the ideal follower of principle should resign moral responsibility altogether, claiming, "Fain would I bring myself chearfully to conform to my mother's will, for I have no will of my own. I never knew what it was to have one, and never shall, I believe; for I am sure I will not contend with a husband" (p. 85). One price Sidney pays for her acquiescence to the force of example is the gradual withering of her own interpretive abilities. When at first she is quick to detect the figurative language her mother misses, the source of this interpretive skill appears to be feeling, what she calls her "heart" (pp. 85, 340). Since the interpretations of the heart are associated with the passions, Sidney is suspicious of them when they come into conflict with the duty prescribed to a virtuous daughter. According to the opening of Johnson's *Rambler* essay, however, the interpretations of the heart might just as well be heard as the voice of experience which tests theoretical and decontextualized knowledge. From this point of view, Sidney's error is to cast herself as Johnson's young, ignorant, and idle, hence passive, reader, rather than as his shoemaker, a dynamic and therefore truly educable reader.

Indeed, the tendency of such mid-eighteenth-century writers as Johnson and Richardson to view fiction as an ideal vehicle by which to disseminate desirable moral values and codes of conduct to receptive readers reflects a preliminary and optimistic response to an expanding print culture, with its potential for the standardization and dissemination of ideologies.[61] That this response was widespread is illustrated by such eighteenth-century educational projects as Hannah More's *Cheap Repository Tracts.* Conversely, Sheridan's portrayal of the exemplary, with its frequent recourse to the metaphor of "literality" and its intertextual relationship to Richardson's novels, reveals a suspicion of the very reifying tendency of print that promised to make fiction such a powerful instrument of education. Yet this suspicion does not put her work in the camp of a Scriblerian satirist, lamenting the deluge of print that laps even at the barricaded doors of the elite poet's retreat. Rather, as the triangulation of *Sidney Bidulph* between *Douglas* and *Clarissa* demonstrates, Sheridan credits her readers with the capacity to read interpretively for themselves. Thus, as I have noted, the sequel to *Sidney Bidulph*, a second-generation story, neatly sidesteps the standard conclusion of the exemplary tale by "chus[ing] to omit" the tale-teller's "many serious reflections" as the "Editor's" "compliment . . . to the judgment of his readers." It seems fitting that the sequel's plot is resolved, after the faulty conduct of Sidney's children has embroiled them in irretrievable catastrophes, not with the deaths of those children, but rather, with the death of Sidney as the embodiment of the inflexible code that has become a straitjacket rather than a guide. Sheridan's second generation of decidedly unheroic characters (Sidney's two daughters and Orlando Falkland, Junior, who between them make errors of passion that step far beyond the bounds of propriety so carefully respected by their elder) perhaps points out of the text toward a second generation of readers of exemplary fiction, readers more worldly and sophisticated than the ignorant and idle young persons Johnson worries about, and therefore more prepared to engage in the sort of dynamic reading which Richardson invites for his *Clarissa*, yet at times attempts to withdraw.

FRANCES SHERIDAN VS. SIDNEY BIDULPH

It might appear that Sheridan's argument for Sidney Bidulph's heroic disinterested virtue in the context of Home's *Douglas* is in tension with the novel's critique of the rigid application of principle, or imitation of exemplary femininity. Some of Sidney's sufferings indeed arise from the practice of disinterestedness in a sinful world: she and her mother place the good of unacknowledged or unborn children and weak-willed men ahead of their own desire, while suffering at the hands of unscrupulously self-gratifying women. At the same time, Sidney's very self-consciousness in imagining herself playing the role of heroine points to the act of will involved in choosing her role models, just as does Sheridan's tantalizing invocation of the heroic Douglas and the helplessly passionate Lady Randolph. Indeed, the novel is something of an extended study in the psychology of heroism: as we have seen, Sidney herself is aware that pride and a desire to please her mother strengthen her heroic impulses. This human touch still clearly places her above the other characters who label her a hero for their own manipulative and accusatory purposes (pp. 307, 462), and even further above the villainous Mrs. Gerrarde, the aunt who "sells" Miss Burchell to Falkland and misapplies the title to herself (pp. 201–3). Nevertheless, in her refusal to take on personal moral authority, Sidney does not rise to her fullest heroic potential, a potential that might simply have made her tragic fall the greater – or might have forced her author to portray a greater congruence between public duty and private reward. For if Sidney had been allowed to follow her better judgment, of course, the novel would not have been a tragedy, and Sheridan's challenge would have been that of celebrating a fully identified female virtue in its public implications.

Would Sheridan have got away with it? I think so. From the evidence of the *Critical Review*, it is clear that separate and gendered public and private spheres were not understood by all contemporary readers or viewers as the fundamental categories of response to the two works. While we have seen that *Sidney Bidulph* is identified by the *Critical*'s reviewer as a skillful and heightened copy of *Clarissa* and *Sir Charles Grandison*, the novel's characters are praised as being "eminently amiable, noble, and heroic," terms which had been applied to Home's Douglas, and Sheridan is invited to "continue to exert those talents, so honourable to herself, so useful, so entertaining to society, and particularly so beneficial to the republic of letters."[62] Presumably, then, Frances Sheridan inhabits that same republic of letters by whose laws David Hume was called to account in 1757 for allowing his private "bias of friendship and affection" in favor of John Home's *Douglas* to overwhelm what is "due to truth, taste, and judgment, which we cannot think any man hath a right to sacrifice, even to the most intimate private connections." The *Critical* concludes its review of *Douglas* by admitting that "We should not indeed have dwelt so long on the little obvious faults to be found in this tragedy, had not Mr. *David Hume*, whose name is certainly respectable in the republic of letters, made it absolutely necessary."[63] The standard of judgment invoked here is neither the sex of a writer, nor the "gender" of the tradition within which a work places itself, but rather, the extent to which each represents a mutually reinforcing balance of disinterested, resigned, private heroism with a courageous, honorable, and patriotic sense of public responsibility.

What, then, has this brief examination of space and language in Frances Sheridan's life and work suggested about her as a mid-eighteenth-century woman writer? First, we have seen that, rather than being adequately identified as one of Richardson's daughters, she was part of several London professional communities whose membership and boundaries were fluid. Indeed, she was highly successful in forming the professional connections so essential to the ambitious writer, adapting those connections in response to need and opportunity, and using them to further her aspirations to influence and patronage. Secondly, in the textual parallels she explicitly drew, as well as in implicit allusions, she acknowledged the existence of gendered assumptions about virtue and appropriate spheres of action, but challenged those assumptions by asserting the responsibility of every individual, male and female, to practice a self-denying private virtue for the public good. Her portrayal of heroism asserts its availability to both women and men, while elaborating on the complex mix of social role-playing, pride, and misunderstanding which can coexist with principled virtue. Finally, contemporary reception of Sheridan's work indicates a climate of acceptance for such a model, proposed by a woman, suggesting that the "republic of letters" ideal of the 1750s and 1760s allowed for a public dimension to women writers' lives that was not entirely acceptable to Sheridan's early nineteenth-century biographer and has been invisible to many late twentieth-century feminist historians. Like John Home, Sheridan sought for herself a place in a political and literary-professional, publicly significant sphere. Again like Home, she did so through a text that could be read in an intimate private setting while promising its readers access to a public virtue. Our model of the public sphere of eighteenth-century English letters, then, ought to be modified to accommodate both "masculine" and "feminine" embodiments of the virtuous citizen. In other words, we need to acknowledge that participation in the overlapping political and publishing spheres could transcend gender and genre for writers who claimed membership in the republic of letters. Indeed, for Sheridan's contemporary Frances Brooke, to whom I turn next, there was no literary engagement distinct from political engagement, and to read her work effectively, as I will show, we must be prepared to erase the boundary between the two.

CHAPTER 2

The politicized pastoral of Frances Brooke

> But whither am I wandering? I am got, without knowing how, into politics, a subject of all others the least agreeable either to my sex or to my disposition.
>
> (*The Old Maid* 31 [June 12, 1756])[1]

> I understand Mrs. Brooke has been a Devilish instrument against you, but has done no harm, and is blown up.
>
> (Patrick Murray, Lord Elibank, to General James Murray, March 24, 1765)[2]

A comparative examination of eighteenth-century women writers and their texts clearly shows wide variations in the degree to which these writers envisioned themselves as what H. T. Dickinson calls "political agents."[3] Once we have moved beyond an oversimplified notion of mid-century women as restricted to a domestic, or private, sphere of action distinct from the public spheres of politics and letters, we can begin to see some variations in agency represented in records of professional lives, in paratextual statements, or in actual publications. Some writers clearly saw their publications, *pace* Habermas, participating in a public sphere that was overtly political, and not merely literary.[4] Whereas I will argue in my third chapter that Sarah Scott intervened in a self-conscious but deliberately disembodied and fragmented sense in a republic of letters, focusing in her historical biographies on the social responsibilities of the "private" gentleman of property, I have shown that Frances Sheridan more explicitly connects Sidney Bidulph's story with the public genre of tragedy in the politically resonant form of John Home's *Douglas*.[5] On the spectrum of political engagement represented in this study, however, Frances Brooke's stands out as the most explicit and particular. She is the sort of political agent of whom Dickinson writes, lending her support to specific public policies and using her writing to advocate particular positions within a broadly defined Country ideology.

Nevertheless, there has been a tendency, in the limited critical discussion of the work of Frances Brooke, to label that work as "sentimental," and therefore as by definition eschewing engagement in the political sphere. Although our understanding of the theory and literature of sensibility has in recent years benefited from a deepening awareness of its social and political investments, sentimental novels by women have tended to be dismissed as a homogeneous and generically typical mass, not taking significant positions on any matter other than marriage choice, as the issue of presumably greatest importance to all women. In G. J. Barker-Benfield's detailed study of *The Culture of Sensibility*, for instance, Brooke's first novel, *The History of Lady Julia Mandeville,* is the only one of her works to be mentioned, as a passing illustration of a "virtually prefabricated" representation of peasants that suggests unselfconsciously clichéd and derivative writing.[6] Brooke admittedly published four novels easily classified as sentimental: two popular novels of her own, *The History of Lady Julia Mandeville* and *The History of Emily Montague*, and two novel translations, *Letters from Juliet, Lady Catesby, to her Friend, Lady Henrietta Compley* (by Marie-Jeanne Riccoboni) and *Memoirs of the Marquis de St. Forlaix.* Moreover, other works share devices and themes with the literature of sensibility: a later novel, *The Excursion*, blends the style and ironic tone of Sterne's *A Sentimental Journey* with the worldly third-person narrator of Henry Fielding; the two tragedies *Virginia* and *The Siege of Sinope* celebrate suffering female virtue; and the early pastoral odes and two later comic operas (*Rosina* and *Marian*) celebrate the rural simplicity so commonly idealized in sentimental novels.

Merely to group these works as sentimental, however, is to raise complicating questions: *Emily Montague* contains detailed discussions of the newly acquired colony of Quebec, the two tragedies are structured around the ideals of civic virtue represented for many eighteenth-century Britons by the Roman republic, and the ironic portrayal of a sensible, yet enterprising, young lady's entrance into the London "world" in *The Excursion* surely complicates the literary conventions of the novel of sensibility. Then there are the publications that do not fit the category in any way: *The Old Maid*, a periodical published weekly from November 1755 to July 1756, and the translation of Claude Millot's *Elements of the History of England*, with a substantial translator's "Advertisement" and notes throughout.

Where Brooke's commentary on public affairs has been acknowledged, it has often been explained as motivated by purely personal concerns.

Discussion of *Lady Julia Mandeville* by Canadianists is restricted to noting that Canada is mentioned as a useful colonial acquisition; Lorraine McMullen, Brooke's biographer, typically comments in introducing the relevant passage that "Frances Brooke's initial interest in Canada no doubt stemmed from her husband's chaplainship."[7] Thus *The History of Emily Montague*, often labeled the "first Canadian novel," is even more likely to be found to reflect the Anglican and assimilationist views of Frances's husband John, chaplain to the English garrison of Quebec immediately after the Conquest. In such a view, the work's commentary on race, religion, comparative culture, and colonial governance is borrowed, momentarily opportunistic, and poorly thought out. Robert Merrett, in an illuminating analysis of the "politics of romance" in *Emily Montague*, which clearly outlines Brooke's use of sensibility as a means for "the lesser, Anglican rural gentry" "of healing their own political displacement," nevertheless argues that Brooke "defends the Crown and attacks the Court . . . in simple-minded, conventionally middle-class ways."[8]

A less narrowly biographical, but initially limited body of criticism has focused on Brooke's feminist politics. Beginning with Canadian literary criticism of *Emily Montague*, such readings first tended to search for an anachronistic feminism against an assumed backdrop of prejudice against women writers.[9] Turning more recently to Brooke's first known publication, her 1755–56 periodical *The Old Maid*, and her later novel *The Excursion*, however, this work has begun to put pressure on the notion of Brooke as "mere" sentimental writer by representing her views of women's involvement in public life. Paula Backscheider and Hope Cotton, editors of *The Excursion*, have noted that Brooke launched her career at an auspicious time for women writers, and that Maria, *The Excursion*'s heroine, represents a sympathetic portrait of a writer's aspirations and experiences in the London literary marketplace. Min Wild, writing on *The Old Maid*, has argued that in the persona of "Mary Singleton, Spinster," Brooke, using the discourses of "civic humanism, politeness, and sensibility," "attempts to negotiate herself into the position not only of a legitimate speaking individual, but also of one capable of independent judgment and criticism in spheres far removed from the domestic." And predating such feminist criticism was the refreshing claim by Kevin Berland, in a 1986 article on philosophical influences on Brooke's *History of Emily Montague*, that "Brooke's own version of sensibility suggests that she developed it more or less independently [of Richardson, Sterne, and Mackenzie], though drawing on common sources" from "literary, religious, and philosophical traditions."[10]

The latter half of this chapter, then, will look at the full range of Brooke's known publications in order to trace her adoption of a consistent and outspokenly political stance which can be broadly described as a feminist Country ideology, expressed through a recurring use of the pastoral mode in her work, even though her specific positions on contemporary events and culture may vary across a spectrum of socially conservative "Tory" and more politically radical "Whig." But first, as a starting point for identifying and interpreting this stance, I will show that Brooke's contemporaries responded to both her texts and her public activity primarily in terms of her views, and only secondarily in terms of her gender. I will also outline Brooke's background, circumstances, and connections to show her links with segments of society characteristically adhering to a Country ideology. Ultimately, my chapter will show that Brooke practiced the greater part of her career in a climate of significant openness to women's involvement in the public sphere of letters, and that she exploited this openness to engage much more fully in the intellectual and political and artistic life of her day than has generally been recognized.

CONTEMPORARIES READ FRANCES BROOKE

A categorization of Brooke as nonpolitical is clearly at odds with the complaints of some of Brooke's contemporaries. The second epigraph to this chapter is from a letter written to General James Murray, appointed military and then civil governor of the new colony of Quebec after the 1759 Conquest. Although a longtime friend of John Brooke, and a supporter of a 1761 petition to the Society for the Propagation of the Gospel in Foreign Parts (SPG) to have him appointed as its missionary to Quebec, Murray had been expressing growing frustration at Brooke's tendency to "interfere with things that do not concern him," adding, "I was in hopes the Ladys [Frances and her sister Sarah, recently arrived] would have wrought a change, but on the Contrary they meddle more than he does."[11] While the immediate reference here seems to be to the family's relations with the Quebec garrison officers, Murray and his supporters resented the Brookes' efforts, in Canada and in London, to further the cause of an Anglican establishment in Quebec and, more broadly, policies aimed at subordinating and assimilating the resident French. On Frances's part, these efforts involved not only publishing *Emily Montague* and, accompanied by Samuel Johnson, personally carrying a second petition on behalf of her husband to the secretary of the SPG, but also presenting her own detailed account of the state of Protestant-"papist" relations in Quebec, an account which explicitly criticizes Murray's handling of those relations.[12]

It is at this point, with Murray and the Brookes increasingly at odds over the former's conciliatory policies toward the French, that Murray complains in 1765 of a "Cabal" against him which is "assisted by the Revd. Doctr. Brookes" and which will be represented by "the Friends of these people" in London, eliciting Lord Elibank's reassurance that Mrs. Brooke, though a "Devilish instrument," has not succeeded in doing him harm. Elibank's assessment notwithstanding, Murray was recalled in 1766. The comment of one of his supporters, writing to him from Quebec about the adherence of the Brookes and their "Connections" to the new Governor, Guy Carleton, may represent Frances's political influence more accurately: "particular Attention is paid to Mrs. Brookes either from fear of her bad Tongue, or from Gratitude for the good offices she rendered in retailing the Scandal of Quebec at the Tea Tables of London."[13] The statement reflects a common trope in *ad hominem* criticism of Brooke: the motive of the attack is a political contest, but its mode is the invocation of a negative female stereotype – here, that of the malicious female tongue.

Some years before Brooke's Canadian episode, she had "meddled" publicly in the politics of what she later represents as "the important empire of the theatre; an empire on the faithful administration of which depend[s], not only national taste, but in a great degree national virtue."[14] This time her target was David Garrick, manager of the Drury Lane Theatre and by far the most powerful figure in the London theater world at the time. The suspicions Brooke gave voice to in the preface to her self-published tragedy *Virginia* – that in addition to rejecting her play, Garrick had deliberately held her manuscript in order to prevent its being produced anywhere else as a rival to Samuel Crisp's version of the same story, staged at Drury Lane in 1754 – were, as I noted in my previous chapter, of the sort regularly aired by mid-century authors seeking access to the London theatres.[15] What was perhaps more unusual was the pointedness of Brooke's attack – John Rich had subsequently rejected the play for Covent Garden, but is not identified in the preface – and its continuity with a similarly weighted attack on Garrick's performance of the title role of *King Lear* which appeared in a 1756 issue of her *Old Maid*. This discussion of the Nahum Tate version of the play, although occasioned by a performance of it in the rival Covent Garden Theatre with the actor Spranger Barry as Lear, nevertheless manages to excuse Barry's choice of the version and praise his superiority as an actor, while taunting Garrick for betraying his vaunted idol Shakespeare: "one cannot help remarking particularly, and with some surprize, that Mr. *Garrick*, who professes himself so warm an idolater of this inimitable poet, . . . should yet prefer the adulterated cup of *Tate*, to the pure genuine draught, offered him by the master he avows to serve with such fervency of devotion."[16]

Brooke's opponent appears to have found her intervention threatening; not only did he restore a considerable proportion of Shakespeare's original lines some months after the attack,[17] but the bitterness continues in his summary narrative to the novelist Marie-Jeanne Riccoboni almost ten years later: "I am not acquainted with Mrs Brooke: she once wrote a play, which I did not like, & would not act, for which heinous offence, she vented her female Spite upon Me, in a paper she publish'd call'd ye *Old Maid*, but I forgive her as thoroughly, as her Work is forgotten."[18] Like General Murray, Garrick belittles Brooke's criticisms and their efficacy by feminizing them, but his very gesture belies his words. And so also does his private meddling here in Brooke's career: he uses this letter to insist that Riccoboni not agree to use Brooke as translator of her future novels, despite the French novelist's view that Brooke's 1760 translation of her *Lady Juliet Catesby* was superior to any other.

The feud with Garrick was exacerbated no doubt by Brooke's becoming manager of the rival King's Theatre together with Mary Ann Yates in 1773, and it is documented in several short-tempered notes between the two.[19] Its final episode was a public one, however, and its publicity was again instigated by Brooke in a notorious satiric representation of the recently retired Garrick in her 1777 *Excursion*. Here Brooke does not claim that Garrick rejects female playwrights on the basis of their sex alone, rather accusing him of choosing on the basis of influential connections; it is Garrick, once again, who genders the issue in his anonymously published review of the novel. He defends the theater manager (himself) at length for producing the works of "female writers" when they were "unprotected and unpatronized," as a proof that he "was always more readily influenced by the feelings of humanity than by the recommendations of the great," and finally challenges Brooke to produce "the name of the great *beauty* who wrote it [the novel]," insinuating that "Mrs. Brooke's person" is not sufficiently attractive to motivate the manager's habitual chivalry.[20]

Interestingly, if attacks on Brooke use her sex – or more precisely, her supposedly unattractive appearance and stereotypically feminine spite and scandal-mongering – as one of their weapons, accounts of her work as author do not adopt a condescending tone. Although the *Monthly*'s commentator on Brooke's first published volume, containing *Virginia* and a collection of poems, does hint that he would have pointed out some faults in the tragedy, had the author not expressed diffidence on the basis of her sex and youth,[21] this follows a favorable comment on Brooke as a new addition to "the number of learned and ingenious Ladies whom we have had the honour of celebrating." Indeed, "ingenious" is the adjective for the author which occurs most frequently in both complimentary and negative reviews, and her work is typically described, here in a review of *Lady Julia Mandeville*, as "distinguished from the common productions of the novel tribe, by ease and elegance of style, variety and truth of character, delicacy and purity of sentiment."[22] These descriptions of style accord with the personality reflected in contemporary accounts, whether from the Quebec colony: ("Mrs. Brooke is a very sensible agreeable woman, of a very improved understanding and without any pedantry or affectation") or from *Town and Country*'s "Biographical Sketch of the late Mrs. Brooke" ("she was as remarkable for her virtues, gentleness, and suavity of manners, as for her great literary accomplishments. She was esteemed by Johnson, valued by Miss Seward, and courted by all the first characters of her time").[23] After their first meeting, when Brooke was fifty, the twenty-two-year-old Frances Burney wrote, "Mrs Brooke is very short & fat, & squints, but has the art of shewing Agreeable Ugliness. She is very well bred, & expresses herself with much modesty, upon all subjects. – which in an *Authoress*, and Woman of *known* understanding, is extremely pleasing."[24]

It would seem, then, that criticism of Brooke's publications arose not out of their aesthetic limitations or their "feminist" positions, but out of her readiness to take public and partisan stances that others saw as opposing their policies and achievements, whether in the newly acquired colony of Quebec or in the theatrical empire of London. Even when Brooke herself uses her sex as a disclaimer, or as an explanation for negative responses to her work, I suggest that we ought to retain a skeptical stance regarding the objective validity of her statements. Whether it be a case of the first epigraph's Mary Singleton, the "Old Maid" persona of Brooke's early periodical, coyly denying a taste for politics after a rousing call for Britons, engaged in a new war with France, to value fame as a means of reviving "our ancient military Spirit" (*OM* 31 [June 12, 1756], pp. 255–58), or the self-professed coquette Arabella Fermor in *Emily Montague* claiming that "For my part, I think no politics worth attending to but those of the little commonwealth of woman,"[25] or the author in her own voice, in the preface to the second edition of *The Excursion*, asserting that her work has been subject to criticism because of "an illiberal spirit of prejudice, and perhaps of affectation, which has lately endeavoured to exclude from the road of literary fame, even by the flowery paths of romance, a sex which . . . is perhaps, when possessed of real genius, most peculiarly qualified to excel in this species of moral painting" (p. 1), such statements ought to be taken as localized rhetorical devices, perhaps even intended as blinds to the explicit and partisan position being elaborated in the surrounding text. It should be noted also that Brooke spent almost her entire career based in London, frequently separated for long periods from her husband as he pursued his professional duties, not only in overseas colonies, but also in country livings. Given the tendency of her enemies to attack her weak points, their silence on this subject suggests that her furthering of her career in this way was judged respectable and not worthy of remark.

BROOKE AND COUNTRY IDEOLOGY

Frances Moore was born into a family of Anglican clergy; her father, both of her grandfathers, and the uncle in whose household she was raised after she was orphaned all held Lincolnshire livings. At about thirty-two years of age, she became the second wife of an Anglican clergyman who held several positions in Norwich and Norfolk, as well as later military chaplaincies; later her only son took orders and held several livings in Lincolnshire, though she would have preferred to have him go into the law. Todd's conclusion that these connections created the "public image" of Brooke, guaranteeing that she would be viewed as "utterly respectable," does not tell the whole story of such a background in the first half of the eighteenth century.[26] As historians of the period's political and religious history have shown, the subculture of traditional country clergy families was a site of instability, where self-interest and principle mingled in competition for livings, under pressure from Catholics, Dissenters, and then Methodists, and accompanied by debate over the function of an Established Church in an era of growing nationalism and colonial expansion. In general, the clergy were a substantial force in the "Country party" of early and mid-eighteenth-century politics, that shifting coalition of Tories and Opposition Whigs whose rhetoric idealized a traditional, hierarchically structured agrarian past in contrast to the urban bourgeois culture gaining increasing socioeconomic and government (Court) influence in the period.[27] With respect to social station and economic means, both Brooke's family and her husband fit the profile of the country clergy whose status was genteel, but whose often limited incomes made it increasingly difficult to maintain a comfortable style of life in an age of growing consumerism and transformation of the rural economy.[28] This sense of tension between a traditionally elevated status and an economic descent is of course represented in numerous contemporary fictional portraits of clergymen, most famously Henry Fielding's Parson Adams.

Women of country clergy families were often privileged with a good education that enabled them to contribute to the rhetoric emanating from this group, whether in the form of pamphlets, sermons, or behind-the-scenes lobbying.[29] In Brooke's case, for example, when we read in Arabella and William Fermor's words that "the church of England [religion is] like an elegant well-dressed woman of quality, 'plain in her neatness,'" is "best adapted" "to a limited monarchy like ours," and "is so much more calculated to make [the French habitants] happy and prosperous as a people" (pp. 80, 210, 209), the phrases closely echo those of her husband in his own 1766 petition to Governor Murray for a grant of the Roman Catholic bishop's land and buildings in Quebec in support of the Church that, "besides its being the Establishment by Law, appears to his clearest judgment and conscience . . . to be better and more happily constituted, than any Christian Establishment that he hath known or read of, to be subsisting now or ever to have taken place in the World."[30] Brooke was surely, however, speaking from a position she herself had a long-term familiarity with, and allegiance to, in her own right. In addition to her background, we know that her active campaign for her husband's appointment as SPG missionary to Canada included statements of her own to the Society characterizing the religious views of the French priests and religious orders, the Lorette Indians, the French Canadians, and the governor (he "gives every Discouragement to Protestants, is indifferent to all Religions, an excellent Officer, but cannot govern his passions").[31]

Hopes of a financial establishment for her family and friends certainly played a part in this position-taking, since we know that Brooke used, or tried to use, her connections to secure places for her husband, her close friend Richard Gifford (also a clergyman), and later her son, both before and after the Canadian sojourn.[32] Thus her dedication of *Emily Montague* to Sir Guy Carleton, the governor who replaced Murray in Quebec, does not necessarily, as Merrett suggests, "[mirror] the facts behind the reversal of British policy" (i.e. toward appeasement of the French populace), while "it fails to grasp this policy."[33] Rather, Brooke presents as established, and to Carleton's credit, precisely the sort of "balanced constitution" of military leadership, British law, and unity under the Church of England that she believed needed to be fought for in the new colony: "Were I to say all your excellency has done to diffuse, through this province, so happy under your command, a spirit of loyalty and attachment to our excellent Sovereign, of chearful obedience to the laws, and of that union which makes the strength of government, I should hazard your esteem by doing you justice" (p. 1).

Critics have associated the Country ideology with eighteenth-century pastoral modes, which nostalgically celebrate a bygone rural order and lament the degeneration of the times, a degeneration emanating outward from the urban monster London and represented by the predominantly georgic long poem and the novel of individual self-improvement.[34] As April London has explained:

> georgic and pastoral are transformed in the eighteenth-century novel from contrastive modes to combative ones that are both mutually informing and antagonistic. . . . Because their meanings emerge from such defined positional contexts, pastoral and georgic in contemporary novels always implicitly invoke the competing mode. For those writing within the georgic mode, pastoral thus comes to stand for an effeminate, pleasure-seeking aristocracy; conversely, for those who align themselves with pastoral, georgic signals the undifferentiated embrace of change and male acquisitiveness, qualities associated with a new middling class (pp. 5–6).

London argues further that the conservative writers of the 1760s and 1770s novel of sensibility used the pastoral for the sake of "its high cultural associations," adding that it had "acquired additional appeal to the hierarchically minded by virtue of its decline in literary fashionability over the previous fifty years." The choice of the pastoral mode is thus in part a reaction against the Richardsonian model of the self-made heroine who reforms the man of property to create a forward-looking, middle-class, patriarchal community. The pastoral in these conservative novels, London claims, "comes to stand for an elite ideal of male communion made possible by withdrawal from an interested world."[35]

This reading offers a point of approach to an author like Brooke, whose works consistently employ pastoral landscapes and motifs in politically conservative ways, from the components yoked together in her first volume, *Virginia* and the poems, to her late comic operas whose self-enclosed pastoral romances were performed against a 1780s backdrop of revolutionary political and social debates. It also raises questions, however, about how a woman writer might participate in, and modify, this celebration of elite male community. I will argue that Brooke works to make the traditional and clichéd mode of the pastoral responsive to a continually changing climate, whether personal, professional, or political – as the patriot hopes centered on Prince Frederick move into the Seven Years' War, then the accession of George III, the peace negotiations, the Wilkite crisis, and the war with the American colonies. Throughout these shifts in the political landscape, as I will show, Brooke consistently speaks to the specific situation. As a result, Brooke's adaptations of the pastoral through the course of this body of work produce what I see as a dynamically feminist and particularized Country ideology, one that insists on making room in the pastoral mode, and by implication, in a series of conservative political positions, for female and middle-class professional aspiration.[36]

This consistent stance may go far, indeed, to explain Brooke's little-understood relationships with several citizens of the literary-professional world well-known for their conservative social and political stances: Tobias Smollett, Arthur Murphy, Samuel Johnson, and Anna Seward. The first two of these connections have a known political dimension. James Basker, Smollett's biographer, has linked Smollett's very encouraging review of Brooke's *Virginia* and poems in one of the earliest issues of the *Critical Review* not only with his empathy over Brooke's failure to get the play staged, so parallel to his own experience with *The Regicide*, but also with Brooke's own endorsement, in her *Old Maid* periodical, of Smollett's project for an academy for the regulation of English language and letters.[37] Like Smollett, Arthur Murphy was a journalist actively supporting the administrative status quo against the voices of "the mob" through the years of the Seven Years' War.[38] At this time, Brooke was writing to her friend Richard Gifford that "Murphy has promis'd me now & then a Paper: if you have read his Gray's Inn Journals you will know this is an offer not to be despis'd."[39] Murphy's political and professional leanings appear to have been very compatible with those of Brooke; with the advent of peace negotiations in 1762, for example, Murphy's journalism argued for the expendability of the sugar islands Martinique and Guadeloupe, just as Brooke did in her 1763 *History of Lady Julia Mandeville*.[40]

Johnson, in turn, appears several times in Brooke's letters of the 1750s, cited as a professional authority to lend weight to her advice to Gifford for the furthering of his own career; thus, "Believe me for Johnson says so an Author's first two or three Works must be in a Manner given away to get a Name."[41] By implication Brooke was herself benefiting from

Johnson's expertise and contacts in the London publishing world; that their relationship was a comfortable one is suggested by Johnson's mirroring comment, in a 1756 letter to Charlotte Lennox, "I have seen Mrs. Brookes, and Miss Reid, since I saw you, and I heard of you at bothe houses, yet, what much surprised me I heard no evil."[42] As we have seen, this link goes beyond the purely professional: when Brooke returned from Canada in 1764 bearing a petition to the SPG, Johnson accompanied her, implying his support for this initiative.

The claim for Brooke's connection with Anna Seward is based not only on an often repeated anecdote about a gathering of wellwishers before the former's departure for Canada, which names Seward, in addition to Johnson, Hannah More, George Keate, and James Boswell as among the company present,[43] but also on the poet's warm praise of Brooke's achievements in letters to the author and to other friends in the 1780s and 1790s.[44] It seems reasonable to conclude that Seward's and Brooke's mutual understanding was based, despite their contrasting provincial-amateur and urban-professional modes of life and their ostensible Whig versus Tory sympathies, in their shared allegiance to a literary sensibility founded upon a Country ideal of patriotism and private virtue.[45]

Nonexistent connections are also revealing in their absence. Unlike her colleague Charlotte Lennox, whose career I trace in chapter 4, Brooke appears not to have cultivated patrons in high places; the only dedications to her works are those of *Virginia* to Lady Elizabeth Cecil, a friend to the family in Tinwell, where Frances's uncle, brother-in-law, and cousin were successive incumbents, and of *Emily Montague* to Governor Guy Carleton, a dedication clearly serving a specific political function, as I have argued above. These dedications, then, assert a reciprocity – by means of a claim of friendship or of a statement of political support – that departs from the traditional dedication's deferential emphasis on the social and cultural distance separating the author and the dedicatee.[46] In her first novel, Brooke explicitly extols the independence of the country gentleman as ideal, and critiques the behavior of "great men" who deceive worthy gentlemen in reduced circumstances with promises of preferment, whether ecclesiastical or political. Her rhetoric in these passages is not only typical of the Country party, but also differs again in its basis in political principle from the thinly disguised personal attacks of contemporary authors such as Charlotte Lennox on Lady Isabella Finch in her *Life of Harriot Stuart*,[47] or Samuel Johnson on Lord Chesterfield in his dictionary definition of a "patron." It is to the political arguments intrinsic to Brooke's works that I now turn.

POLITICAL OPTIMISM AND THE FEMINIZED PASTORAL

Although published in 1756, after the launch of her periodical, Brooke's tragedy *Virginia* and the accompanying odes and pastorals were composed in the early 1750s, if not earlier. The story on which the tragedy is based, Livy's account of the virtuous young Virginia whose father, the Roman centurion Virginius, kills her by his own hand rather than allowing her to become the mistress of the tyrannical decemvir Appius, clearly struck a chord with those espousing the themes of civic humanism in the early 1750s, judging from the simultaneous production, by the rival Drury Lane and Covent Garden theaters, of two other plays based on the same story.[48] Brooke's play, unlike that of at least one of her rivals, makes such themes very explicit: Virginius is beloved by his soldiers for his "brave, plebeian, honest Deeds" despite their general loss of courage under "th'oppressive Hand of Tyranny"; Virginia acts as "a Roman Maid / Who loves her Honour and her Liberty"; "her Cause is the Cause of Rome, / Of Liberty, and Virtue."[49] The patricians who "arrogate all Honours" to themselves and "scorn Alliance" with the plebians in marriage are in fact "Luxurious Slaves" whose actions prove them unworthy of "the purer Blood of our Plebians" (3.2). The blame for this situation ultimately rests on the plebians, who "rais'd this Power. . . / To give us Laws, the Wonder of the World," but made the mistake of allowing the patrician Tarquins "Power unlimited," which is "only fit for Jove" (1.7). Livy's celebration of heroic courage in the face of oppressive rulers is highlighted in Brooke's version to emphasize the key Opposition themes of superior plebian virtue, liberty through respect for the law, and the erosion of that liberty by too-powerful rulers.[50]

Brooke, however, also enhances the role of Virginia from that of a silent and passive victim to that of an active individual preparing to take her own life rather than dishonor herself, her family, and her class. Rather than the surprised acquiescence of Livy's and Crisp's Virginia when her father seizes a butcher's knife at the story's climax, Brooke's heroine displays cool forethought in providing a dagger, and freely expresses her sense of pride and outrage.[51] Nor does Brooke shy away from a story that calls first for passive resistance to tyrant rulers, and then for active rebellion. In Virginius's words, "'Tis not for me, but for yourselves, O, Romans! / That Freedom bids you wake the glorious Flame; / To save your blooming Virgins from Pollution: / I have no Interest in these Tyrant's Deaths: / What can I lose? Alas! I have no Daughter!" (5.12). With this portrayal, Brooke engages contemporary debates about the legitimacy of working to overthrow an existing political order, taking, it appears, a position significantly more radical than that of most mid-century Country critics; in Dickinson's analysis, this position on resistance would place Brooke rather closer to the radical Whig than to the Tory pole of the Country party spectrum.[52]

Brooke furthermore inserts into her play a temple scene in which Virginia, her friend Icilia, and a train of virgins seek the aid of the goddess Diana. Their hymn invokes Diana as "beauteous Goddess of the Grove," "Goddess of the rural Plain," and "Guardian of the woody Glades," rising toward the plea that she lend them her aid, together with that of her "sweet Companion, Liberty": "Leave the peaceful sylvan Scene, / And in awful Terrors drest, / Pierce the Tyrant's impious Breast" (4.1). As Brooke's original insertion into the historical account, this scene works to link both female chastity and the defense of liberty to a pastoral source. The poems which accompany the published tragedy further explore speaking positions within the pastoral tradition that allow an elaboration of the perspectives of a woman with literary ambitions. The themes include aspiration to emulate Sappho's poetic achievements and a turn away from the world to a female companion significantly named "Sabina" (after the heroic Sabine women), with whom the speaker, Delia, can toast "the Goddess Liberty" over a punchbowl (Ode IV, lines 11–12), a delight more precious than ambition, wealth, and even love. The culminating ninth ode addresses "thou, my lov'd, my latest Choice," Fame, which will "crown with deathless Bays thy raptur'd Bard" (lines 1, 6). The bard, of course, is a public, political poet, who turns from "the languid, Lesbian String" of Sappho to the "nobler Themes" of "godlike Britain's Liberty and Laws, / And Heroes bleeding in her beauteous Cause" (lines 8–12). Despite being clearly identified as female, this bard insists on her right to address such subjects: "Nor be my weaker Sex deny'd / To breath the glorious Patriot Strain; / Since we can boast, with pleasing Pride, / The Virgin Queen's triumphant Reign: / When Tyranny forsook th'enfranchis'd Land, / And Freedom rose beneath a female Hand" (lines 25–30).

After a review of the great men associated with Elizabeth's reign, the speaker turns to prophesy "A Patriot-Monarch, who shall find / His Safety in his People's Love: / Unbrib'd, around, his grateful Subjects stand, / While base Corruption blushing leaves the Land" and both peace and the arts flourish (lines 63–66). A note attached to the "Patriot-Monarch" reference explains, "The Author wou'd not be misunderstood as meaning any disrespect to a Name for which she has the greatest Veneration: all she meant was to express the Hopes almost universally conceiv'd, at the Time this Ode was wrote, of a most amiable Prince, who dy'd not long after, lamented by a whole People; and like Titus, left behind him the Character of, the Friend of Human kind." Brooke's decision to print the poem unaltered, five years after the death of Frederick, Prince of Wales, and despite this need to smooth over the implicit insult to George II, surely indicates her determined alignment with the Country Opposition that had until recently coalesced around the Prince.

As I have already shown, Brooke's periodical *The Old Maid*, presented in thirty-seven numbers as proceeding from the pen of Mary Singleton, spinster, has been examined primarily for evidence of Brooke's "apprentice feminism."[53] It is therefore of note that Robert Spector, in his study of literary periodicals in this politically volatile early period of the Seven Years' War, finds that of those "essay-journals" not specifically political or economic in nature, *The Old Maid* is one of only two to include political commentary. While Spector describes this commentary as "cursory remarks" limited to the periodical's penultimate numbers 35 and 36,[54] Brooke's interventions in contemporary political debates are in fact continuous throughout the periodical, shifting only from a generalized patriot rhetoric at the outset to more pointed commentary in the spring of 1756, when Admiral John Byng's conduct at Gibraltar had become the public obsession. Mingled assertions of female citizenship and of English liberty imbue *The Old Maid* from its first number, where Mary Singleton argues that it is her duty to offer "service to the community" through public observations as a compensation for her domestic uselessness, claiming her "natural right" as an Englishwoman to expose her ideas, while her readers may exercise "the same liberty of reading or not as they shall think meet" (*OM* 1 [November 15, 1755], p. 1); in the second number, she is "too much a freeborn Briton to submit" to establishing a "regular plan" for the paper (*OM* 2 [November 22, 1755], p. 11).

With the same facetious use of political rhetoric, Singleton canvasses such controversial and public topics as the best means of funding a charity like the Foundling Hospital, the importance of poetry to national greatness, the need for an institutionalized academy of criticism, the theologically and politically appropriate response to the Lisbon earthquake, the nature of true patriotism, the dangers of Methodism, and the true extent of clergy poverty. Nor are her characteristic attitudes hidden in favor of concessions to an urban consumer audience. In the first number's account of her own failed betrothal, for example, Singleton's fickle lover is ruined by the extravagance of the wife he chooses over the Old Maid with her impeccable country pedigree: "she was a city fortune," who "because she would not be thought to have had a confined education, . . . gamed, intrigued, and in short, practised all the vices which, she had read in those blessed helps to female virtue, modern memoirs, were the requisites of a woman of distinction" (*OM* 1 [November 15, 1755], p. 7). What might be mere cliché is particularized and made contemporary: the idealized country residence of Singleton's young friend Rosana is "among the *Dryads* that people the embowering shades of *Rutland*" (*OM* 17 [March 6, 1756], p. 136) and the seventeenth-century memoirs of Rochefort can serve to teach contemporary readers the importance of national unity against the French enemy (*OM* 20 [April 10, 1756], p. 188). It is not surprising, then, that a series of letters from "An Antigallican" proposing a scheme of using Amazonian Englishwomen to defend the nation from a threatened French invasion escalates from a generalized satire on weak British forces, to an increasingly specific taunting of the navy, and of Admiral Byng in particular. Although she claims to end the *Old Maid* in part because "the present confused state of public affairs" renders literary efforts "ill-timed" (*OM* 37 [July 24, 1756], p. 302), Singleton has in fact ranged well beyond the "literary," seeing with a self-proclaimed "*political* and *moral* eye" as much as with a "*poetical*" one (*OM* 36 [July 17, 1756], p. 296). This freedom from generic and gender restraints would remain characteristic of her creator's fictional efforts in the coming years.

Lady Julia Mandeville, Brooke's 1763 debut novel, is described by its 1930 editor as the product of her experience of translating Riccoboni's *Lettres de Milady Juliette Catesby*; there she was "taught by this example how to apply that sensibility which was a genuine part of her character to the production of works of fiction, and profit[ed] by the close study of a simple and unified story."[55] While not disputing this claim, I wish to emphasize here the journalistic topicality of Brooke's epistolary novel, dated very precisely from July 3, 1762, to some days beyond September 19 of that same year. The story is punctuated by continual references to the controversial peace negotiations at the end of the Seven Years' War, and even, on the latter date, to "this event in Russia," presumably the deposition, murder, and succession of Peter III by his wife, Catherine the Great, and her supporters (p. 181). Brooke's discussions of the terms of peace take a clear position in favor of the Tory ministry's policy of pursuing

such a peace as equally provides for the interest and honor of Britain, and the future quiet of mankind. The terms talked of are such as give us an immense addition of empire, and strengthen that superiority of naval force on which our very being depends; whilst they protect our former possessions, and remove the source of future wars, by securing all, and much more than all, for which this was undertaken; yet, by their just moderation, convince the world a British Monarch is governed only by the laws of honor and equity, not by that impious thirst of false glory, which actuates the laurel'd scourges of mankind (pp. 119–20).

It is in this larger context, rather than the narrow one of the Brookes' self-interest, that this novel's mention of Canada as already "of more national consequence to us than all the Sugar-islands on the globe," and potentially, through assimilation and further settlement, "an acquisition beyond our most sanguine hopes!" (pp. 156–57), should be read.

By supporting the current ministry, under enormous pressure from Pitt and the London merchants to prolong the war, or at least to push to retain more of the conquered territory,[56] the novel's idealized patriarch Lord Belmont links that ministry to the continued independence of the country gentleman, the key to maintaining England's balanced constitution. Lord Belmont is characterized by "a liberality which scarce his ample possessions can bound, a paternal care of all placed by Providence under his protection, a glowing zeal for the liberty, prosperity, and honour of his country, the noblest spirit of independence, with the most animated attachment and firmest loyalty to his accomplished sovereign," and a full array of "domestic virtues" as "the tender, the polite, attentive husband, the fond indulgent parent, the warm unwearied friend" (p. 44). The novel's central characters are united in their disdain of "cits" and new-made aristocrats; thus Lord Belmont's perfect fulfillment of his role as the local social leader includes inviting his wealthy citizen neighbors to a celebration of the birth of an heir to the throne on August 12, 1762, even "though he observed, smiling, 'this was a favor, for these kind of people were only gentlemen by the courtesy of England'" (p. 123). Another particularly explicit passage, though presented as a sketch of an elderly and eccentric aunt's views, clearly summarizes the novel's opinion of these groups as colluding to abuse their power for private gain:

She is a great politician, and sometimes inclined to be a tory, though she professes perfect impartiality; loves the King, and idolizes the Queen, because she thinks she sees in her the sweet affability so admired in her favourite Queen Mary – forgives the cits for their opposition to peace, because they get more money by war, the criterion by which they judge everything: but is amazed that the nobles, born guardians of the just rights of the throne, the fountain of all their honors, should join these interested 'Change-alley politicians, and endeavor, from private pique, to weaken the hands of their sovereign: but adds with a sigh, that mankind were always alike, and that it was just so in the Queen's time (p. 156).

In this context, Lord Belmont's estate, cited by Barker-Benfield as the stereotypical site of rustic dances, hermitages, and other rural amusements, takes on the weight of representing all that is valuable in the English political and social culture. The first in a series of "utopian, agrarian space[s]" in Brooke's fiction,[57] Belmont is continuous with the "shining and amiable example" of "Royalty itself" (p. 64); the sensible hero Henry Mandeville's, and presumably the author's, hopes for a renewed correlation between place and worth are centered in George III as "a Prince to whom the patriot glow, and that disinterested loyalty which is almost my whole inheritance, cannot but be the strongest recommendations" (p. 96). While these hopes with respect to the hero are dimmed when he discovers the falsity of great men who promise favors, and completely dashed when he is killed in a duel over love, the novel's extended modeling of a social ideal based in the rural, and its explicit support of the new king's policies, leave the reader with the impression that positive political change is imminent.

From this perspective, Brooke's 1769 *The History of Emily Montague* represents a continuity of political engagement as much as of sentiment. Again set very particularly in Quebec City over the year beginning in the summer of 1766 with "a kind of interregnum of government" (p. 7) between Murray and Carleton, *Emily Montague* is the Brooke novel in which political commentary is most explicit. It is no accident that at the same time, one of the novel's principal narrators, the sentimental hero Edward Rivers, discusses his courtship of Emily Montague in a manner that pits the clichés of sensibility against contemporary economic and status issues: their marriage is obstructed, not by lovers' misunderstandings or parental resistance, but by Rivers's inability to maintain himself and his future wife in England in the life of privilege for which their birth and upbringing has prepared them. Rivers's Canadian journey, therefore, is motivated by the desire to improve his economic situation through colonial adventure; the eighteenth-century novel's structuring of colonial episodes in terms of "an existing, dehistoricized pastoral order invigorated by georgic industriousness," identified by London,[58] is made explicit here by Rivers's statement of his qualifications for the venture: "I have studied the Georgicks, and am a pretty enough kind of a husbandman as far as theory goes; nay, I am not sure I shall not be, even in practice, the best *gentleman* farmer in the province" (p. 24). However, the domestic ideal achieved by the two central couples is ultimately defined as more narrowly pastoral: whereas Rivers initially comes to Canada intending to work hard, and then fantasizes about his labors to cultivate a rural "paradise" while Emily "adorn[s] those lovely shades" (p. 260), the pair's eventual return to England is accompanied by an increasing emphasis upon the rural landscape as a locus of leisured "variety" and "amusement," rather than labor to improve the land and increase one's wealth. Rivers's final letter asserts that "my only plan of life is to have none at all," wherein there will be "no rule but inclination" (p. 407). Brooke's pastoral, then, is presented as an informed, economically determined choice, rather than as a denial of the reality or importance of economic considerations.

What makes this apparent retreat from active life morally positive is its prioritizing of female economic and status concerns. The demands of women – his sister, his mother, his wife – are a drain on Rivers's standard of living; his heroism therefore consists in his insistence upon providing for them not only fairly, but generously. He consigns, first his own estate, then his half-pay and a post-chaise to his mother, denying himself these comforts in order to ensure not only her comfort, but her independence. While some women are a source of great expense – his sister Lucy, for example, needs magnificent jewels and fine clothes – these expenses are shown as resulting from the vitiated, luxurious tastes of the men they are associated with. Thus Lucy must be "an exquisite politician" in her marriage, making a showy appearance and planning amusements such as masquerades, because her wealthy and formerly philandering husband can be kept faithful only through continual variety and display on her part (p. 378). The married Emily, on the other hand, is presented by Rivers with "a dressing room and closet of books, into which I shall never intrude," because "there is a pleasure in having some place which we can say is peculiarly our own"; Rivers wants Emily to have such a space, in a remarkably ungendered line of reasoning, because it "is a pleasure in which I have been indulged almost from infancy" (pp. 336–37).

Brooke's portrayal thus differs from the country idylls marred by bourgeois female consumerism in Tobias Smollett's 1771 *Expedition of Humphry Clinker*, for example, or even in her own earlier works, in that the idealized pastoral mode of life toward which the novel moves is explicitly feminized. When the two central couples first turn their backs on Canada, Arabella Fermor, Emily's witty friend and the second principal narrator, laments the loss of her dream of "a little society of friends" in which she and Emily

> should have been continually endeavoring, following the luxuriancy of female imagination, to render more charming the sweet abodes of love and friendship; whilst our heroes, changing their swords into ploughshares, and engaged in more

substantial, more profitable labors, were clearing land, raising cattle and corn, and doing every thing becoming good farmers; . . . In one word, they would have been studying the useful, to support us; we the agreable, to please and amuse them; which I take to be assigning to the two sexes the employments for which nature intended them (p. 269).

By the very end of the novel, however, the masculine georgic impulse has become entirely undesirable to Arabella, if still characteristic of all but the domesticated male: "You men are horrid, rapacious animals, with your spirit of enterprize, and your nonsense: ever wanting more land than you can cultivate, and more money than you can spend . . . I should not, however, make so free with the sex, if you and my *caro sposo* were not exceptions" (p. 347).[59]

But how does this idealization of a feminized pastoral community fit into the larger context of political argument in the novel? As I have already noted, the political issues represented in *Emily Montague* are very specific and contemporary: far from being obvious and widely accepted, Brooke's views of Church establishment, the management of colonies, and French-English relations were controversial and partisan. Her family's desire for an increased income was a particular manifestation of the grievances of the country gentry, especially the lesser landowners, who felt themselves taxed unfairly and underappreciated as the bedrock upon which England's social and political stability and growing international strength were founded.[60] Brooke's prescriptive approach to these issues in the novel, as well as her founding of a youthful and forward-looking rural community at its conclusion, suggests again that at this point in her life, with the recent accession of George III and the successful conclusion of the Seven Years' War as a backdrop, the pastoral ideal of her novels is meant to project a possible future rather than a distant and irrecoverable past. While her central characters reject the hurry and luxury of London life, they maintain cordial relations with the likes of Lucy and her husband John Temple, hoping eventually to convert them as well to their rurally based, domestic ideals.

Late in the novel, the old Earl of ———, patron of Arabella's father William Fermor, writes to the latter that his youth and optimism have been renewed by a day spent making the acquaintance of young Rivers; while the sequel to this encounter remains a vague projection, it is possible to imagine that this representative of the established Whig oligarchy may in the future turn to the country gentleman Rivers to infuse new vigor into an ossified ruling class. At any rate, Rivers insists that the private interests of the tree-planting country gentleman and the public interest, embodied in a constitution wherein "liberty and prerogative are balanced with the steadiest hand," and which is metaphorically "the lovely and venerable tree under whose shade he enjoys security and peace," are in perfect accord. As a result, "I believe we country gentlemen, whilst we have spirit to keep ourselves independent, are the best citizens, as well as subjects, in the world" (pp. 342–43). Such explicit polemicizing is characteristic of the novel's conclusion; its strenuousness in itself, however, points to Brooke's sense that the message needs constant reiteration, even at what is the most politically optimistic point of her career.

THE FEMINIZED PASTORAL AS RETREAT

While I cannot discuss Brooke's translations from the French at any length in this chapter, I now turn briefly to one of these, the 1771 *Elements of the History of England*, translated from the Abbé Claude Millot, as significant both in choice and in the textual apparatus of her translation. In a letter of this period to her publisher James Dodsley, Brooke expresses her concern upon learning that he has lost money with *Emily Montague*, and, as one explanation for the limited success of the novel, speculates that genre and intended readership were not in alignment: "One of the best judges of literature I know, a man of exquisite taste, told me soon after it was publish'd that it wou'd be liked by literary people, but that it wou'd not be so popular a book by much as Julia Man. That it wou'd be better liked by men than women; it has prov'd so I am afraid. Now a novel to sell shou'd please women because women are the chief readers of novels, & perhaps the best judges."[61] In the same letter, quoted in the epigraph to my introduction, Brooke offers to share with Dodsley the profit or loss of her upcoming translation of Millot. Demonstrating business confidence and easy collegiality, this letter also reveals that Brooke wants to continue to produce political commentary, but in a genre more identified with such content. The translation of Millot's history, she hopes, will provide such a forum. That the genre of history is attracting her at this point is also made clear in her hint, in the "Advertisement" to the first volume, that "she may possibly insert, at the beginning of the third volume, some cursory observations on history in general, and that of England in particular."[62]

In the Millot, Brooke was making widely available to the English reader a work of French and Roman Catholic origin that nevertheless portrayed the English movement toward a balanced constitution as reasonable, even admirable. Brooke's notes to the translation are thus few, and worthy of note. They often consist of counter-representations where she feels English Protestantism and the seventeenth-century transition away from absolutism are being criticized.[63] Regarding the latter, when Millot in his preface draws the moral that history teaches the reader to be content with the law and with the existing authority, exclaiming, "What disturbances and misfortunes has [the leaven of dissension] not produced in England! That unquiet, turbulent, factious nation; what has it gained by so many attacks on the government so many violent shocks given to the royal authority?", Brooke replies smartly, "We will answer Mons. Milot's question in his own words: Finally, from this chaos, full of horrors, there arose a form of government which excites the admiration of all of Europe" (vol. I, pp. xxvi–xxvii, my translation). Later, when Millot explains Henry VIII's resistance to ongoing church reform as partly due to "that spirit of liberty which their sect respired, as much calculated to make republicans as heretics," Brooke notes:

> Far from meriting this reproach, whoever is perfectly acquainted with the doctrines, the forms, and the spirit, of the church of England, will, the translator persuades herself, readily allow, not only that it is peculiarly adapted to a mixed monarchy like ours, but that it is of all establishments the most favorable to rational obedience, as well as to well-regulated freedom. It ought to be remembered, and remembered with gratitude, that this church has ever stood foremost to defend both the rights of the prince, and the liberties of the people, when attacked (vol. II, pp. 226–27).

Clearly, Brooke's preoccupations in 1771 are similar to those of 1769; she continues to defend the existing English constitution for its balance of authority and liberty, and the established Church as ideally congruent with such a constitution.

In the course of this defence, however, Brooke by implication also acknowledges the legitimacy of resistance, even violent resistance, to excessive authority. In the new era of Wilkite riots and more broad-based arguments for Englishmen's liberty, Brooke's stance is potentially more controversial than it was two years earlier. With respect to more recent history, Brooke agrees with Millot's assertion that the high Tory Bishop Thomas Atterbury was unfairly convicted of treason in 1725 – "Without entering into the question of the bishop's guilt or innocence, every impartial reader must allow the evidence on the trial to have been very insufficient, and the proceedings irregular and dangerous to liberty" – and continues to condemn partisan politics in general: "It is the misfortune of England, that each party, though jealous of power in the hands of its adversaries, is very little scrupulous as to the use of it in its own.

The Whigs, when in power, are the partizans of prerogative; the Tories, when out, the zealous advocates of freedom" (vol. IV, p. 310). If Brooke believes heartily in the status quo, in other words, she also sees it as currently subject to pressures from the politically self-interested which are much less defensible than the agitations of past forces for change.

Over the next six years, Brooke was preoccupied with branching out into the theatrical sphere, comanaging with the leading actress Mary Ann Yates the King's Theatre (generally known as the Opera House), which her brother-in-law James Brooke and Yates's husband Richard had purchased in 1773. As I have already indicated, the theatrical world of the 1760s and 1770s was politicized in both the specific and broader senses of the term. Brooke and her partners hoped to be granted a license to perform plays, as well as operas, at the theater, and it is not grasping at straws to suspect that interference on the part of Garrick, who was well connected with the Court (see chapter 1) helped to prevent the licensing.[64] Brooke may well have felt that she was a perpetual outsider to Garrick's court, even as a seasoned London literary professional who currently enjoyed warm relationships with Garrick friends such as Samuel Johnson and the Burney family; she hailed Garrick's retirement from the stage in 1776 as a victory for liberty just as the Country Opposition might welcome the fall of a powerful government minister.

In this spirit of perceived political and theatrical corruption, Brooke's 1777 novel *The Excursion* is constructed around a framework of values that is essentially that of *Emily Montague*, in its movement toward the final establishment of a select rural community of well-born but economically reduced gentry. Nevertheless, the story is told by a third-person narrator whose self-consciously cynical tone is darker and more all-pervasive than the flirtatious irony of the earlier Arabella Fermor. Although this narrator has been described as Fieldingesque,[65] the method is as much that of Laurence Sterne's 1768 *A Sentimental Journey*, where the minute shifts of feeling in the individual of sensibility are detailed at length, complicating simple dichotomies of character.[66] Similarly, the pastoral environment that has nurtured the heroine, Maria Villiers, is self-consciously stylized and represented with irony, albeit gentle. Typically, the obsession of Maria's uncle, Colonel Dormer (who has raised and educated the heroine and her sister Louisa in every virtue and accomplishment, and who might be an elderly Colonel Rivers), with his garden is ostensibly harmless, but nevertheless prevents him from tearing himself away from home in order to supervise Maria's journey.

That excursion is taken, not into the wilds of Canada, but, in another ironic twist, into London, represented as a savage social world where wealth buys status, whether for Lady Hardy the housekeeper-mistress turned rich widow, "whom (to borrow the admirable definition of Fielding) every body knew to be what nobody chose to call her" (p. 22) or for the heiress of the wealthy nabob for whom Lord Melvile, the object of Maria's infatuation, rejects her. This degeneracy is modeled by a corrupt aristocracy, represented by the cynical Lord Claremont, Melvile's father, who "had stood high in administration; and, on a change of men, had figured not less conspicuously on the side of opposition: the school of modern politicks not being the purest school of rectitude, he had found a great part of those with whom he co-operated knaves, and therefore, naturally enough, though very falsely, concluded knavery to be the characteristic of mankind" (p. 23). This father, who has "spared no expence or trouble to improve and adorn his [son's] person, polish his behaviour, cultivate his understanding, and corrupt his heart" (p. 23), finally arranges his son's marriage for money as a means of recovering his bankrupt estate. In other words, political and social hierarchies have been subverted at every level by the predominance of self-interested values, and Maria learns the hard lesson that, though she can defend herself with dignity to Lord Claremont as "a woman whose family is not inferior to your own, whose virtues do not disgrace her birth," she is living in an "age of unexampled venality," wherein "[her] fortune [gives] her less right to aspire" to marriage with an aristocrat "than those who are in every other respect infinitely below [her]" (p. 114).

In this age, those who choose to live by traditional ideas of hierarchical order and true worth, as represented in the ancient bloodlines and inherited estates of the country gentleman, can afford no illusions about challenging the prevailing forces of corruption. Rather, their solution is to form a select rural community of contiguous estates, bound together by the marriages of Louisa to the neighboring squire's son and Maria to Colonel Herbert, the dutiful son of Lady Sophia Herbert, a lady "with an air which [speaks] her birth to have been the most distinguished," but whose "inclination, and the mediocrity of her fortune, [have] preserved her from mixing in the *ton*" (p. 139). Since Colonel Herbert, like *Emily Montague*'s hero, has insisted upon dividing the income of his impaired estate with his mother, arguing "that he was a single man, and that whilst he continued so, a handsome lodging, and a hired chariot, were all the exteriors for which he had occasion, and that his pride was much more interested in her ladyship's appearance than his own" (p. 140), this plan for a sociable retreat is conveniently assisted by Dormer's inheritance of wealth and title at the death of an estranged kinsman.

This resolution again parallels Smollett's creation of a nostalgic Welsh retreat for Matthew Bramble at the conclusion of his travels in *Humphry Clinker*, a journey which passes through, and firmly rejects, a similarly corrupt and socially unstable urban landscape. Again, however, Brooke's pastoral retreat does not match the misogyny of Smollett's (or of the sentimental pastoral in general, as discussed by London): rather than working to minimize the negative influence of easily corrupted women, Colonel Dormer's "little domain," where "every thing around him" reflects his admiration "of truth, nature, and genuine beauty," is an ideal spot for the nurture of strong and sensible women. Thus the novel plays constantly with the double sense of Dormer's garden as one that cultivates both flowers and young women, where "delicate in his choice, attentive in his culture, his flowers bloomed more fair, his fruit had a more delicious flavour, than those of his more opulent neighbours" (p. 8). By contrast, Lord Claremont has, "in the variegated garden of human life and manners, . . . industriously pointed out the weeds to his son's observation, and concealed from him with not less sedulous anxiety the flowers with which it at least equally abounds" (p. 24). The "little paradise of Belfont" (p. 9), the Colonel's home, is an ideal nursery of the feminine in that it is characterized by moral and social qualities which transcend narrow gender definitions. Although Maria's nearly disastrous London excursion reveals his poor judgment and her naive vanity, it also affords her the opportunity to demonstrate the strength of character gained in this pastoral setting.

The competitive jungle of London society is mirrored and supported by a literary marketplace that is corrupt, again, from its patrons downward. Maria's talent and ambition as a writer (she has come to London with an epic poem, a novel, and a tragedy in manuscript in her trunk) meet with the same inability to recognize true worth as do her social qualifications. The city's reigning theater manager, a Garrick caricature, dismisses her tragedy in a manner that exposes his dishonesty, his love of sycophancy, and his selection of plays on the basis of playwrights' social connections.[67] In a literary marketplace unable to recognize true value, falsehood is a profitable commodity. The greatest risk Maria faces in London, therefore, is not the loss of her actual virtue, which she has the moral strength to protect, but the loss of her reputation in a shadow world of nonreality, that of the slanderous gossip page. Significantly, the false "*tete-a-tete* history of Lord M-lv-le and Miss V-ll-rs" (p. 116) is composed not by a starving hack, but by an aristocrat, the malevolent Lady Blast, "a pretty good scribbler" who has "more than once enriched the ——— Magazine with little anecdotes of her most intimate female friends; anecdotes which [want] no recommendation except the very useless one of being true" (p. 116).[68] To this "murderer of reputation" (p. 118), the poor compositor who prints such work to feed his hungry children is ultimately morally superior, refusing despite his state of dependence to print the story in question.

While Brooke continued to pursue her London career, then, she used her pastoral mode of representation to signal a turn away from her earlier, more optimistic brand of conservatism. This novel contains neither celebration of the balanced constitution, nor projection of improvements through political change. Rather, the aristocracy are revealed to be hopelessly corrupt and in collusion with false, money-bought gentility, while the public sphere of letters reflects this corruption in "the licentious malignity of [the] press" (p. 117) and in the active obstruction of genius. Where true public spirit exists, as in the form of the elderly Mr. Hammond, Maria's London mentor, it serves only to render impotent particular instances of falsity, like that of Lady Blast against Maria, and to contemplate with nostalgic, "reverential delight" the past "public virtues of the great, the wise, the uncorrupt, minister [William Cecil, first baron Burghley], who raised the glory of his country to its summit" under Elizabeth I (p. 126).[69] Interestingly, however, though no virtuous characters attempt to change the political system and its parallel theatrical world, the narrator makes a direct, impassioned appeal to the reader to exercise his or her consumer power to halt the abuse of print. To quote only briefly from the passage:

> Do you not – unfeeling as you are – by encouraging such detestable publications, wantonly plant yourself the envenomed dagger in the bosom of innocence? It is in your power alone to restrain the growing evil, to turn the envenomed dart from the worthy breast. Cease to read, and the evil dies of itself: cease to purchase, and the venal calumniator will drop his useless pen . . . You wish to be amused; I pardon, I commend your wish; but you may be amused without wounding the better feelings of your soul (p. 118).

Despite the apparent political cynicism and nostalgia of so much of *The Excursion*, then, Brooke is not prepared to withdraw entirely from her engagement in shaping the public through print.

The author's preface to her next published work, the 1781 text of her tragedy *The Siege of Sinope*, confirms more specifically that Brooke was unwilling to back away from her earlier criticism of Garrick's reign, while at the same time being willing to acknowledge generously the assistance she did receive. In 1779 the King's Theatre had been sold to Richard Brinsley Sheridan, son of Frances, and Thomas Harris, a change that seems to have freed Brooke again for writing, and also to have created a theatrical outlet for her pen. Thus Brooke thanks Harris as one to whom

> my obligations are great: his good sense and taste called my attention to more than one impropriety in the conduct of the piece, when first offered; his liberal turn of mind gave it every advantage of decoration; whilst his candour and politeness removed the dragons which have been supposed to guard the avenues to the theatre, and which have too long deterred many of our greatest writers from taking this road to the Temple of Fame.[70]

The prologue to this play was written by the Rev. William Collier, husband of a close friend of Brooke, and so is likely a fair representation of Brooke's own view of her tragedy. It announces a turn away from satire's "misguided rage" to an appeal to nature and the heart as a means of correcting the age.

Indeed, the play appears to turn away, not only from *The Excursion*'s satire of corrupt manners, but also from Brooke's early *Virginia*, in that tragedy's celebration of a union of feminine and masculine, public and private virtue in an idealized father-daughter relation. Here Thamyris, daughter of Athridates King of Cappadocia, and wife of Pharnaces King of Pontus, is torn between the competing identities of daughter, wife, mother, and queen. Her attempt to reconcile these identities through dutiful behavior to all is marred by the devastating conflict, both public and private in origin, between her husband and her father as rival monarchs. While the most grievous fault at first appears to be in Pharnaces' elopement with her, as his betrothed wife, from her father's court, this fault is minimized by the revelation of Arthridates' ambitious attempt to use his daughter as a means of alliance with Rome and by his unremitting thirst for vengeance against the house of Pharnaces for past wrongs. As an unnatural father, Athridates turns all of Thamyris's attempts at mediation, motivated by her "unsuspecting, woman's, heart" and "weak, mistaken, filial piety" (3.6), to his own evil purposes. It is not a stretch to read in this play the psychic ruptures of the recent war with the American colonies and a disillusioned comment on hardline policies that forced the nation's colonial "children" to rebellion in self-preservation.[71]

While such familial parables were common in the 1780s, of particular interest here is Athridates' self-destruction in a vindication of the justice meted out by the gods; as he is the only central character who dies at the conclusion of this tragedy, his faults are expiated in a cathartic movement that leaves an intact family unit in control of two newly united nations. Once again, Brooke is also here significantly altering a precursor, Thomas Hall's 1765 opera *Pharnaces*, to which she refers in her preface. In that work, the Roman commander Pompey is the peace-bringing hero who, through the mediation of Pharnaces' sister Selinda, saves Pharnaces and his family from the villainous Athridates. Commentary on Brooke's play, from its first performance to the twentieth century, has assumed, typically, that her plot innovations are motivated simply by her desire to highlight the dramatic skills of her friend Mary Ann Yates. The central unifying role of Thamyris, however, together with Brooke's colonial model of the domestic family, are deliberately underscored by a concluding prayer of thanks, which blames the conflict on political interference from the outside – "the arts of Rome, / Whose wild ambition sets the world in arms" and has turned "The kindred nations" against one another – while celebrating the establishment of a newly "firm, united bond" of peace between those nations (5.10).

From the perspective of this attempt to salvage relations between kindred states through self-enclosure and the expulsion of the father figure corrupted by ambition and a foreign empire, it is perhaps not surprising that the author's next major work, *Rosina*, should be a comic opera characterized by a simple plot of rural romance contained within a benevolent landlord's estate. Perhaps also not surprising is the great success *Rosina* enjoyed from its first performance on December 31, 1781, and throughout this decade of general anxiety and soul-searching in Britain; as late as 1789, the *European Magazine* describes this work as Brooke's "most popular performance," and one for which "the simplicity of the story, the elegance of the words, and the excellence of the music, promise a long duration."[72] Between her conservative support of a traditional social hierarchy and her distaste for those with entrenched political power, and given her increasing ill-health, Brooke's inclination may have been to turn her back on political engagement and retreat into a more self-contained artifact than any she had constructed in her previous works. Yet even *Rosina*'s stylized pastoral fable, with its songs set to folklike melodies, gestures toward a recognizable political heritage.

Rosina's plot draws on the biblical romance of Ruth and Boaz, significantly through the mediation of the early eighteenth-century poet James Thomson's retelling, as the story of Palemon and Lavinia, in his enormously popular poem *The Seasons.* Not only was Thomson closely associated with the Country Opposition around the Prince of Wales whom Brooke had celebrated in her first book of odes, but this version of the story affirms arguments for natural gentility in the person of Lavinia/Rosina, whose "graces of . . . form" and "native dignity of . . . mind" are only two of the "thousand circumstances" that "concur to couvince [*sic*]" the admiring Mr. Belville that she was "not born a villager."[73] Nevertheless, the social elevation of Rosina and her lover is carefully limited to the level of the lesser gentry and professional classes: she is the daughter of Colonel Martin, "the friend of [Belville's] father's heart" (Act 2), while he is the local landowner, whose brother is a captain. *Rosina* thereby declares its allegiance to the Country principles which served as the ideological frame of Brooke's earliest works; now, however, the absence of commentary on contemporary public affairs and the throwback to the 1740s suggest a pastoral ideal which has become culturally isolated and nostalgic, existing only in the realm of popular entertainment. One might go so far as to label this entertainment "escapist" but for the congruence of *Rosina*'s pastoralism with the well-known efforts of a great landowner like Elizabeth Montagu to keep her laborers contented through the revival of old rural customs such as the harvest feast.[74] Mr. Belville is idealized as a generous and fair landlord whose brother comes down to the estate to assist in the September first harvest celebrations; his workers are reminded by their overseer not only that "What would gilded pomp avail / Should the peasant's labour fail?", but also that "Ripen'd fields your cares repay / Sons of labour haste away; / Bending, see the waving grain / Crown the year, and chear the swain" (Act 1).

Brooke's final publication before her death in 1789, besides the 1785 second edition of *The Excursion*, was a second comic opera, *Marian*, produced in 1788 to more moderate success than that of *Rosina*.[75] Once again owing their happiness to "a rare land, . . . and a kind landlord," who is recognizable as "a gentleman born, by his not having a morsel of pride," the story's principal pastoral characters learn to marry for true love rather than wealth, and are variously rewarded by bequests and by their landlord's generosity in dispensing fortunes perfectly appropriate to the gradations of their respective births and educations.[76]

While Brooke's views here, as in her entire body of work, can in some respects be seen as clichéd, they remain significant to anyone looking to understand an eighteenth-century woman writer's sense of public responsibility and voice. The response to her views in turn can enrich our understanding of her peers' notions of the place of women's voices in the political public realm. By 1788 Brooke was residing in Sleaford, Lincolnshire, not with her husband, but near the two parishes of which her son Jack was rector. Her final decade of life is recorded in generally sympathetic references to her in the press and in private correspondence. Certainly nothing suggests that readers or critics had turned against her as a woman writer. Yet two incidents hint at a possible shift in the political climate for a woman writer as well as for an advocate of a feminist Country ideology. One is the refusal by Frances Burney in 1783 of Brooke's invitation to join her in joint-editorship of a periodical paper. Burney assigns no reason for her refusal of the offer, which must at the least have been flattering coming from this seasoned and admired writer, beyond the statement that she has nothing left to write in the aftermath of her exhausting work on *Cecilia.* It is hard to imagine Burney having nothing to contribute to the periodical genre, given her constant and voluminous production of short set-pieces in her letters and journals. Brooke's reply, "I am sorry you are *disinclin'd* to writing at present, but I have that opinion of your Sincerity, that I do not believe you wou'd have given that reason if it had not been a true one," implies some suspicion of this explanation as less-than-candid.[77] Burney may indeed not have felt up to the drudgery of producing material for a constant deadline, but she may also have felt that such work would assign to her a feminized literary identity that, as my final chapters will argue, she was trying to avoid.

Secondly, as noted earlier in this chapter, Brooke asserts in her preface to the second edition of *The Excursion* that there is a move afoot to deny the competence of women writers even in the field of novel-writing, one where their natural sensibility and domestic talents would presumably be put to good effect. This formulation is unexpected at the end of a career in which Brooke has unapologetically published a periodical paper, managed a theater, written for the stage, translated history, and addressed contemporary political and social issues in her novels.[78] Indeed, Brooke launches this preface with a rhetorical move that insists on the alignment of the political and literary public spheres: "'I APPEAL TO THE PEOPLE,' was the celebrated form in which a citizen of ancient Rome refused his acquiescence in any sentence of which he felt the injustice. On giving a new edition of The EXCURSION to the public, I find myself irresistibly impelled to use the same form of appeal" (p. 1). As I have speculated earlier, the complaint may well be a red herring, planted to turn the public's attention away from Brooke's attack on Garrick as the reason for criticism of the first edition, and in the process to exploit audience sympathy for the victim of unjustified censure. But if it is generally untrue for Brooke's mid-century career, now drawing to a close, it may nevertheless serve as a very early sign of a new reality, of the sort that at once made Frances Burney anxious and to which she contributed: the raising of new barriers of self-consciousness to women's unapologetic implication in the literary marketplace.

In the penultimate and final chapters of this study, I will return, first, to Burney's negotiation of her entrance into this new literary world, and second, to the agency of Brooke, Burney, and other women readers and writers themselves in the restriction, and sometimes even the obliteration, of other women's writing. But now I wish to turn to Sarah Scott, a writer who contributed actively to the formation of the ideal citizen of the public sphere, yet who, unlike Sheridan and Brooke, used the disembodied medium of print to obscure deliberately her own participation therein.

CHAPTER 3

Sarah Scott, historian, in the republic of letters

> . . . to converse with historians is to keep good company: many of them were excellent men, and those who were not such, have taken care however to appear such in their writings.
>
> (Lord Bolingbroke, *Letters on the Study and Use of History*, 1752)[1]

> . . . you make so good use of history it wd be strange not to be glad to furnish you with it.
>
> (Elizabeth Montagu to Sarah Scott, [1759])[2]

Although there can be few historians of eighteenth-century British literature who remain unfamiliar with Sarah Robinson Scott, woman novelist and utopian writer, she was in her day something of a recluse, living in genteel poverty in provincial England, and choosing to keep her distance from the glittering and conspicuous salon circle presided over by her bluestocking sister Elizabeth Robinson Montagu, where she might have attained a higher public profile for her wit and intellectual accomplishments. Indeed, Sarah Scott appears to have consciously sought to live out her life in the role of private gentlewoman, called upon to perform quietly the Christian duties of her social station to the extent afforded by her kinship relations, a few long-term friendships, her limited means, and her poor health. To this identity, private in multiple senses, she sucessfully subordinated her activities as published professional author. Thus at the age of seventy she writes to her sister, in the context of the political stresses of the Warren Hastings trial, "If I were to write any thing it must be a Satire on Juries . . . , it is therefore lucky for me that I am not a Writer."[3] Even if ironically intended, such a comment suggests a model of identity very different from the emerging professional model of the writer in eighteenth-century print culture.[4] Far from being a vocation to be pursued – or, for that matter, a shameful association with the marketplace, and, therefore, an essential element of her identity – "author," for Sarah Scott, seems to have been a merely occasional label that could remain for the most part unclaimed.

Since Scott's place in the history of women's writing is secure on the strength of her utopian fiction *A Description of Millenium Hall* (1762) and its sequel *The History of Sir George Ellison* (1766), grounded as they were in her own experiments in alternative community living,[5] it might seem best to leave well enough alone, to acknowledge the novelist and respect the place she herself appears to have been content to hold as a modest footnote to the main text of eighteenth-century literary history. Yet the figure behind the footnote is more complex than such a solution would imply. In contrast to considerable interest over the past several decades in *Millenium Hall* and its sequel, little attempt has been made to place Scott in the republic of letters as the author of at least three book-length histories published over a thirteen-year period encompassing the two fictions: *The History of Gustavus Ericson, King of Sweden* (1761), *The History of Mecklenburgh* (1762), and *The Life of Theodore Agrippa D'Aubigné* (1772).[6] But Scott apparently valued herself more for these histories than for her fictions and translations. In 1763, for example, finding that her father knows she is the author of *Millenium Hall*, she writes to her sister Elizabeth, "You may if You please tell him in confidence that he bears the same Relation to Gustavus, for I am surprized he does not feel some apprehensions, lest if I apply myself only to Novels, I may endeavour to arrive at a denouement myself in spight of my *mature* years." As for the translation of French novels, she calls this being "the interpreter of nonsence," and declares that she would be satisfied to earn £40 a year in that capacity.[7]

A highly educated and well-read intellectual, a frequently published author in a range of genres, and the co-author of a 55-year-long correspondence with Elizabeth that records the details of her domestic, social, readerly, and authorial life, Scott offers the literary historian an opportunity to test models of the English public sphere, or republic of letters, for their ability to illumine the practical realities of professional authorship in eighteenth-century England. In short, what shall we make of the paradox of Scott, as formulated by Gary Kelly: "Sarah Robinson Scott . . . was the most published yet one of the least known of the first-generation bluestocking writers in their time?"[8] And what light does this paradox shed on the experience of authorship in a rapidly expanding print culture distributing its products, whether books, pamphlets, or newspapers, on a national scale?

Q5

I have already shown that reviewers responded to Frances Sheridan, upon her debut as a novelist, as a welcome and contributing citizen of the republic of letters. For the purposes of this chapter, I conceive of the "republic of letters" in its eighteenth-century British manifestation to be constructed of individual subjects connected primarily through reading and writing (whether circulated in manuscript or disseminated through print) about ideas and values. As Sheridan's case illustrates, the intellectual exchanges of these individuals were not limited by constraints of genre, gender, geography, social status, or national origin to the same degree as were embodied social interactions. In a parallel argument for these women's French contemporary Marie-Jeanne Riccoboni, Elizabeth Heckendorn Cook has suggested that print authorship in the republic of letters offered a woman an escape from the embodied sexual contract in favor of a disembodied textual contract.[9] Nevertheless, access to the means of exchange, whether in the form of theater contacts, connections with Court favorites, or proximity to the London publishing trade, overlapped with, and to some extent was informed by, these classifications.

On a similar note, in her examination of "the institutions of the urban renaissance," whether printed materials or social organizations, in English cities and towns of the eighteenth century, Kathleen Wilson has cautioned against overly optimistic accounts of the inclusivity of these modes of public engagement. While they may indeed have provided opportunity for "a wide range of residents, men and women, artisans and merchants, shopkeepers and patricians to associate and subscribe money and time in order to refashion and regulate their physical and cultural environments," they "also advanced definitions of subjectivity that supported the prerogatives of middle- and upper-class men."[10]

It is in this paradoxical light that one must view recent studies of the lively activity of provincial literary circles consisting chiefly of women,[11] or descriptions of networks of female intellectuals or bluestockings which have suggested that they constructed a unique "version of humanist and Enlightenment intellectual culture" that was "mainly sustained by epistolary networks," but also shared in a general "Whig" recognition of "the power of print to form a social coalition."[12] For if the medium of writing was remarkably accessible, its socially embedded institutions could prove challenging to negotiate.

Thus Wilson's caveat applies to this study of women writers: while I am arguing that there was ample space for their activity in the literary marketplace of the day, the option of remaining hidden from the spotlight, at one extreme, held its attractions, while that of forming a publicly identified coalition of women writers, if it existed at all, was never taken up. The professional identity of the individual writing subject might manifest itself in a range of disembodied and embodied forms, controlled by the individual to some extent, but also to some extent beyond her control. I will suggest that Scott as reader and writer participated in an intellectual community which to a significant degree transcended the limitations placed upon her by her sex, her relative poverty and ill-health, and her geographical isolation from London as cultural center. At the same time, Scott's reluctance to embrace the identity of author impeded the construction of a coherent position for her as a citizen of the republic of letters who would be recognized as such not only by her immediate acquaintances, but also by the larger intellectual community. Her reluctance was matched by the apparent inability of many of her contemporaries to assign the author-function (in Foucault's sense of a coherent explanatory structure for a body of publications)[13] to a woman writer who published both fiction and history, both popular and more scholarly work.

EIGHTEENTH-CENTURY USES OF HISTORY

Scott's relative pride in her history-writing, noted above, no doubt stems in part from the prestige of history in the received hierarchy of genres at the height of the century, what Mark Salber Phillips refers to, in *Society and Sentiment: Genres of Historical Writing in Britain, 1740–1820*, as "the dignity of history" when understood as a narrative of "events of a certain order of public importance." Yet even if we assume that Scott accepted the generic elevation of history, her lifelong propensity for reading and writing it raises questions, for as Phillips goes on to explain, the "lessons" of such narratives were understood to be "addressed primarily to those in a position to profit by them";[14] the political, social, and gendered exclusivity of the target audience for traditional history was a given. Indeed, D. R. Woolf has argued that an increasing awareness and elevation of a distinctly political and public *genre* of history-writing in the period was inherently linked to a *gendering* of its authorship, subject matter, and readership as masculine.[15] As Lord Bolingbroke phrased it in his 1752 *Lessons on the Study and Use of History*, in the statement which serves as an epigraph to this chapter, "to converse with historians is to keep good company: many of them were excellent men, and those who were not such, have taken care however to appear such in their writings."[16] Scott read Bolingbroke appreciatively in 1758,[17] shortly before publishing

Gustavus Ericson, her account of the sixteenth-century Swedish king also known as Gustavus Vasa, who converted that nation to Protestantism.

But she would also have been aware of the challenges to this traditional view as outlined by the likes of Samuel Johnson in his recent *Rambler* No. 60: "Histories of the downfal of kingdoms, and revolutions of empires, are read with great tranquillity," whereas it is in "narratives of the lives of particular persons" that lessons are found "applicable to private life." In Johnson's view, to benefit from such lessons necessitated a revolution in values, away from "false measures of excellence and dignity" toward an appreciation of "learning, integrity, and piety," on the principle that "what is of most use is of most value."[18] Johnson's tendentious formulation thus exemplifies Phillips's claim that "the eighteenth century was a critical moment in the adaptation of classical understandings of history to the needs of a modern, commercial, and increasingly middle-class society." Phillips argues that "history" for the eighteenth century is most accurately understood as "a group of overlapping and related genres," that its subject matter had become "a much wider, but less easily defined set of concerns for which contemporaries did not really have a name."[19] Woolf and Devoney Looser have shown that numerous writers promoted women's reading of history, and Woolf and Phillips note that Hume, for example, clearly signalled in his correspondence and publications the belief that history's appropriate audience was a broad group of individuals who could claim a legitimate interest in the origins of contemporary society – certainly this included bourgeois male readers, and to a large extent women as well.[20]

Nevertheless, inclusive assertions about subject matter, style, and readership often slipped into more narrowly traditional, gendered, and elitist ones, just as did the institutions of the public sphere described by Wilson. Thus in his essay "Of the Study of History," Hume argues that it is "an unpardonable ignorance in persons, of whatever sex or condition, not to be acquainted with the history of their own country, together with the histories of ancient Greece and Rome." Yet he begins this short essay with two substantial paragraphs attacking female readers for their "aversion" to history, as opposed to their persistent "appetite" for falsehood in the generic form of novels, romances, and secret histories. Bolingbroke similarly opens up the readership of history "to all the members of every society that is constituted according to the rules of right reason," but it becomes clear that "the people" essentially means "Free-men, who [although they] are neither born to [the aristocracy], nor elected to [the House of Commons], have a right however to complain, to represent, to petition."[21] In this landscape, historical biography held a mediating position. More suitable than traditional histories for the private and general reader, as Johnson's *Rambler* essay indicates, yet without the threatening formlessness of the memoir or "secret history," it attained its own "distinct, if subordinate, dignity."[22] Donald A. Stauffer has suggested that eighteenth-century biographies of royalty and other significant political figures helped establish the "respectability" of biography "by showing that a career, even in its trivial and anecdotal aspects, might be narrated seriously in elevated prose."[23]

Sarah Scott, who at least twice chose biography as her form of historical composition, was as self-conscious as her contemporaries about the realm of historiography as one in which issues not only of legitimate membership in the public sphere, but also of the nature of public identity itself, were being played out. She is clearly invoking discussions of the status of history, its writers, and its readers, when as the published author of several histories of her own, she reports to her sister in 1767 that she has been the recipient of a visit from the historian Catharine Macaulay, adding slyly that this was "a pleasure I wishd I cou'd make over to my Father as I am unworthy of it."[24] Like Macaulay, Scott used this contested space, with its debates about the relative uses of scholarly fact and coherent narrative, entertainment and instruction, and public versus private lives, for elite versus general readers, as a fertile field for the development of her own theory and methodology of history-writing. And yet her comment on the celebrated Mrs. Macaulay suggests as well a significant divergence between paths that might initially seem parallel.

As childhood acquaintances from privileged Kentish families, both women emerged as successful writers of history in the early 1760s and were most active over the following decade. Scott, in fact, was about ten years older than Macaulay and published her first history three years before the appearance of the first volume of the latter's *History of England from the Accession of James I to that of the Brunswick Line*.[25] In 1763 she wrote to Elizabeth, "Have you seen our old acquaintance Mrs. Macaulay's (once Kitty Sawbridge's) book, the first volume of an English History; she seems to have a noble spirit, & has taken great pains, & as far as I have seen I think acquits herself well" – this though she goes on to disapprove of Macaulay's republican politics.[26]

Scott recognized and credited the work of this fellow female historian, but she clearly chose a different authorial trajectory. While Macaulay's *History of England* was published under her name, Scott's *Gustavus Ericson* carried the pseudonym "Henry Augustus Raymond, Esq."; while no portraits of Scott are known to survive, Macaulay's third volume was fronted by an engraving, and she was the subject of numerous poems, portraits, and caricatures. This is the writer of whom Horace Walpole wrote, "She is one of the sights that all foreigners are carried to see,"[27] and whose 1777 birthday celebration in Bath was described by Elizabeth Carter to Elizabeth Montagu as a "farcical parade of foolery" in which Macaulay appeared as "a queen in a puppet show."[28] For Scott, the writing of history, particularly of biography, was of great public importance, but she rejected utterly the theatrical, embodied authorial identity created by and for Macaulay in favor of the disembodiment afforded by print as she managed it.[29] The remainder of this chapter will therefore focus on Scott's authorial management of history-writing, ranging from her practical use of booksellers and target audiences to achieve her financial ends, to her methodology and manipulation of historical genres as a historian, to her theory of how history should be read, and finally to the implications of all of this for her self-identification as an active, yet unidentified, participant in the formation of useful and virtuous members of the public.

SCOTT'S HISTORICAL PRACTICE

The writer of history is of course preceded by the reader. Scott's correspondence with her sister exemplifies Woolf's conclusion that eighteenth-century women "contributed . . . to what might be called the 'social circulation' of historical knowledge by reading history, by acquiring familiarity with its details and certain documentary sources, and by discussing this knowledge conversationally or in private writings."[30] Scott, however, further reveals a breadth and depth of historical sense as a reader which surpasses that of the well-informed Elizabeth; Sarah's is the more authentically intellectual and critical practice.[31] Reading a voluminous *Universal History* in 1755, she comments, "tho' I cou'd find many faults in it, yet upon the whole it is entertaining, but woud be more so if I had lost my memory."[32] It is she who many years later explains to her puzzled sister the historians' veiled references to Henry VI's insanity, which are being discussed as a precedent for managing George III's episodes of mental illness.[33] And while Elizabeth tends to be very swayed by what she is reading, Sarah maintains a determinedly critical perspective. Thus when Elizabeth in the 1750s is very taken with Mme. de Maintenon upon reading her memoirs, Sarah responds that she cannot accept her treachery to Racine, Fenelon, and Noailles, concluding, "She will never be my Heroine."[34]

In a much later moment of highly wrought public sentiment over events in France, Elizabeth enthuses over Edmund Burke's newly published *Reflections on the Revolution in France*, calling it "Mr Burkes admirable, excellent, incomparable pamphlet," while Sarah simply comments drily, "the news papers have . . . treated me with some Extracts [from the pamphlet] by way of Sandwhich's to prevent my being famish'd, & among them such a rhapsody about the Queen of France as must have given a little shock to the delicacy of Mrs Burkes conjugal sensibility."[35] Thus, on the basis of reading alone, one might concur with Elizabeth, when she writes to Sarah upon sending her a parcel of reference books, that "you make so good use of history it wd be strange not to be glad to furnish you with it."[36] But Elizabeth's phrase gestures beyond reading toward the broader mid-century preoccupation with the educational utility of history already noted. Scott, her sister implies, not only reads history to her own profit, but also makes it useful to others – and thereby financially profitable to herself.

After the 1752 breakup of her brief marriage to George Lewis Scott especially, Sarah Scott lived in precarious financial circumstances and looked to authorship as a means of earning money.[37] Despite ill-health, the secrecy in which she enveloped her projects, and the challenges of negotiating manuscript sales from provincial locations such as Batheaston, Scott worked hard at writing saleable copy and marketing it to appropriate booksellers. Thus she writes to Elizabeth soon after the publication of her 1762 *Millenium Hall* that "I am much obliged to you for recommending it & shall be exceedingly so if you cou'd set Gustavus on foot a little; my reason for which is that I am in treaty with Millar, for my Geography, not yet finished which he is to have in Summer, and if a little sale cou'd be procured for Gustavus, which he published, it wou'd go far towards getting me the price I ask." She continues with the statement:

> I get but very little by *Millenium Hall*, much less than ever I did by any thing, but I bargained for the price in an agreement for a more extensive scheme, . . . in truth *a thing like that* takes so very little time in writing that I can not say but my time was sufficiently paid for; it was not a month's work, therefore it brought me in about a guinea a day; more than I cou'd gain by *a better thing*.[38]

Surely one of the "better things" referred to is *Gustavus Ericson*. With this biography, Scott likely hoped to capitalize on the eighteenth-century British reading public's ongoing fascination with the histories of Swedish monarchs as Protestant military heroes.[39] Andrew Millar used the end-piece of *Gustavus Ericson* to advertise eight other books lending the dignity of public history to Mr. Raymond's biography; these books included Hume's and Robertson's histories, a complete edition of Milton on royal paper, the fourth edition of Thomas Stanley's *History of Philosophy,* and the second edition of Jonas Hanway's *Historical Account of British Trade over the Caspian Sea, illustrated with Maps and Copper-Plates.* In 1762, on the other hand, Scott published, with apologies for "this hasty performance" and an accompanying "Errata" notice, an anonymous *History of Mecklenburgh, from the First Settlement of the Vandals in that Country, to the Present Time.* This book enabled Scott to turn her *Gustavus* research to further professional and political advantage, in an explicit attempt at "imparting satisfaction to" "the general curiosity of the nation" about the new Queen Charlotte's ancestry. Scott and her bookseller Newbery had read their market well: the history went into a second edition the same year.[40]

Errata sheets notwithstanding, Scott set a high standard of scholarship for her work. Although, like Hume, she relied on published sources, she annotated her narratives more extensively than he did, providing a full apparatus of footnotes and glosses for her two more "serious" histories, *Gustavus Ericson* and *The Life of D'Aubigné* (in the first case in Latin, in the latter in a more anglicized style), as well as an alphabetical index of names and places for *D'Aubigné,* and an editorial preface for *Gustavus* which discusses the merits of various sources. In the conclusion to her *Gustavus* preface, she comes down firmly, though gracefully, on the side of antiquarian accuracy over narrative elegance:

> The Abbe Vertot is so approved an author, that I do not know whether I shall easily be forgiven the liberty I have been obliged to take of relating some facts entirely contrary to his representation of them. There is so much elegance and spirit in his history, that I could not have pleased myself so well, as by a faithful translation of what he relates of Gustavus; but some of his facts are so contradictory to those recorded by the best authors, and others so misplaced in time and order, that I could not avoid differing sometimes entirely, at others in part, from him . . . . it would ill have become a writer who could not imitate him in his graces, to copy him in his defects. The authors on whose authority I have chiefly relied, are Puffendorf, Loccenius, Pontanus, Meursius, Cramero's Compendium of the History of Sweden, and Des Roche's History of Denmark (p. xiii).

Scott's apparatus, indeed, is significantly more elaborated than that of the rival Vertôt translation. In her Mecklenburgh history, Scott accommodates her more general audience by providing a simple introductory explanation of the political structure of the German states, limiting the number of footnotes, and employing marginal glosses merely to signal changes of date and ruler. Yet the apparatus remains as a mark of her commitment to scholarly standards and to acknowledging the work of her fellow historians. When Elizabeth suggests that Sarah write a history of Francis I, her reply indicates a combined professional pragmatism and awareness of developing standards of authorial integrity; she speculates that such a history "might easily be so compos'd from different authors as not to require the name of a translation, only acknowleging in a preface the great use Gailliard had been of."[41]

Perhaps more interesting in light of the period's lively debates about the nature and role of history and its contiguous genres, Scott's publications are generically self-conscious. Her preface to *Gustavus Ericson*, for example, includes a comparative and detailed analysis of the pitfalls of writing history and biography. Her choice of biography is more than a matter of conveniently available materials. "General histories," she argues, tend to a kind of false representation of cause and effect, whereby "great actions appear to arise from great motives; kingdoms seem to quarrel with kingdoms, and every thing is represented as the effect of the foresight of wisdom, the rage of ambition, the arts of the acute politician, the passion of an headstrong prince, or the imbecillity of a weak one," even though actions may in reality have been "inconsistent" and motives "contrary." "The biographer," on the other hand, "enters into a detail which more properly developes the human mind," "thus teaching the knowledge of men in a superior manner, while [he] acquaint[s] us with facts" (pp. iii–iv). In this formulation, Scott shows herself alert to Enlightenment writers' turn against the high narrative traditions of classical history, Bolingbroke and her own regal subject notwithstanding. Yet she manages to have her biography and her conventional history, too – in a double irony, Scott inserts a 94-page political history of Sweden as a preamble to her 307-page biography, thereby not only writing a substantial piece of traditional history without precisely asserting that she is doing so,[42] but also subordinating that history to biography in an inversion of standard generic hierarchies. In effect, Gustavus Ericson's lifestory becomes in Scott's hands what Phillips has called "philosophical biography," wherein biography serves as a more flexible instrument than traditional history for organizing the materials of religious, political, and social history.[43]

A similar repudiation of the narrative traditions of classical history becomes more politically bold in the preface to *The History of Mecklenburgh*, where Scott laments the necessity of working with histories of the

German empire as source materials and hints at the excessively bloodthirsty nature of the new queen's ancestors: "few events," she writes, "occur while they [the principalities of the empire, including Mecklenburgh] remain in amity; and the history of *Germany* thus becomes entirely military; and consequently unentertaining" (p. xi). In this formulation, the dichotomy is not one of history versus biography, but the Johnsonian one of the newly valued, less glaring domestic virtues subsuming the traditional *vertu* of the public hero.[44] With respect to Mecklenburgh, the domestic unit is the nation: "An ambitious man may spread his renown through many nations, while peaceful virtues are seldom wafted by the voice of fame, beyond those confines which set bounds to the Prince's power" (p. xi). But as Scott moves from Sweden and Mecklenburgh to rural England and France, the "private" man, biography's ideal subject, comes to signify not the private motives and domestic behavior of the public figure, but the individual beneath notice on the basis of his birth, title, or wealth (*D'Aubigné*, p. xi). Thus Scott claims to be led to write her 1766 fictional *The History of Sir George Ellison* because "the life of a man more ordinarily good, whose station and opportunities of acting are on a level with a great part of mankind, might afford a more useful lesson than the lives of his superiors in rank or piety, as more within the reach of imitation"; she will tell the story of a life "which in some particulars every man, in all particulars some men may imitate, his actions being confined within the common sphere of persons of fortune, in several articles within the extent of every gentleman's power" (p. 3).[45] It is from this sort of life, she tells us again in the 1772 *D'Aubigné* preface, that the reader may learn that "virtue is within the reach of every station; it cannot, in all, wear a dress equally splendid, but it is alike respectable in its plainest garb, and in its richest attire" (p. xiv).

As Scott's biographical subject has come more "within the reach of every station," she has clearly been elaborating her notion of history's readers. Even when writing in the male voice of Henry Augustus Raymond, Scott regrets that

> many of the particulars of his [Gustavus Ericson's] private conduct are buried in oblivion, while his public actions are preserved with sufficient exactness: his behaviour as a father, a husband, and a friend, are passed over in silence, and his conduct as a king only recorded. We admire the virtues of a monarch, but the social graces win our affections, and we are more apt to be charmed with benefits showered down on one miserable family, than with those which are dispensed through a whole nation: as we are more affected by a private distress than by public misery (p. xi).

To fill the gap for this affective reader, Scott speculates about motives, invents dialogue, and inserts generalized moral sentiments in the hallmark mid-century style of a Sarah Fielding, Samuel Richardson, or Samuel Johnson. Thus, in Gustavus's conversion to Lutheranism, "His reason acquiesced in the doctrines of Luther, and his inclinations welcomed them. He was half persuaded of their truth, by his wishes that they might be true; and he who desires to be convinced is seldome far from conviction" (p. 216). In this respect Scott's history departs significantly from the Vertôt, which is characterized by detailed analyses of revenues and power balances, with little personalization of relationships or internalization of motives.[46] With respect to Gustavus's "peaceful virtues," she dares not "expatiate," for fear that "few readers would patiently proceed through (what would be called) a lifeless detail of such actions" (p. 376). Yet she ultimately subverts her own account of the traditional military hero with the concluding assertion that

> the writer records with pleasure, and his readers peruse with admiration, those facts, which in reality render the vanquished miserable, and distress the conquerors; for while the prince gains renown, his subjects are oppressed with taxes to supply the expence of his wars, and sacrifice their lives to raise his fame. . . . These are the real sufferings of a people, who, for their sins, are visited by that cruel punishment, an heroic prince (pp. 375–76).

In the 1772 D'Aubigné biography, on the other hand, there are increasing hints that, in a culture where the distinction between history and biography parallels those constantly drawn not only between public and private, great and common, but also between male and female, history and novel, Scott is quietly carrying out a territorial incursion not only by elaborating on individualized states of mind, but also by valuing the domestic and the common as the materials of history. Thus the preface quotes from the "private memoirs" of her subject, in which he "addresses his children." In this context, D'Aubigné argues, he can "lay open every action, which it would have been a shameful impertinence to have inserted in my Universal History." Only in his memoirs can the speaker "recount every minute particular as if you were still sitting on my knee, and listening to me, with the amiable simplicity of childish attention." The anonymous author concludes that "D'Aubigné's address to his children I may apply to my readers" (pp. xi–xiii).

While not explicitly gendering her authorial voice as female, Scott uses the model of an intimate domestic exchange, and the text recording such an exchange, to overcome the limitations of the public historian of the past, who, seeing only through "the gross mist of dullness, distinguishes only great and glaring objects," and "void of the refinements of taste, and delicacy of understanding," cannot appreciate the "sentiments . . . expressed in familiar conversation," the "beauty of elegance," and "the amiable part of a character, which appears in mild colours and delicate touches" (*Gustavus*, p. x). Scott is evoking the terms of mid-eighteenth-century confidence in the progressive refinement of civil society, but she is also clearly elevating the domestic and the feminized as integral to such a society's greatest achievements. Again, biography manifests less a modest reluctance to aim so high as historiography than an assertion that the hierarchy of genres ought to be leveled, or even inverted.

READING THE GENDER OF SCOTT'S HISTORIES

My discussion of Scott's histories, and particularly her biographies, as elaborating a theory and practice of history-writing that is scholarly yet appealing to the general reader, and that values the private over the public as the sphere of individual motives and of universal virtues, cannot of course be uninfluenced by my knowledge of her sex and social status. Yet we have also noted that many of her historiographer contemporaries, including Bolingbroke, Hume, and Johnson to varying extents, participated in what might be called a feminization of history-writing. What of Scott's original reviewers, who encountered her as "Mr. Raymond," or as an anonymous author? First, they pay virtually no attention to her claim to value the less glaring public virtues of Gustavus Ericson or Theodore D'Aubigné – in their choice of extracts and summaries of the importance of these biographical subjects, they emphasize military and sensational exploits. They do, nevertheless, endorse the appeal of these histories to the general reader: "Whatever portion of reputation the learned may think proper to assign our author, we doubt not but the public in general will approve of his labours, as he has not only rendered his narrative [of Gustavus Ericson] entertaining, but selected his subject with judgment." They agree with their mid-century colleagues that the historian's primary task is to tell a story, to shape the facts into "a beautiful edifice," not produce a dull chronicle. Indeed, the *Critical Review* calls *The History of Mecklenburgh* "entertaining" three times.

Only one review, again in the *Critical*, comes close to adopting Scott's position on the exemplary value of the private life; not surprisingly, it is a review of *The Life of D'Aubigné*, which notes approvingly that the writer "undertakes . . . to hold forth to public view his character, which ought not to sink into oblivion, and which has not yet met with an historian who has done it justice in those essential points where it merits most," for "to relate the actions of a virtuous man, especially those in the trials of adversity, is to give mankind the properest lesson for becoming virtuous, as it may induce them to imitate such amiable examples."[47]

Most striking, however, are the multiple manifestations of gender assumptions in these reviews. As an "amiable example" of virtue, D'Aubigné's story is told by an author "admiring the spirit and constancy with which he exposed his fortune and his life in defence of his religion":[48] admiring writer, virtuous actor, and imitating reader are held together by a shared value for spirited action and by the assumed possession of fortunes and lives to be disposed of honorably. The reviewers' attention to the author's use of source materials, noted above, further indicates an assumption of mutual membership in the company of "the learned," who will ultimately decide "Whatever portion of reputation [they] . . . think proper to assign our author." But most importantly, the terms used to describe Scott's style form a virtual catalogue of those Laura L. Runge has defined as coding masculinity in the critical lexicon of the eighteenth century: "judicious," "spirited," "animated enough," "rapid and fluent, though sometimes flippant and unchaste," "the liveliness of his diction," "peculiar strength and vivacity both of style and sentiment," and so on.[49] A passage from the *Monthly Review* on *Gustavus Ericson* bears quotation in full:

> Indeed, the life and reign of Gustavus, is marked throughout with the most striking and interesting events. All is spirit and motion: and the description of such busy scenes, demands an Historian possessed of no common degree of energy and vivacity.
>
> Our Author, it must be admitted, is far from being deficient in these qualities. His style is, in general, easy, spirited, and manly. His remarks are always distinguished by a peculiar freedom and vigour of thought, and are frequently made with great judgment and propriety.

If anything, this review finds that *Gustavus Ericson* errs on the side of masculinity of style: "Mr. Raymond's History . . . if not elegant and correct, is nevertheless animated and entertaining."[50] Such language may seem inevitable with respect to a text purportedly by a Mr. Raymond, but the *Critical Review* concludes in turn, for the anonymous *The History of Mecklenburgh*, that "as Mr. Newbery's name stands at the bottom of its dedication to the queen, we have no right to refuse him the honour of being its author." One cannot help but wonder how the reviewer's tone in describing one incident from the *History* might have changed had he known that Mrs. Scott, rather than Mr. Newbery, was the author: "Our Author then gives an entertaining account of the imprisonment of a king of Denmark, by a count of Schwerin, a Mecklenburgh prince, for having violated his bed while he was upon an expedition in the Holy Land."[51]

Scott's reviewers, then, appear to have assumed that history was written by men, for an audience consisting mostly of men. Some recent critics have seen *Millenium Hall*'s framing device, and the fact that *Sir George Ellison* is its sequel, as implying that Scott's model of a Christian society is directed at such a public political sphere.[52] These inferences would seem to be borne out by Scott's repeated choice of male biography, whether factual or fictive, as her genre; implicitly, she would appear to agree with Charlotte Lennox, as Judith Dorn has formulated it, that while women may properly read and even write history, they can only be scandalous and improper "subjects of history."[53] However, a closer examination of what Scott did with her biographies, as a professional seeking a public readership, as a theorist of historical genres, and as a writer selecting, shaping, and compensating for her sources, leads one to conclude that Scott was articulating a developing model of who should make use of history, and how. Emerging from a highly circumscribed private sphere, her biographies were nevertheless acts of engagement, through the disembodied mode of anonymous or pseudonymous publication, in a public discussion of what made lives useful.

By these actions, Scott took part in the British Enlightenment project of writing a refined, socially responsible, pacific, and honorable Protestant public sphere into being. Her views appear to have resembled those of her contemporary Elizabeth Carter during the third quarter of the eighteenth century, as outlined by Harriet Guest, in a simultaneous commitment to a "quite extreme personal self-effacement and the obligation [both moral and financial] to publish exemplary work."[54] An account of Sarah Scott in the republic of letters, then, reconfigures that which has focused on her fiction, in particular *Millenium Hall*, and thereby emphasized her partly autobiographical concern for the position of women in a restrictive patriarchy. Her career as a whole suggests rather that a print-based republic of letters extended an invitation to women, to provincial writers, to those excluded for various reasons from the clubs and salons of London as cultural center, to contribute to the creation of an ideal political subject. Yet the tendency, often, was to use these contributions to reinforce the ideal of an English reading subject who was "activist, virtuous, [and] *masculine*."[55]

ANONYMITY AND THE REPUBLIC OF LETTERS

As we have seen, Scott consistently erected a screen of anonymity between her private identity and the public sphere of print, despite evidence suggesting that she valued her historical writing highly. In this she was unlike even Elizabeth Carter, whose career and social position paralleled hers in a number of ways, and who worried much more explicitly and at length about the issue. She seems to have shunned relationships that might have identified her as an intellectual; her resistance to being drawn into her sister's bluestocking salon in London, of which Carter was a part, is of a piece with her above-cited response to the Macaulay visit and with her insistence that to appear on a printed subscription list as "Madame Scott, Soeur de Madame Montagu" was "a distinction in my opinion more honourable than any title in his list, tho' there are some very splendid ones."[56] Scott's social position, below that of Elizabeth's cousin by marriage, Lady Mary Wortley Montagu, yet above that of Carter, the daughter of a provincial clergyman, may well have played a significant role in this reluctance to acknowledge the title of author. At any rate, Bridget Hill's generalization about the double bind of anonymity for the female author in the eighteenth century – "Anonymity, while protecting women writers against attacks based on their sex, also deprived them of any identity"[57] – though clearly not accurate for all of the writers in this study, conveys a truth for Scott that nevertheless presupposes the desirability of an authorial identity in a manner not applicable to her.

While it is unlikely to be the only explanation, Scott's wish for obscurity must have been one factor in her constant change of booksellers. Her colleagues in the publishing world appear to have been content to help her maintain the split between private gentlewoman and public intellectual. The reviews of *Millenium Hall* and *Sir George Ellison* make this especially clear. The former is presented rather uneasily as improving, cautionary material for young women, if not precisely a novel, while the reviewer of its sequel recommends it to "every man of fortune, who has more money than he can rationally employ, except in generous and beneficent acts."[58] The *George Ellison* review makes only one buried reference to the place Millenium Hall, as though the assumed shift in target audience, from young women to landed gentlemen, establishes an unbridgeable chasm between the two halves of this continuous social project. On April 17, 1772, James Boswell notes a conversation at "Mr. Dilly's" wherein he and a Dr. Gibbons "talked of George Lewis Scott, who published the continuation of Chambers's *Dictionary*, and of his separation from his wife (Mrs. Montagu's sister), who writes novels."[59] Twenty years after the Scott marriage breakup, Boswell recalls both that fact and Sarah's novels, of which Thomas Carnan had just printed her fourth. But he is sitting in the home of one of the Dilly brothers, who are at that precise moment printing Scott's *Life of D'Aubigné*, published May 19. Since Dilly recommended Boswell as attorney to Catharine Macaulay, whom he was also publishing at the time, he seems unlikely to have been reticent regarding Scott's authorship of histories without such secrecy being at her own insistence. Whether he told Boswell or not (and the very fact of this conversation hints that the imminent publication of *D'Aubigné*, though suppressed in this account, may have prompted it), he, or he and Boswell, colluded with Scott in obscuring her identity as historiographer.

As a result of such fragmentation of her body of work, Mrs. Scott the author, even when named, never gains coherence as an author-function of print culture, let alone as a historian or intellectual. This is further indicated in a *Gentleman's Magazine* account of Miss Mary Scott's poem *The Female Advocate*, published in 1774. Although Sarah Scott had already published three works in the 1770s alone, more than her sister Elizabeth published in her lifetime, this poem's author, the reviewer notes, has named Elizabeth Montagu (and Catharine Macaulay) among the English female muses, but has not "recollected" a "namesake of her own, and the sister of Mrs. Montagu (Mrs. Scott), the author of Millennium Hall, the History of Sir George Ellison, and the Life of Theodore Agrippa D'Aubigné."[60] The reviewer, whose business it is to know such things, connects the name "Scott" with a publishing career including both fictional and historical biographies, but the more general reading and writing public, even when listing outstanding women writers of the time, cannot recollect her. Eleven years later, when Clara Reeve's *Progress of Romance through Times, Countries, and Manners* sets out consciously to name women as among the "capital writers" of fiction, Scott's disappearance into anonymity and the dispersal of her oeuvre seem fully accomplished, for Reeve speaks approvingly of both *Millenium Hall* and *Sir George Ellison* without linking them together, without attributing either work to Scott, and without showing any awareness of their author's achievements in history-writing – all contrary to her practice of crediting women writers at every opportunity.[61]

So a reading of Sarah Scott's history-writing through a model of the republic of letters leads me to conclude that, when held in counterpoise to a narrative of female authorship as increasingly gendered and essentialized in the eighteenth century, the notion of an intellectual exchange that could to a significant extent transcend barriers of gender, geography, genre, and status in forming a public sphere serves as a valuable corrective. Yet the print culture which enabled the membership of a writer such as Sarah Scott in a disembodied, inclusive English republic of letters simultaneously contributed to the obscuring of a coherent public identity. It would appear that in England, at least, the republic of letters was prepared to grant citizenship to those living a life of the mind, incarnate in a body of published work that engaged the issues being debated in the public sphere, while collaborating with those citizens in denying their very existence. Another option for the female author, of course, was to bring her private identity as a woman with her into the public sphere of letters. In this case, such tangible markers as geographical location, gender, and station became factors that could either be exploited as assets or struggled against as impediments to the establishment of a desirable public identity. The next two chapters juxtapose two sets of authors' negotiations of such challenges in the face of shifting structures of the public sphere of print.

CHAPTER 4

The (female) literary careers of Sarah Fielding and Charlotte Lennox

> Sally [Fielding] has mended her style in her last Volume of D[avid] Simple, ... The Art of Tormenting, the Female Quixote, and Sir C. Goodville are all sale work. I suppose they proceed from her pen, and heartily pity her, constrain'd by her Circumstances to seek her bread by a method I do not doubt she despises.
>
> (Lady Mary Wortley Montagu to Lady Bute, 1754)[1]

> [Mrs. Fielding] has really found great advantage from being of a sex which has a title to politeness from the other, for she has received the genteelest Letters accompanied with more substantial services from most of the scientificks & beaux Esprits of our Kingdom, those especially who are highest in reputation.
>
> (Sarah Scott to Elizabeth Montagu, *c.* 1760)[2]

The fragmentary nature of Sarah Scott's literary reputation, both in her own time and now, despite her numerous, varied, and relatively well-received publications, invites the question of whether a literary career as we would recognize it was achievable for a woman writer at the height of the eighteenth century. But ahead of this gender-specific question stands the even more fundamental one of the relation of the "person of letters" to the literary professional, and the applicability of the term "career" to each. In his analysis of David Hume's career, Jerome Christensen insists that from its Renaissance origins, the term "man of letters," though "generally honorific, . . . was never entirely free of the stigma of commerce, for the condition of possibility for the man of letters, and the basis for all his subsequent claims of independence, is the existence of the printing press and the publishing business." Christensen allows for a vestigial eighteenth-century resistance to commercialization and professionalization in this idealized identity, which incorporated images of exchange and specialized service, but in the benign figure of the middleman or mediator, distinct from the slave of the booksellers. He suggests, nevertheless, that in the second half of the century the gap between the person of letters and the professional author was fast closing. For both of these types, Christensen claims, the career was a practice that produced a narrative, an "intelligible course" modeled upon and made possible by the repetitive and distributive qualities of print publication and by the mutually reinforcing relation between "the influence of the writer" and "the induction of society." Frank Donoghue expresses this relation in less abstract terms by defining the career as a collaborative narrative involving the writer and those principal readers, the reviewers.[3] In this chapter, I will rely on this collaborative model of the career, illustrating with two examples how a career trajectory might be determined by a writer's apparent self-identification and conception of her professional goals and societal position, acting on and reacting to the social and economic conditions represented by her particular and local situation.

As I have indicated in my introduction to this book, Christensen's argument elides the presence of the female author in the republic of letters, a presence similarly obscured by Donoghue's 1996 pronouncement that, for the eighteenth century, "the literary career was an exclusively male form of social practice."[4] In the background to the discussion, indeed, is Sarah Scott, who refused to participate in the creation of an identity understood in terms of a career, rather entering into, and withdrawing from, the literary marketplace at discrete intervals without signalling a continuity between her interventions. While the model of a self-conscious practice of career is therefore inappropriate for Scott, Sarah Fielding and Charlotte Lennox by contrast clearly encouraged the creation of a continuous career narrative through internal indicators in their texts and through private and public representations of their work. This chapter therefore situates these two female authors on either side of Christensen's narrowing gap. Fielding's approach was that of the "person of letters," representing her work as arising out of a self-generated impulse, but one that was induced by the perceived needs of the society around her, whereas Lennox lamented the "slavery to the Booksellers"[5] that externally drove her continuous output. Yet both pursued and achieved a cumulative professional identity that resulted in greater audience recognition and economic reward than Scott ever achieved.[6] In other words, gender, while one determinant of a woman writer's career, was far from the only, and perhaps not always the most significant determinant of that career's trajectory. My comparison of Fielding and Lennox will show that not only should these two writers be understood as professionally "successful" in mid-eighteenth-century terms, but also that the differences in their career patterns suggest important variables – namely, those of geographical location, mode of publication, professional connections, and patronage networks – in determining their professional experiences.

This chapter thus argues that eighteenth-century British women writers were faced with a range of choices that, if limited and involving risk, nevertheless required their active engagement in the mapping of their writing careers. While this claim may not seem startling, a tendency of literary historians to remember only one or two texts (generally novels) of a woman writer's oeuvre, and to assume that women were merely reactive, responding initially to financial pressures in their attempts to publish, and then with a uniform lack of self-confidence or ambition to a fixed set of societal obstacles, has resulted in a map of women's writing covered with disconnected points rather than career trajectories. In Fielding's case, this has taken the form of a repeated focus on the supposedly self-deprecating advertisement to her first novel, *The Adventures of David Simple*, and her brother Henry's condescending preface to the second edition, in which he assures the reader that he has "endeavoured, tho' in great Haste" to correct Sarah's "small Errors" of style as what "no Man of Learning would think worth his Censure in a Romance; nor any Gentleman, in the Writings of a young Woman."[7] Donoghue's citation of this example as recently as 1996, while feminist in its intent, arguably does little to advance Robert S. Hunting's 1957 discussion of "this very busy man," Henry Fielding, reading "affectionately, patiently, whimsically, ironically, . . . through the brave and bungling efforts of a loving, trusting sister."[8]

For Lennox, the problem is more subtle, and perhaps therefore more insidious. Catherine Gallagher, for example, speculates in her 1994 *Nobody's Story: The Vanishing Acts of Women Writers in the Marketplace, 1670–1820* that "Lennox became the center of a remarkable circle of (mostly male) collaborators and promoters" because her situation as an unhappily married woman made her "a representation of deserving, dispossessed authorship." Separating the conditions of Lennox's authorship from her professional achievements, which rivalled those of many of her male colleagues, Gallagher explains these colleagues' support in terms of gender relations, concluding that it was provided because Lennox skillfully "broadcast her dispossession and thereby invited the investment of time, labor, and money in her career."[9] Given, first, the fact that Lennox's greatest marital discord seems to have coincided with a later period in which her appeals *failed* to mobilize supporters effectively, in contrast to a relative absence of explicitly gendered appeals in Lennox's extant correspondence of the 1750s and 1760s, and given also the collaborative nature of so much writing in the Johnson circle at the time,[10] I question an explanation that attributes Lennox's attraction of supporters solely to mid-century gender restrictions and domestic circumstances, and not at all to her proven authorship and professional collegiality. Such a reading in effect only rings changes upon the frequent critical conclusion already noted in my introduction to this study, namely, that the shape of works such as Lennox's *The Female Quixote* can be explained in simple terms as the outcome of censorship of the female writer.

The comparative method of this chapter will help set these two literary careers in relief against the background of eighteenth-century print culture, making more visible the components used in their original construction. Noting differences between careers will thus make clearer how these differences served to limit, but were also exploited in an attempt to maximize profits, build a reputation, and map a professional direction. In other words, the interrelationship between the agency of the individual writer and the subcultures of a rapidly modernizing print culture becomes the focal point when we attend to differences between careers, rather than assuming their uniformity – or, indeed, their nonexistence. Ultimately, it will appear that Fielding's career path represents that of the person of letters, balancing traditional models of the writer's social place with a developing print culture's modes of economic support and audience appeal. Lennox, on the other hand, practices both by choice and by necessity a more professionalized model of the writer, one that is more prescient of the future of authorship. In the final section of this chapter, I will suggest how an acknowledgment of these differences might be brought to bear on discussions of influence – specifically, on the question of Fielding's and Lennox's responses to Richardson (and Johnson) in their *Remarks on "Clarissa"* and *The Female Quixote*, respectively.

SIMILARITIES

Sarah Fielding's life as an author, which likely originated in 1742 with an anonymous contribution to her brother Henry's novel *Joseph Andrews* (the letter "from Leonora to Horatio"),[11] was publicly launched as a career with the success of her fiction *The Adventures of David Simple* in 1744, presented as "By a Lady." While critics have made much, as we have seen, of the prefatory material, one might focus rather on the success of this novel, which led to its almost immediate reissue. Janine Barchas has argued that the novel appealed stylistically to a broad popular audience, and suggests that Henry Fielding's corrections represent in part "an objection to a writing style labelled as lower-class and ephemeral by prominent authors such as Swift and Johnson" – Sarah was "importing . . . typographical gimmickry into the novel."[12] Whatever her brother thought, Fielding appears to have planned her career moves as effectively as fluid and shifting conditions could allow. Sequels, for example, offered the most immediate means of reproducing an initial success and capitalizing upon a familiar work, and a number of mid-century women novelists seized upon this device.[13] Thus Fielding published, in 1747, *Familiar Letters between the Principal Characters in David Simple*, an epistolary collection only loosely related to her first novel but obviously drawing on the recognizable name, and in 1753 *The Adventures of David Simple, Volume the Last*, a narrative continuation of the original story, but with a significantly darkened atmosphere and social outlook. In the preface to *Volume the Last*, a no-nonsense statement of purpose written by "a Female FRIEND of the AUTHOR," likely Fielding's fellow-author Jane Collier, no traces of apology or feminine modesty appear. Rather, Fielding's work is compared favorably to that of Shakespeare; other parallels are drawn to the traditionally masculine domains of music composition and history painting (pp. 241–42). Her 1757 *The Lives of Cleopatra and Octavia* is carefully researched in a range of classical and modern sources, and the introduction asserts in the author's own voice the superiority of biography to the fanciful stories of "a *Joseph Andrews*" or a "Sir *Charles Grandison*."[14]

After eight substantial works of fiction which included the "moral romance" *David Simple*, the first children's novel (*The Governess*, 1749) and other journalistic forays, a highly experimental combination of narrative and chorus in *The Cry: A Dramatic Fable* (1754), and the already noted fictional autobiographies of figures from classical history, as well as the important critical pamphlet *Remarks on Clarissa* (1749), Fielding's career culminated twenty years after "Leonora to Horatio" with a 1762 translation from the Greek of Xenophon's *Memoirs of Socrates*.[15] The latter was immediately acknowledged as a fine translation, placing Fielding among the select group of eighteenth-century English female classicists, and it has been critically respected since its publication.

Fielding thus followed, if not the classical and Renaissance trajectory of the poet's career, the eighteenth-century version of it, in her rough progression from miscellaneous pieces, to the relatively demotic fictional and familiar letter genres, to the more prestigious forms of criticism, educational writing, historical biography, and classical translation. Given the caution of mid-century booksellers with respect to new publications, remarked in my introduction, it is noteworthy that Fielding was able to convince them to risk the production of work that was generically wide-ranging and innovative; both her contemporaries and subsequent critics repeatedly note, though not always favorably, this tendency to experiment.[16] And she maintained a recognizable profile throughout; from the time of *David Simple*'s initial success, she was provided with her "public literary signature" as "the Author of David Simple,"[17] used on the title page of six of her works. No real attempt at anonymity, this signature was invoked as a badge of achievement rather than a proof of coy modesty or transgression, since Fielding's publishing activity was an open secret to her contemporary subscribers and readers. Lady Mary Wortley Montagu's tendency to make false attributions of works to Sarah Fielding is a typical effect of Fielding's having achieved an author function, an effect complained of as well by such contemporaries as Alexander Pope and her brother Henry.[18]

If Fielding's literary signature was a marketing ploy, booksellers clearly found her work marketable. She appears to have sold the copy of *The Governess* for at least four times the price of any of her novel copies. Even in the novel genre, for which G. E. Bentley estimates the average payment for a copyright in the eighteenth century to have been, variously, between £5 and £27 (lower than payments for almost any other category of publication, and certainly the lowest in proportion to length[19]), it is significant that copy prices for Sarah Fielding's later novels not published by subscription were at the 50- to 60-guinea mark. She seems to have become increasingly experienced in negotiating her price, continuing to handle such arrangements even when living in Bath: Fielding's letter of December 14, 1758 to Richardson providing details of the sale of the *Countess of Dellwyn* copy to Andrew Millar indicates that she conducted this transaction herself, including provision for an additional payment if the novel went into a second edition; her delegation of the proof-reading of the novel to Richardson or his nephew in London therefore seems more a matter of pragmatism than of a reluctance to engage in the business aspects of publication.[20]

Fielding also felt considerable confidence in the loyalty of an established readership. One indication of this is in her use of the subscription method, a means of publication which Linda Bree notes as innovative for a novelist and a woman writer when Fielding first adopted it for her *Familiar Letters.* Nor was she proven wrong: Peter Sabor counts 507 subscribers for *Familiar Letters*, 440 for *The Lives of Cleopatra and Octavia*, and 611 for *Memoirs of Socrates*, all very healthy numbers.[21] In the above-cited preface to *Volume the Last*, though it was not a subscription publication, Fielding is described as "introduc[ing] to her Readers their old Friends, with whom if they were once pleased by them, they will undoubtedly not be displeased to renew their former Acquaintance" (p. 241). Reviewers were equally supportive. In a typical reflection of her acquired reputation, one reviewer greeted *Cleopatra and Octavia* with the words, "It were superfluous to compliment the Author of David Simple upon her merits as a Writer." Sabor has noted that Fielding's translation of Xenophon, her last published work and the only one with the name 'Sarah Fielding' on the title page, "is probably the one for which she would most wish to have been remembered."

The picture, then, is one of a literary career brought to a satisfying conclusion. Sending a note of thanks and affection to her benefactor Elizabeth Montagu just months before her death and five years after her last publication, Fielding ostensibly downplays her achievements, while in effect recalling them as the basis upon which Montagu's support has been extended: "Take from me the fame of any thing I ever wrote, if any fame is due, whilst you cannot withdraw your own approbation I am well contented."[22]

While recognizing arguments which have emphasized Fielding's reputation as a "theorist," an intellectual more likely to serve her guests rarefied conversation than an edible dinner, the literary historian need not choose between financial necessity and intellectual inquiry as the force driving publication for this writer.[23] She herself combines these motives explicitly in explaining her translation goal to James Harris, the classical scholar who was a childhood Salisbury friend: "I have a double view in this Translation the Improvement of the Greek as well as the *Substantial* Utility which my Situation makes Needfull." Fielding refused to avail herself of a French translation for this edition, writing that "I believe I once had it in my hand half an hour, but would not read it or look in it so as to mark any perticular passage till I have gone through it the rough Copy with the Greek and Latin only, because . . . if I had the French before me it might encline me not so thoroughly to search the Greek Lexicon, for to spare pains, and more especially at my time of Life, is natural."[24] Characterized by projects chosen primarily, it appears, for the intellectual and creative challenges they offered, yet managed to generally good effect within the publishing system of the day, Fielding's sequence of works fits the "person of letters" career model particularly well, combining as it does a sense of self-development with external affirmation in the form of financial remuneration and achieved reputation.

In the 1770s and 1780s, Fielding's *David Simple* and *Ophelia* (1760) were reprinted in abridged or collected editions of novels, in the company of such works as Lennox's *The Female Quixote* and *Henrietta*, and novels by Henry Fielding, Richardson, and Smollett. Cheryl Turner points out that circulating library catalogues highlighted the names of authors such as Fielding and Lennox as writers whose "public status" made it "advantageous for the [library] proprietors to name them." In 1774 Mary Scott's poem *The Female Advocate*, which had neglected to name Sarah Scott, praised both women: "Twas FIELDING's talent, with ingenuous Art, / To trace the secret mazes of the Heart," while Lennox, "'in various nature wise!'" is described as "virtue's friend," who "Bid[s] the coquette in blushes hide her face" and "Bid[s] virtue . . . / Press on, and keep perfection still in view." Hester Thrale in 1778 ranked Lennox on a "Scale of Novel Writers" as superseded only by Richardson and Rousseau (though "at an immeasurable Distance" beneath them), and on a par with Smollett, slightly ahead of Henry Fielding. And in 1785 Clara Reeve paid particular attention to each of these two writers in her *The Progress of Romance through Times, Countries, and Manners*, emphasizing their production of considerable bodies of work by naming several texts by each – seven titles for Fielding, including the Xenophon, "which is reckoned her capital work," and three for Lennox, in addition to a general mention of "works of a superior kind, which are above our retrospect, though we can only speak here of her Novels."[25]

Charlotte Lennox's contemporary professional reputation was thus comparable to Fielding's; indeed, it might be said to be even higher in that it was less genre-specific, and references tended to be made back to more than one previous work. Thus the *Monthly Review* notes, for the *Memoirs* of Sully, "that the present translation is judiciously executed; that the language is easy, and proper for the subject, and such as may well become the fair hand to which the public is obliged for the *Female Quixote* and *Shakespear Illustrated*."[26] As late as 1797, the bookseller J. Bell considered it worth his while to advertise a new novel, *The History of Sir George Warrington; or, the Political Quixote* as "By the Author of the Female Quixote," though the second printing of title pages suggests that he found the marketing power of this link to have waned, since he now claimed the anonymous work to be "By the Author of the Benevolent Quixote."[27] Nevertheless, Lennox's biographer Miriam Small has compiled an impressive list of casual references to *The Female Quixote* indicating its familiarity to readers right up to 1861.[28]

Clearly, Lennox had also established a "public literary signature." In her case, this was again achieved through an early novel, though not her first individual publication: more precocious (or financially pressured) than Fielding, she published a volume of poems at the approximate age of eighteen years, in 1747, and her first novel, *The Life of Harriot Stuart*, in December 1750. The *Poems on Several Occasions* were accompanied by a dedication to Lady Isabella Finch, signed "Charlotte Ramsay," and *The Life of Harriot Stuart* was presented as "*Written by Herself.*" It was Lennox's 1752 *The Female Quixote*, however, that made a mark comparable to that of Fielding's *David Simple*, and which was most often called upon to introduce her later works. These comprised, to name only the most certain attributions, a number of ambitious translations: the five-volume *Memoirs of Maximilian de Bethune, Duke of Sully* (1755), *The Memoirs of the Countess of Berci* (1756), and *Memoirs for the History of Madame de Maintenon* (1757); *Shakespear Illustrated*, a three-volume translation of Shakespeare's source-texts accompanied by critical commentary (1753–54); *The Greek Theatre of Father Brumoy* (1760), also involving commentary as well as translation; a periodical, *The Lady's Museum* (1760–61); three further novels, *Henrietta* (1758), *Sophia* (1762, previously serialized in *The Lady's Museum*), and *Euphemia* (1790); and three plays, two of which were staged. In all, this is a remarkably substantial oeuvre, not just for a woman writer, but for any eighteenth-century author.

In this body of work, Lennox, like Fielding, displayed a broad and growing range of authorial skills, recognized by her contemporaries as beyond the merely mechanical. This included in particular an ability in fluent, elegant translation that was regularly remarked by the reviewers at a time when translated works were a publishing staple and by no means uniform in quality. The positive reception of Lennox's translations matches her own 1752 statement of preference for such work as "a good deal easier then Composition."[29] According to Small, there had been eight editions of the *Sully* by 1810, when it appeared, still attributed to Lennox, in a revised and corrected edition with a historical introduction by Sir Walter Scott. For the *Brumoy*, Lennox not only did the largest part of the translation but also supervised an all-male team of translators that included Johnson, the Earl of Orrery, James Grainger, and Gregory Sharpe; the *Critical Review* describes the finished product as "valuable in the original, but rendered more valuable by the translation," with an English that is, "with respect to stile, almost faultless," improving on

Brumoy's unwieldy "metaphors and forced allusions" so that they "assume an air of gentility . . . in the translation."[30] Her *Shakespear Illustrated*, while controversial – Garrick, for example, chided her for "a greater desire of Exposing [Shakespeare's] Errors than of *illustrating* his Beauties" and for "a kind of severe Levity & Ridicule" – was groundbreaking enough to be remembered fifty years later by one reader, after the great flood of late-century Shakespeare criticism, as a "book I have not read for half a century, but which entertained me very much when I *did* read it, though I have no doubt that she was a dashing Critic, and a superficial Historian."[31] While there is no record of Lennox knowing the classical languages, producing this work involved the remarkable feat of learning Italian, apparently in a period of less than a year, well enough to translate Shakespearean sources with facility and appeal.[32]

Lennox was adept at reading the public taste, not merely in order to elicit reader support, but as a necessary skill in proposing marketable materials to the booksellers. The bookseller Andrew Millar has been praised as one of the new eighteenth-century patrons (though both Sarah Scott and Sarah Fielding had stories to tell about being bested by him[33]); he could be persuaded to publish unknown authors, but also clearly continued to invest in new work by authors who were successful for him. Eight of Lennox's works, from *The Female Quixote* to *The Greek Theatre of Father Brumoy*, were published by Millar (sometimes together with others); for the initial agreement on *The Female Quixote*, this involved considerable behind-the-scenes effort on her part,[34] but the five multi-volume translation projects included in this group reflect Millar's confidence in her abilities not only as translator but also as leader of a team of contributors. Lennox couches later correspondence about invoking the law to regain copyright control of her very popular *Memoirs of Sully*, which had come into the hands of James Dodsley, in terms of "Mr. Lennox . . . [being] so desirous of recovering his property out of the hands of the booksellers, that he gives me leave to take any measures that shall be judged proper," but it is clearly Mrs. Lennox who is conducting this process. Small argues plausibly that the dispute was settled amicably, with Dodsley bringing out a "New Edition" by "the Author of the Female Quixote" in 1778 on terms presumably involving financial remuneration more advantageous to Lennox than the regaining of her copyright would have been.[35]

The most-discussed feature of Lennox's literary life, however, is her success in attracting the support of influential male authors, especially Samuel Johnson and Samuel Richardson. These writers clearly viewed her individual publications as components of an overarching career strategy.

While they were no doubt responding in a measure to her own goals and ambitions, they also appear to have been instilling or reinforcing (or in Christensen's term, "inducing") such a model in her. Thus as Lennox prepared *The Female Quixote* for publication, she received a letter from Richardson which encouraged her to think of the long term in making her revisions:

You are a young Lady have therefore much time before you, and I am sure, will think that a good Fame will be your Interest. Make therefore, your present work as complete as you can, in two Volumes; and it will give Consequence to your future Writings, and of course to your Name as a Writer.

Four years later, Lennox's comparative stature in the profession is beyond doubt in Johnson's view, despite the "Wrath" she has apparently expressed about reviews of her *Berci* translation:

I do not believe that either of the Reviews, intended you any hurt, it is certain that if they meant to hurt you they will be disappointed, and if you were not too proud already, I would tell you, that you are now got above their malice, and though you cannot expect to be always equally successful, have such a degree of reputation as will secure you from any neglect of readers or Stationers.

This reassurance reveals Johnson's sense that a high reputation is an appropriate and achievable goal for Lennox, but also implies her understanding of the degree to which a career is dependent on external acknowledgment. Her self-consciousness about keeping her name before the public is shown by her urging Johnson in the late 1770s, for example, to deal expeditiously with the printer William Strahan, probably about a proposed edition of her collected works dedicated to Queen Caroline, "as it is of great consequence to me to have the book presented to His Majesty, before I am quite forgot."[36]

The biographical narrative constructed of such expressions of anxiety and other accounts of financial struggles has arguably overemphasized Lennox's personal unhappiness, poverty, and abortive publishing projects – thus the private correspondence has overshadowed the public record of significant and tangible successes.[37] It should be remembered, for example, that when Lennox complains of her "slavery to the Booksellers," it is in a private letter to the duchess of Newcastle, where it forms part of an appeal to the duchess for permission to dedicate *Henrietta* to her and for remembrance of her promise to find a place in the civil service for her husband Alexander Lennox.

Lennox's achievement was such that by 1761 she could boast published dedications of her works to the Lady Isabella Finch, the Earl of Orrery, the Earl of Middlesex, the Duke of Newcastle, the Duchess of Newcastle, the Countess of Northumberland, Viscount Charlemont, and the Prince of Wales (now George III). The 1783 "Memoirs of Mrs. Lenox" in the *Edinburgh Weekly Magazine* reports that she had received in the late 1750s the offer of recommendation for a royal pension; Dustin Griffin conjectures convincingly that Lennox's choice rather to request a post for her husband was based on the gamble that, because a pension might well end with the aged king George II's death, such a position would provide more permanent support. The fact that this place, obtained through the Duke of Newcastle, proved an impediment to later patronage with the eclipse of the duke's influence, while tying Lennox to the wellbeing of a husband with whom her relationship appears to have been increasingly strained, does not change the fact that a pension likely signified an annual income of between £200 and £300 in recognition of her achievements, and a highly unusual form of recognition for a female writer.[38] A conservative estimate of Lennox's earnings would have to include (in addition to money gifts accompanying the permissions to dedicate and the salary earned by Alexander Lennox as a result of his wife's literary reputation) subscriptions purchased despite the nonappearance of the books proposed, copy payments for at least five novels, and translation rates for works of considerable length. As a married woman living in London with two children, Lennox's costs would have been higher than Fielding's, but she likely earned more money than her counterpart in the productive decades of her career.

DIFFERENCES

There is no denying, however, that for Lennox even more than for Fielding, the contingencies of social and marital status and simple longevity conspired to diminish the material satisfactions which might have accrued to someone with her professional reputation.[39] I wish to turn now to a more detailed examination of the effects of other, less personal or domestic factors – those of geography, professional/social networks, and modes of publication – to bring into focus the differing directions in which these woman writers chose to take their literary careers in this transitional period, and why.

Both Fielding and Lennox came to London sometime in the 1740s and made it the base from which they launched their active publishing periods. Clearly, Fielding was in close communication with her brother at this time, quite possibly there on the spot to provide materials for his

Joseph Andrews and *Miscellanies*, when he was calling on those around him to help fill out manuscripts produced under pressure. Henry in turn assisted her in selling subscriptions to her *Familiar Letters* through his connections.[40] Lennox's early career circumstances are even more obscure, but it is clear that she needed to find means of support, and moved from an unhappy attempt at using the patronage system to contact with the printer William Strahan, publication of poems in *The Gentleman's Magazine*, the friendship of Samuel Johnson, and an ever-widening professional network. It was likely residence in the city, then, which brought both women into contact with important male literary professionals such as Millar, Richardson, and Johnson; while the roles of some of these men may have been overstated or misinterpreted subsequently, there is no doubt that they provided various forms of encouragement and practical assistance in launching the two careers.

Lennox, however, appears never to have left the city for any significant period, while Fielding moved permanently to the Bath area sometime around 1753. Why was Lennox's career pursued so entirely from London, when life in a provincial town was cheaper and, thanks to steady eighteenth-century improvements in the transportation and postal systems, allowed for the continuance of a career once the key London connections had been established? One of her few accounts of a venture out of the city provides a clue: in 1760 she writes to thank the Duchess of Newcastle for providing the financial support that has allowed her to leave the city to regain her health after an exhausting series of publications – in order to recover enough to make more money back in London.[41] For her, in other words, the city was apparently the only viable locus for pursuit of her trade. The extant correspondence reveals that the network of contacts Lennox established was fundamentally collegial, though cordially so, and depended very much on urban proximity, whereby individuals might meet accidentally in a printer's shop or even on the street, send one another complimentary copies of new publications and quick notes about a mislaid book or a recent conversation, and mention a translation possibility recently spotted at a bookseller friend's. Such modes of interaction make the most efficient use of oral and print communication channels in a relatively stable society with a limited population size, as David Kaufer and Kathleen Carley have demonstrated.[42]

Lennox appears to have been adept at exploiting such opportunities,[43] arguably more adept than Fielding, but she also clearly had to work hard to remind others of her existence, needs, and location. Thus a one-sentence note thanking Thomas Birch for an "agreeable present" (probably of one of his works) and for a favorable review modulates into the hope that "you may approve of my plan for a new work which I am advised to publish by subscription, I send you one of my proposals and shall be extremely obliged to you if you will recommend my undertaking," and a 1778 letter to her most loyal friend, Johnson, expresses concern at having had "no answer to my last letter," twice begs an appointment about the urgent matter of Dodsley's threatened reissue of *Sully*, and ends with a reminder of her current address: "if the bearer is so fortunate as to find you at home he will bring me your answer, but if that should not happen I send my direction again lest my former letter should be lost."[44] Even after Johnson's death in 1784, continued connections with members of the Johnson network such as James Boswell, Mary Gwyn, Bennet Langton, Frances Reynolds, and Frances Chambers proved useful; these individuals wrote subscription proposals for her, sought out royal patrons, provided lodgings, and gave her money. And at the end of her long life, Lennox benefited substantially from one of the earliest institutions of the authorial profession, the Royal Literary Fund, through the mediation of Langton and Chambers, among others.

Throughout most of her career, however, Lennox also relied upon London's proximity to the Court in order to pursue the traditional avenues of patronage. The 1760 letter to the duchess of Newcastle cited above, which also serves the purposes of reminding the duchess of her "favourable intentions with regard to Mr. Lennox" and requesting permission to dedicate the second edition of *Henrietta* to her, concludes with her London address as a convenient means for the duchess of dispensing those favors: "If your Grace will do me the honour to signify Your pleasure to me with regard to the Dedication of *Henrietta*, a Message directed for me at the Mineral Water Warehouse in Bury Street St. James's, will come safe to my hands."[45] Similarly, Lennox's first patron, Lady Isabella Finch, was a member of the royal entourage; when this avenue to further patronage closed for reasons that remain obscure, Lennox was able to gain access through Johnson to the Earl of Orrery and the Earl of Middlesex, and perhaps through her New York childhood as a colonial officer's daughter to the Duke and Duchess of Newcastle.[46] This account indicates, in fact, how closely integrated were the traditional patronage patterns and the new networks of the literary profession, and how this integration was in part dependent upon geographical centralization.

If geographical stability and proximity to the cultural center were enabling conditions of career continuity and success in mid-eighteenth-century England, Sarah Fielding relinquished these assets, leaving behind the printer and congenial fellow-author Richardson as well as Andrew Millar, her publisher for most of her novels. Yet Fielding's career path suggests that her move to the Bath area proved a positive one even in terms of her profession.[47] For one thing, the diminished expense of her provincial location may have allowed her greater latitude for pursuing her own inclinations in the publishing projects she took on. Moreover, she possessed the asset of the sort of social connections that not only helped maintain London business links, but also helped her insert herself into local support networks. Mid-eighteenth-century Bath was a major social center with an increasingly lively cultural and publishing dimension to its civic life. Social historians have outlined its importance to the so-called "urban renaissance" of the eighteenth century, and Elizabeth Child has argued persuasively that this optimistic, forward-looking, essentially bourgeois and genteel civic character enabled, and was reflected in, the writings of a number of women of the period, among them Sarah Fielding.[48] Basing herself in Bath, known for its relatively permeable boundary between gentry and middling status,[49] seems to have permitted Fielding to practice an authorship synthesizing the social claims of the gentlewoman, albeit impoverished, to support and acceptance, with the claims of the accomplished professional to encouragement of her projects on the basis of her established reputation.

Fielding's connections in Bath included both permanent residents of the area – the bookseller James Leake (Richardson's brother-in-law), Sarah Scott, Lady Barbara Montagu, the patron Ralph Allen, and the poet Esther Lewis[50] seem all to have been important to her as a writer – and its occasional visitors, among them the aforementioned classicist and dialogue-writer James Harris and his family, Frances Sheridan, Elizabeth Montagu, and Andrew Millar. The foundation of this extensive network seems to have been friendships forged in her Salisbury childhood, where her circle included Harris, the three Collier siblings (Jane, Margaret, and Arthur), Dr. John Hoadly, and John Upton. These links were to some extent mediated through her brother and sisters during her London period, but the deaths of all her siblings made the connections, augmented by new acquaintance, more direct and visible in the Bath period. Here Harris, for example, not only encouraged and advised her by letter on her Xenophon translation but also loaned her his copy of the Greek text and, through family connections, assisted her in the purchase of a cottage. Alicia Lefanu, Sheridan's biographer, tells us that in Bath Fielding's "company was much courted, and she spent a good deal of time at the house of Allen, of Prior Park. This man . . . highly valued Sarah

Fielding's acquirements and agreeable conversation, and allowed her a small annuity."[51] The influential bluestocking Montagu's correspondence with her sister Sarah Scott indicates the former's often secret contributions to the elderly Fielding's income, designed to repair the financial neglect of her half-brother John and the loss of the annuity with Allen's death.[52]

Fielding's hybrid social and literary identity as author is reminiscent of the terms often used to describe the subscription method of publication as a synthesis of a traditional patronage system and a market-based print culture. It is therefore not surprising that, of Fielding's four major publications of her Bath period, two were highly successful subscription projects. While the subscriptions for *Familiar Letters* had been sold from London and relied heavily on Henry Fielding's efforts as well as on the recent success of *David Simple*, proposals for Fielding's *The Lives of Cleopatra and Octavia* had first been printed in London in 1748, but apparently did not sell. It was from Bath that this project finally took flight: Fielding's immediate circle of like-minded friends and professional mentors linked her to valuable patrons, who in turn accorded Fielding the respect due a well-known literary figure and energetically advocated her work.

The self-consciousness of the strategy is indicated by Sarah Scott's letter to her sister about the Xenophon subscription drive, quoted in the first epigraph to this chapter: "[Mrs. Fielding] has really found great advantage from being of a sex which has a title to politeness from the other, for she has received the genteelest Letters accompanied with more substantial services from most of the scientificks & beaux Esprits of our Kingdom, those especially who are highest in reputation."[53] The "strikingly attractive" subscription volume of the 1757 *Lives*, printed on royal paper and selling for the relatively high price of half a guinea for one volume, signals an appeal to well-heeled patrons,[54] in contrast to her more generally marketed six-shilling novels, *The Countess of Dellwyn* and *Ophelia*, and the relatively accessible six-shilling subscription to the Xenophon translation which was broadly supported, as Scott notes, by the intellectuals of England. Clearly, Fielding chose her methods of publication carefully. The subscriber system thus synchronized well with the model of her audience that Fielding reveals in this strategy and in her prefaces: a group of discriminating but well-disposed friends, at the forefront of a broader readership earned by the quality of the work with which she has previously presented them. Such a system worked ideally in the provincially based literary culture of Fielding's day, where traditional loyalties to place and family combined with modern pride in local improvements to great effect. Evidently, however, it was not a professional mode of publication in the modern sense because of the high degree of permeability between social networks and those based upon shared skills and reputation. Thus, while Sheridan likely sought out Fielding in Bath because of her reputation as a writer, a contact that seems to have been facilitated by Richardson as a colleague, Harris's connection with Fielding conversely broadened from simple friendship to include professional collaboration; Fielding and Scott seem to have been united in social projects that encompassed their writing; and Montagu never lost her sense that Fielding was as much an object for charitable patronage as a writer worthy of support on the basis of her accomplishments.[55] The sum of these varied, but interwoven, modes of support is greater than its parts, as Lennox's story illustrates by negative example.

Although Lennox conducted her career effectively within the relatively narrow and disjunct confines of a middle-class urban professionalism and a traditional Court-based system of patronage, as I have shown, she apparently failed in her attempts to move beyond the bounds of these models and draw upon a more socially based model of authorship. The absence of any acknowledged English kinship network or local roots, her transient upbringing in Gibraltar and New York, and her husband's apparent lack of useful connections beyond the print trade[56] seem to have combined to work against her fashioning something like Fielding's system. Thus, while she initiated a subscription publication on at least four occasions,[57] not one of these publications was seen through the press, at least not in subscription form. This lack of completion does not signify total failure: Lennox secured prestigious writers for her proposals (Samuel Johnson, James Boswell) and also obtained prestigious subscribers and/or dedicatees to head her lists, as I have already shown.

However, these results indicate a disjunction between her ability to work effectively with her colleagues and her inability to forge similarly successful relations with those beyond her immediate circle. Johnson's letter justifying his failure to sell subscriptions to her projected 1775 edition of *Original Works* is almost comically plaintive in tone:

> You tell me of a numerous acquaintance, and of the vain and the gay, who will be proud of standing in the same list with the Queen. Among these whom I know how many are there to whom I should be welcome if I asked them for a Guinea? With the Vain and the Gay I cannot be supposed to have much conversation, nor indeed with any who will enquire the opinion of the court on the matter.

Finally, he spells it out: "The work must be done principally by the great Ladies."[58]

Twenty years later, Mary Gwyn is again explaining the social nuances of the subscription system to Lennox, but in much sharper terms, implying the author's direct responsibility in making it work:

> Madam, I send the Opera which you wish'd me to see – and am sorry to say I can not be of any service on the occasion. Mrs. Bunbury can not with any propriety speak to the Duchess of York on the subject – as she has already mention'd to hr a work of yours – and for which we collected subscriptions, which work you do not now mention. give me leave to say; you should put it in my power, by publishing your first book; to acquit myself of the promises I made to those, whose subscriptions I receiv'd – before you Employ me again.

By contrast, Fielding's success with subscription can be credited in large part to her sense of personal obligation to her audience as her friends. Implying James Harris's efficacy as a subscription distributor, she thanks him "for those Names you was so kind to send me, which will greatly credit my List," and "for your kind Offer of trying to make the fine Gentlemen and the Ladies forgive me this Attempt," with reference to the Xenophon project. But later, writing again to Harris, at a point where the work had been delayed by illness, she worries that "the irrecoverable Treasure of time that I lost by ill-Health last Summer, a good deal distressed me, and its a disagreeable Circumstance to have one's Friends, who have kindly exerted themselves, questioned when the Book will come out."[59]

Unlike Fielding, Lennox chose not to submit to the blend of interpersonal and professional expectations that made this hybrid mode of publication work. Rather, she appears to have viewed subscription as a means of obtaining the traditional sort of patronage, but at one remove; once obtained, she saw such support as a completed, one-way business transaction, wherein her subscribers, if they found they had contributed in vain, were expected simply to write off the loss as a bad investment rather than lodge complaints with her. The fact that three of her four subscription projects involved new editions of earlier works reinforces the impression that Lennox did not see herself as beholden to her subscribers to provide much of anything besides this opportunity to make a charitable donation.[60] Thus Lennox's mode of operation, through necessity as well as choice, resembles that of a member of an economically and socially uncertain artistic profession, according to the summary of sociological analyses of such "reputational" or "incomplete" professions provided by Susanne Janssen. That is, her true social network was an essentially professional one, set apart from the large social structures she inhabited, and it was on this more exclusive or restricted network of fellow authors that she relied for access to resources and opportunities, advice and support, the rituals that established her professional identity, and the maintenance of her reputation.[61] Fielding, on the other hand, appears to have viewed her relation to the public according to the model of the man of letters, as a matter of personal, intellectual, and sociable engagement.

FIELDING, LENNOX, AND RICHARDSON

At this point it is possible to turn again to the crux of the late 1740s and early 1750s, when in the immediate aftermath of the 1747–48 publication of Richardson's *Clarissa*, both Sarah Fielding and Charlotte Lennox, as authors whose own careers were well launched and who were on the brink of their most productive periods, responded with works that explicitly invoked their fellow-writer's high-profile novel. To what extent might Fielding's and Lennox's responses to *Clarissa* and to Richardson's model of reading be a reflection of their particular situations in the literary marketplace? The premise of most critics has been that it was their disenfranchisement and material necessities that led these women to pursue the approval and assistance of powerful figures such as Richardson. This chapter has certainly shown that each experienced economic pressures – Fielding as an unmarried gentlewoman without any reliable source of support, and Lennox as a poorly connected outsider both by upbringing and by marriage – which likely made conformity a temptation. Both women needed the sorts of support which Richardson, as a well-connected and well-intentioned published author, could give to a blossoming career. The question, then, becomes how each of these women responded to the challenge of establishing and maintaining such a valuable connection.

In the light of the dichotomous career patterns I have been tracing, it is significant that Fielding's publication was a critical pamphlet, boldly announcing itself as such with the title *Remarks on "Clarissa," Addressed to the Author*, and appearing a mere month after the final installment of the novel, apparently without Richardson's prior reading of it,[62] while Lennox's commentary is contained in a novel published in 1752 and preceded by an epistolary discussion with Richardson about both the suitability of praising Richardson publicly and the possibility of his assistance in getting the novel published. Fielding's pamphlet not only offers a sympathetic analysis, but also enacts a theory of reading similar to Richardson's, yet bolder in its egalitarianism. Lennox's use of *Clarissa* in *The Female Quixote* is much more derivative in its adulatory, generalized representation – the novel is reified rather than analyzed. In effect, Fielding, while she humbles herself in a private letter to Richardson, "daring . . . but to touch the hem of [*Clarissa*'s] garment," enters into public discussion with him as a fellow-thinker about issues of reading, aesthetic representation, and the social function of fiction,[63] whereas Lennox's heroine Arabella, David Marshall speculates, "is sent . . . back as a hostage to Johnson and Richardson."[64]

Remarks on "Clarissa" begins with the affirmation of an interpretive principle frequently asserted by Richardson himself: both criticisms of the novel and their answers, to be valid, must be based on "an impartial and attentive perusal of the Story" (p. 3). On this basis, one set of readers is immediately dismissed – those who condemn the novel out of hand as "tedious stuff" and "low" without having "had [the] Patience to read it." It is worth noting, however, that Fielding is also elaborating upon a hermeneutical model which she had established well before *Clarissa*, in her 1744 novel *David Simple*. There, even sympathetic characters, male or female, when they interpret a dramatized scene or a narrative on their own, almost invariably draw laughably idiosyncratic conclusions which are corrected by the domestic group's collective conversational analyses. Camilla, for example, who has been driven from home by her stepmother, asks when she meets an obviously unhappy French gentlewoman, "if this *young Lady had not a Father alive*, and *whether it was not probable his marrying a second Wife might be the cause of her Misfortunes*" (p. 152).[65] Thus the bulk of the pamphlet takes the form of conversations between a group of readers of mixed sex and age who, after having read the novel in isolation, exchange idiosyncratic and partial responses to Richardson's text. The responses are then modified through the conversational processes of elaboration, analogy, and debate.

For Fielding, this method is about more than the dramatization of criticism. Embodying Richardson's principles of engaged readership and of interpretation through debate, these conversations also draw on the much longer tradition of the dialogue as a form in itself enacting philosophical and ethical truths. Fielding's sensitivity to the possibilities of the dialogue form very likely reflects also her close association with James Harris, who in this period contributed a dialogue to her 1747 *Familiar Letters* and probably another to Henry Fielding's *Covent-Garden Journal* in 1752, while using the form in two of his 1744 *Three Treatises*; as his biographer has put it, "'moral painting by way of dialogue' (to use Shaftesbury's own phrase), became something of a minor industry for Harris . . . between 1744 and 1752."[66]

If superficial or nonreaders are unworthy of the author's attention, those readers who emerge from this exchange without any modification of their interpretations are subject to comic self-exposure in much the same way as are the *David Simple* characters. One of these, indeed, is a young female reader who, after a lengthy discussion of Clarissa's reasons for retaining her reserve toward Lovelace during which she has remained silent, whether through inattention or disengagement, "mutter[s] out a strong Dislike, that the agreeable Mr. *Lovelace* should not become a Husband" (p. 25). The other, however, is a rheumatic old gentleman, wincing in pain, who criticizes Clarissa's authoritarian father, refuses to acknowledge Mr. Harlowe's gout as an extenuating factor, and then verbally abuses his own meekly submissive daughter before the assembled company. At the other end of the spectrum, Fielding's most accurate reader, a young lady named Miss Gibson, is the only one never required to change her initial response to an issue. This clearly makes her authoritative as the novel's principal interpreter; that authority is reinforced by references to a recent "printed Paper" containing similar observations (p. 13) – an allusion to Henry Fielding's *Jacobite Journal* 5 (January 2, 1748) – and the presence of a male character named "Mr. Johnson" (in Ruth Perry's view, an explicit reference to Samuel Johnson),[67] who chimes in on two occasions to support Miss Gibson's points with examples drawn from classical history and from a visit to a painter's salon with his friend "Mr. Tonson." The inference seems at least partly to be that accurate reading is not the prerogative of sex or age.

Importantly, this point is not made by means of a denial of gendered responses in reading. Miss Gibson is carefully represented as capable of a response colored by heterosexual desire; the one Richardsonian assertion which she refuses to accept, despite an experienced matron's vigorous defence of it, is that Anna Howe's suitor Hickman is an ideal husband – she insists that he is insipid and dull. In fact, this perception is shared by all the young women present, even by those who correctly resist Lovelace's attractions, suggesting that in this respect the generally sympathetic Fielding was one of the first to direct Richardson to his next project of creating a good *and* attractive hero in Sir Charles Grandison.

As an exemplary reader, Miss Gibson is also interesting in her increasing investment in the responses of one speaker, Bellario, to the novel. Although described at one point as the father of a daughter, Bellario enters enthusiastically into discussion of the warmly affectionate nature he looks for in the ideal woman; this and his romance name (an exception among the dialogue's Mr. Johnson, Mr. Singleton, Mr. Dellincourt, and

Mr. Barker) lend an aura of courtship to the increasing congruence of his views with those of Miss Gibson. Bree has noted that Bellario's "Conversion" from an initial position of skepticism to enthusiastic support of the novel reenacts the process of arriving at an ideal reading of it,[68] reinforcing Fielding's explicit claim that the novel can only be judged as a sequential reading experience, whereby the scenes "ris[e] in due Proportion one after another, till all the vast Building centers in the pointed View of the Author's grand Design" (p. 41). Yet at the conversation's end these two characters embark upon an epistolary correspondence in which Bellario endeavors to give "Amusement" and "Pleasure" to Miss Gibson through their mutual admiration of a novel which, at its most elementary didactic level, might be seen to be all about the dangers of corresponding with an unmarried man. Careful readers of moral fiction, one may surely infer, can be trusted to graduate from the mutually improving exercise of interpretive conversation to negotiation of their own relationships with the opposite sex.

The broader social implications of gendered dualities are also tackled explicitly by Miss Gibson in a manner that at first glance might appear to acquiesce to an essentialist ideology limiting women's sphere of action: she agrees that a lack of "all Affection" is "the heaviest Charge a Woman can be accused of; for Love is the only Passion I should wish to be harboured in the gentle Bosom of a good Woman." The succeeding statement, however, indicates that Miss Gibson is urging a conscious repudiation of evils that have universally infected human society, and which men would do well to abandon: "Ambition, with all the Train of turbulent Passions the World is infested with, I would leave to Men: And could I make my whole Sex of my Opinion, they would be resigned without the least Grudge or Envy; for Peace and Harmony dwell not with them, but on the contrary, Discord, Perturbation and Misery are their Constant Companions" (p. 18). The love of which Miss Gibson speaks, a love she sees embodied in Clarissa, is furthermore one that extends beyond heterosexual desire to consider the happiness of family and friends. This is the Sarah Fielding who created the ideally feminized David Simple, and who will soon anatomize his destruction by an inexorably hostile society. By the same token, this goes beyond the Richardson whom Jerry Beasley insightfully describes as critiquing "the corruptions of traditional male authority" by offering his heroines "an authorized language that empowered them as moral agents but that also affirmed rather than counteracted their entrapment within the male culture that created it."[69]

In short, Fielding's model of reading is more precisely termed individualistic than antifeminist: any isolated reader may go astray, and those readers whose positions are the most stereotypical of their sex and social position are in the greatest danger of interpreting wrongly. But the feminist implication is there: a young woman may be as educated and articulate a reader of a novel as any other, and need not defer in her interpretations to any but those whose readings convince her of their validity. In this Fielding challenges the eighteenth-century's developing model of "patriarchal reading" as identified by Patricia Howell Michaelson. Michaelson describes a domestic scene centered on the male reader, perceived as an orator, "a figure of power," who mediates the text for his audience, the assembled familial circle, in an expression of "self-consciously companionate relationships."[70] Thus Richardson imagines, in his correspondence with the young Sophia Westcomb, "I see you, I sit with you, I talk with you, I read to you, I stop to hear your sentiments, in the summer-house."[71] We may conclude that Richardson ultimately had more difficulty than did Fielding in following through the implications of his own model, in treating his (female) reader as an equal partner in the interpretive process, as his own response to comments on *Clarissa* increasingly took the form of prefaces, interpretive footnotes, "restored" passages underlining characters' motives, and extracts of moral sentiments. In this respect, his truest imitator was not Sarah Fielding, but Charlotte Lennox.

Lennox's 1752 *The Female Quixote, or The Adventures of Arabella* at once elevates Richardson's novel and simplifies the reader's task. This work famously, or perhaps infamously, incorporates in its penultimate chapter a discussion of the superiority of a novel like *Clarissa* to the French heroic romance as the basis of a young lady's education in life. Laurie Langbauer, among others, has made the important observation that the novel to some extent subverts this authorization of didactic realism in that it is the pleasures of romance which govern the text and constitute much of its appeal to the reader.[72] The fact remains, nevertheless, that Lennox's resolution of her novel's problem, the socially ridiculous, physically dangerous, and morally suspect reading habits of her heroine, is based on an explicit identification of the truly exemplary in fiction with masculine interpretive authority.[73] This identification has already been established by the novel's prior linkage of Young, Richardson, and Johnson as the authors of the most beautiful, incisive, and ethical "Productions" of the age.[74]

Even earlier, Arabella's inadequate reading has led to a shortlived but dangerous decision in favor of "withdrawing from a tyrannical Exertion of parental Authority" with respect to her marriage choice, when her father wants to marry her to her cousin Glanville for a combination of expedient and affective reasons. In so deciding, we are told, she acts without romance precedents, but also without any cautionary points of comparison, for "she [does] not remember to have read of any heroine who voluntarily left her Father's House, however persecuted she might be" (p. 35). Clearly, Arabella is ignorant of the important example of Clarissa's ill-fated flight from precisely such a situation; at this early point in the novel, it is only Arabella's father's sudden illness that accidentally, in the absence of *Clarissa* as a useful contemporary analysis of such a case, prevents a potentially disastrous "withdrawal" from "parental Authority." It is noteworthy here as well that the parallel Lennox offers to Clarissa's situation simultaneously simplifies the earlier heroine's dilemma; since Arabella's father's choice is a worthy one, and ultimately her own, the interpretive challenge for the reader of *The Female Quixote* is effectively an artificial and temporary one that any reader of comic novels will immediately recognize as such.

Beginning with its title – "Being in the Author's Opinion, the best Chapter in this History" – the conversion chapter itself is heavily encrusted with the sort of interpretive aids Richardson eventually found so desirable for *Clarissa.* Gestures toward authoritative male contemporaries dominate: not only is the dialogue Johnsonian in style and content, and initiated by a "Pious and Learned Doctor ———," a clergyman long viewed as a portrait of Johnson himself (p. 366), but Richardson, as "an admirable Writer of our own Time," is rendered authoritative by a quotation from Johnson, who is in turn described even more superlatively as "the greatest Genius in the present Age" (p. 377). It is no surprise, therefore, that *Clarissa* is portrayed as a sugar-coated moral pill, an "Antidote" to the wickedness of the experiential world (p. 380). Richardson, says the doctor, "has found the Way to convey the most solid Instructions, the noblest Sentiments, and the most exalted Piety, in the pleasing Dress of a Novel" (p. 377). In all, despite Arabella's active role in the dialogue, the scene conveys little of Sarah Fielding's insistence upon readerly initiative or responsibility in the interpretive process. To put it another way, the heroine actively abdicates her right to interpretation; Kate Levin notes that "what matters is that Arabella not only acquiesces in, but invites her own cure." Jodi Wyett has argued, similarly, that the dialogue form is used here as a mode of supervision in its opposition to Arabella's faulty reading, which has been characterized above all as unsupervised. Lennox's reader is a passive one who may be "vitiate[d]" and "pervert[ed]" by what she reads (p. 374), despite her demonstrated moral and social intelligence in other situations.[75]

Indeed, many of the chapter's ideas echo closely Johnson's earlier *Rambler* No. 4 essay on the importance of exemplary characters to the "young, the ignorant, and the idle," the stereotypical readers of the realist novel, and it is perhaps with such essays in mind that Johnson is identified in this passage only as "the Author of the Rambler" (p. 377). The outcome of Arabella's reading lesson is her chastened decision to "give . . . [her] self," as "a poor Present," to her longsuffering suitor, promising to "endeavour to make [her]self as worthy as [she is] able of such a favourable Distinction" (p. 383). Marshall has made the important observation that throughout the novel Arabella shows herself a slavish imitator of romance models, legalistically subjecting herself to the laws of romance; her shift in allegiance to an alternative fictional tradition of realism and to the patriarchal social authority with which Lennox associates such fiction simply reinstates an orthodox hierarchy of gender and reading which has always been latent in the novel's plot. As Levin notes, social consensus, or "custom," is in Lennox's representation an absolute value for a woman;[76] Arabella therefore initiates no potentially open-ended correspondence with an attractive and admirable young gentleman to debate issues of interpretation and conduct, as did Fielding's Miss Gibson.

Langbauer has argued that to take her place in the domestic novel tradition, Lennox "must cease to be a *woman* writer"; Marshall in turn suggests that she indeed indulges in authorial cross-dressing in the novel's dénouement, "disguising herself in order to gain entrance into that republic of letters where writing-masters are in command." In rather tentatively reading this as "an act of surrender and perhaps self-sacrifice" rather than as "an act of self-empowerment," however, Marshall raises without directly addressing the issue of Lennox's choosing to represent a woman's readerly and authorial agency in this way. Lennox chose in *The Female Quixote* to further her own reputation by representing a male author's work as the source and standard of the genre, like the early Frances Burney discussed later in this study.[77] This was a legitimate professional choice on Lennox's part,[78] but, as the contrast to the work of Fielding shows, it was demonstrably not the only option within the mid-century writing context, constraining though that context may have been.

These contrasting strategies for associating themselves with Richardson's novel and his authorial name support my argument that Sarah Fielding's and Charlotte Lennox's career narratives were structured upon different models. Fielding's model blended traditional and modern elements, ultimately in a provincial context, to arrive at an implied self-definition of the writer that is recognizable to us today in its emphasis on self-motivation and direction as well as a sense of obligation to one's public. Lennox is recognizable in another sense, reading the currents of public taste and the needs of the press in order to maximize the success of her works, while insisting upon freedom from personal accountability. Together they represent the interdependent double faces of the modern author: that of the creative artist outside of a productive system of exchange, and that of the producer in the marketplace.

The relative poverty of both women is distressing to contemplate, but can be seen as a reflection, not of prejudice against their authorship as women, but of this precarious and transitional period for authors, without support networks beyond those of family and friends, where longevity beyond the capacity to earn was a misfortune. In this chapter, I have chosen to emphasize the fact that in these circumstances both Fielding and Lennox achieved remarkable things. Both built professional reputations which worked in their favor beyond their period of publishing activity. And both, even in their poverty, were assisted on the basis of the reputation they had acquired, though in different ways: Fielding was cared for by her social circle of intellectuals and patrons, while Lennox was recognized as deserving of repeated assistance from the Royal Literary Fund. At the least, such an account serves as a corrective to those which have tended to emphasize the misfortunes and failures that were largely beyond their control, and to explain those in terms of their gender.

In light of such examples, as I indicated in my introduction, Donoghue's claim for the mid-eighteenth century about "the particular difficulty women experienced not only in writing professionally, but in having a professional life story analogous to those of successful male writers"[79] might in fact hold more true in its latter half: it may be that reading the narrative of the female literary career, at least after its close, has been more difficult than living it was. It can be argued that Sarah Fielding and Charlotte Lennox have both in fact been more ill-served by literary history than by their contemporaries. To borrow a phrase from Sarah Fielding's "Female FRIEND," in the preface to *Volume the Last,* she and her colleague had learned a thing or two about "building . . . [a career up]on public Approbation" (*David Simple,* p. 241). The vicissitudes of cultural memory, to which I will turn in the final section of this study, proved a more complicated matter.

CHAPTER 5

Harmless mediocrity: Edward Kimber and the Minifie sisters

> I brought with me Hurd's Dialogues on Education, which have entertained his Grace very well, and a silly harmless story book called Maria, which serves to entertain myself at minutes when I am fit for nothing else.
>
> (Catherine Talbot to Elizabeth Carter, 1764)[1]

> *Sophronia*: Pray what is your opinion of Miss *Minifie*'s Novels?
> *Euphrasia*: They are in the class of mediocrity, if I were to mention such, it would make our task too long and tedious, I must therefore pass over these, and hundreds beside that are very innocent and moral books.
>
> (Clara Reeve, *The Progress of Romance*, 1785)[2]

While insisting upon the need to reexamine mid-eighteenth-century women writers, this study has to this point taken for granted the importance of the publications and professional lives of Frances Sheridan, Frances Brooke, Sarah Scott, Sarah Fielding, and Charlotte Lennox. Perhaps the implication has even been that they merit this attention simply because their work has not been attended to sufficiently in the past. In a recent plenary presentation, Susan Staves argued that feminist literary critics have been reluctant to make value judgments about the work they are "recovering" or "rereading" or "restoring" for fear of a return to the exclusive universalizations of canon-making.[3] Without by any means claiming to resolve the problems raised by a return to the discourse of aesthetic value, I want to take some steps in this chapter toward acknowledging the issue and determining how early "situated" critical commentary can be used as a guideline for reinstating women writers in a literary history that takes into account what might tentatively be isolated as transhistorical, but generically specific, criteria of aesthetic value. I will approach the question of the stature of Sarah Fielding and Charlotte Lennox, specifically, in their contemporary print culture and, by extension, in the canon of English novelists, through a comparison with the reception of three other eighteenth-century suppliers of novels to the reading public – Edward Kimber and the co-authoring sisters Margaret and Susannah Minifie. My initial basis for the comparison is twofold: each published, between the 1750s and the early 1780s, novels roughly equivalent in number to those of Fielding, Lennox, Scott, and Brooke, and these novels were generally characterized by their reviewers as worthy of public notice and as appropriate for consumption by the increasingly stereotypical "young, ignorant, and idle" novel audience. Kimber and the Minifies also mirror my Lennox-Fielding pairing in the sense that Kimber was a London-based professional with a need to make his living in the print marketplace of the day, while the Minifies were the daughters of a country clergyman, living in Somerset. In addition, Kimber's case allows for further attention to the role of gender in determining reception.

The primary interest of these parallels for me lies in the fact that Kimber and the Minifies are ultimately mere foils to Lennox and Fielding, in that their work, though popular in its day, has consistently been classified as harmless but mediocre and forgettable. A look at the reception of their work thus allows me to broach the fraught task of identifying historically legitimate criteria of value by which a work's merit, and a career's significance, may be judged and compared with those of other works or careers. In other words, Kimber and the Minifies provide an opportunity to place in relief and to test some of the assumptions and assertions of this book: my choice of the principal study group of women writers, my claims about their contemporary stature, and my implication that their work and their cultural position merit further attention, not merely on the sociological basis of their gender and its role in their professional lives, but also on the basis of aesthetic values. In my examination of contemporary responses to Kimber's and the Minifies' work, the increasingly hierarchical classification of imaginative literature, the early establishment of criteria that have persisted through reception history, and the relation of those criteria to circumstantial aspects of the career (including the author's gender) will become visible.

As fiction became a more and more significant consumer product, sometimes-competing models of classification were developed by both "lay" readers and the reviewers – objective criteria, such as relation to exemplars of the genre, vied with qualitative criteria such as entertainment provided, or the morally corrupting or improving characteristics of a work. While the resulting judgments may at first glance seem confused and quaintly antiquated, I will show them in fact to have established a fairly complex and consistent set of evaluative criteria, in which the aesthetic, though modified by the moral, took precedence over it. These criteria have been at once simplified and maintained over time. The surprising continuity of value judgments suggests that aesthetic criteria which can be used to weigh contemporaneous works against each other are themselves coeval with the establishment of the novel as a literary genre. The resulting evaluations have subsequently been flattened out, or simplified, but their original complexity suggests that the work of recovery need not entail the development of entirely new criteria of value, but can in fact usefully attend to original judgments as a guideline to a reintegration of "forgotten" works into a more inclusive literary tradition.

In part, this is true because the author's gender, while creating rhetorical "noise" in many reviews, has in fact less to do with early judgments of a publication's value than has often been assumed. Indeed, Antonia Forster has recently argued that despite a pattern of unflattering and domesticating language in reviews of novels by women, "the most important and well-established of the women writers might find their work reviewed almost without reference to the author's being a woman."[4] Through this examination, I will show that what Jane Spencer some time ago identified as the "terms of acceptance" by which mid-eighteenth-century women gained access to the literary marketplace could in fact serve as a barrier to a male writer and a boost to a female writer's career.[5] Gender, in other words, acted as a kind of free-floating signifier, sometimes irrelevant to the reception of a work, and at other times inflating or deflating its perceived value.

First, however, I will outline briefly what is known about the professional lives of Kimber and the Minifies. Edward Kimber (1719–69) was the son of Isaac Kimber, a Dissenting (Baptist) clergyman who appears to have been known for his tolerance and his learning, and who gave his son a broad education. The senior Kimber's principal career was as inhouse writer for the printer-bookseller Charles Ackers, later joined by his son John Ackers; for them he edited the *London Magazine* from its inception in 1732, while also writing such individual works as a life of Cromwell and a history of England. Edward therefore grew up within the trade, contributing poetry to the *London Magazine* by the age of 15, and a serialized account of a two-year excursion to America published between August 1745 and December 1746. A 1756 posthumous volume of Isaac Kimber's sermons, presumably published for the benefit of his family as well as to honor the deceased divine, reveals a modest network of connections, both in social "quality" and in quantity. The book is dedicated to "John Keeling, Esq;" a Justice of the Peace and friend of the Ackers family, and the subscription list consists of 275 names, with the Ackers family at its head, an array of Ackers relations, the typefounder William Caslon and his family, some *London Magazine* associates, various gentlemen and clergymen, a handful of knights, and a few military and medical men (among the few well-known names are Christopher Smart, M. A., and a George Macauley), M. D., quite possibly the soon-to-be husband of Catharine Macaulay.[6] Edward's context, then, is the geographically and socially restricted sphere of the lower- middling-class urban professional.

Kimber's own working life, after his American sojourn of 1742 to 1744, continued in his father's pattern: he became editor of the *London Magazine* in 1755, after the latter's death, and compiled the magazine's index for 1732 to 1758, while also contributing constantly both to this periodical and to others, on matters as various as the lodestone, recent earthquakes, and "royal instances of humanity." He also produced a wide range of indices and additions to established texts, pocketbooks, and almanacs in the burgeoning field of practical "how-to" books, including, in 1763, *The Ladies Complete Letter-Writer*, which Kevin J. Hayes calls "Perhaps Kimber's most influential work." Interspersed with these writings are seven original novels and an eighth in translation (beginning with *The Life and Adventures of Joe Thompson* in 1750 and ending with *The Generous Briton; or, the Authentic Memoirs of William Goldsmith, Esq.*, in 1765) of which Frank Gees Black has counted a combined total of "about 37 editions, several of them in French or German, between 1750 and 1808." In a departure from the anonymity of much of his work, discussed below, Kimber's last publication, the updated 1771 edition of Thomas Wotton's 1741 *Baronetage of England*, names him as co-author. His career ended with his death in 1769, one year after that of Sarah Fielding. That Kimber was a hard-working and well-respected member of the local professional community is suggested by the posthumous tribute offered to him by his partner in this work, Richard Johnson: "let me not forget the Tribute due to the Memory of my Friend, Mr. Kimber, who fell a Victim, in the Meridian of his Life, to his indefatigable Toils in the Republic of Letters. To him I owe the present Plan of this Work: He was the Architect, I only the Builder. Happy shall I think myself, if I shall appear properly to have executed the Design which he formed."[7]

Margaret and Susannah Minifie, daughters of the Rev. James Minifie of Staplegrove, Somerset, first appeared in print as authors of the 1763 epistolary novel *The Histories of Lady Frances S —— and Lady Caroline S ——*. They immediately claimed their work much more publicly than did Kimber, announcing on the title page that the novel was "Written by the Miss Minifies, of Fairwater, in Somersetshire." Like the book's fashionable London booksellers the Dodsley brothers, contrasting with the obscure John Hinton who published Kimber's *Joe Thompson*, the Minifies' dedication to "Lady Tynte, of Haswell, in Somersetshire" and their list of 774 subscribers displayed the gentility and breadth of their connections. Their list includes numerous names of rank and prominence, such as the Countess of Haddington, Lady North, Lady Onslow, Jonas Hanway, William Strode, and the Bishop of Bath and Wells, in addition to other less certainly identifiable figures, such as the Mr. and Mrs. Allen who may be the Ralph Allens of Bath. At the same time, the *Monthly Review*'s writer indicates that the authors' fame did not yet extend beyond the provincial, referring to them as "the *Miss Minifies* of *Fairwater*, if there are such names";[8] we still know little about their early lives. In all, the sisters appear to have published six novels jointly or separately between 1763 and 1783, with Susannah probably ceasing to publish upon her marriage to General John Gunning in 1768.[9] They are not identified with works of any other genre until the scandal which erupted around the Gunnings' daughter Elizabeth in 1791 led to Susannah's separation from her husband and her publication of a highly dramatized version of these events, a heroic-couplet rendering of the classical Virginius and Virginia story, and further novels.

CONTEMPORARIES READ KIMBER, THE MINIFIES, FIELDING, AND LENNOX

On February 12, 1764, Catherine Talbot wrote to her friend Elizabeth Carter that she was reading Bishop Hurd's *Dialogues on Education* to Thomas Secker, Bishop of Oxford and Archbishop of Canterbury, to whose household she belonged and who was ill at the time. Simultaneously, as the first epigraph to this chapter reveals, she was enjoying a "silly harmless story book called Maria, which serves to entertain myself at minutes when I am fit for nothing else." This comment is not in itself surprising: perfectly capable of reading educational treatises, political memoirs, and moral philosophy for her own interest and benefit, Talbot also enjoyed narratives centered on women's lives, and writes of reading such novels as *The Female Quixote*, Sarah Fielding's *Ophelia*, "a Lady a Julia Mandeville . . ., written by Mrs. Sheridan," and "Bell Fermor" (i.e. *The History of Emily Montague*). Unlike these texts, however, the anonymous *Maria*, we now know, was the work of a male author, Edward Kimber. Four years later, a recommendation of "light summer reading for the ladies" leads Talbot to a comparison between the work of the Minifies and that of the historian Vertôt: "I owed your Light Summer Reading a spite for your preferring it to my Knights of Malta. Indeed I never will give up the point, that the nice geniuses of the nine Minifies, however clubbed and compounded, can ever arrive at the amusement of one Vertôt."[10]

Talbot's letters allow us to determine her own working hierarchy of the mid-century fiction she read right up until her death in 1770. The publication of Richardson's novel of a "good man," *Sir Charles Grandison*, is an important and interesting literary event, dignified like "Mr. Pope, in Mr. Warburton's edition" and Fielding's *Amelia* by being reserved for perusal "en famille," that is, in mixed company in the Bishop's household, after supper. Following upon this most formal and mixed-gender category of domestic amusement is miscellaneous, excerptable material shared with friends in a less formal, more feminized setting. An example here is Sarah Fielding's *Familiar Letters between the Principal Characters in David Simple*, which together with Madame de Sevigné's letters and Mrs. Rowe's "excellent works" leads her to exclaim, "I scarce know a greater pleasure than reading over a book one is fond of with persons of taste and candour, to whom it is entirely new" when she reads it while riding in a coach on an afternoon excursion in the countryside with a group of ladies and one of their sons. The novels of Lennox, Fielding, Brooke, and by inference Sheridan (since Talbot thinks Brooke's *History of Lady Julia Mandeville* is hers) are thoroughly enjoyed as well written, amusing, and generally moral (though *Henrietta* is suspect).[11] With "faults and excellencies enough to raise [them] above this denomination [of nonsense fit for a circulating bookseller]" (regarding *Julia Mandeville*), these she often reads to her mother when they are alone. Finally, Kimber's *Maria*, like "Jemmy Jessamy and Betty Barnes" (the former is Eliza Haywood's *The History of Jemmy and Jenny Jessamy* while the latter, though it has been attributed to Sarah Fielding, is the work of Mary Collyer), are what Talbot is "reduced to studying" when a long sojourn in the country leaves her no other option, or when low spirits drive her to seek emotional escape.

Talbot's account of her fiction reading as broad, yet clearly categorized according to the functions played by the genre and its subgenres in her life, personalizes the treatment of novels recorded in the periodical reviews. Janet Todd has characterized the 1760s to 1780s as a time when sentimental fiction's "fantasy world of powerful feminine passivity" had not yet been relegated to a culture of popular fiction seen as entirely distinct from and inferior to more legitimate or elite literature: "What remains interesting in the eighteenth century, which fashioned the form and the fantasy, is the centrality of this fiction to the culture as a whole. Although repeatedly mocked, the books were noticed in the major literary organs in a way that would be unthinkable for Barbara Cartland's work in our time."[12] If we broaden Todd's comment to include popular adventure as well as popular romance, it points us to contemporary reviews of fiction as a means of observing in process the formation of hierarchies and subcategories of the form. Although brief mention has been made of reviews of Fielding's and Lennox's work in the previous chapter, a fuller account of *Monthly Review* (and later also *Critical Review*) notices of their publications, in comparison to those of Kimber's and the Minifies' work, will be useful here.

Occasionally, both Fielding's and Lennox's productions are treated as original and of the highest calibre: Fielding's 1754 *The Cry*, co-authored with Jane Collier, is described as written according to a plan "entirely different from that of any modern novelist," and as "contain[ing] more literature and good sense, than, a few only excepted, all our modern novels put together"; Henry Fielding describes *The Female Quixote* in his *Covent-Garden Journal* as comparable, and in some respects superior, to *Don Quixote*; and the *Critical Review* "warmly recommend[s]" Lennox's *Henrietta* in part for a style that "sink[s] no where below the level of genteel life, a compliment which cannot be paid to one of the most celebrated novel-writers we have" – a jab that could be directed at either Richardson or Henry Fielding. Although not a review *per se*, an anonymous 1754 pamphlet attacking Richardson's novels contrasts them with Fielding's *David Simple* as "perhaps the best moral romance that we have," and describes Fielding herself as its "ingenious authoress."[13]

More often, perhaps, Fielding and Lennox are taken seriously as writing in the preestablished traditions of Richardson and Henry Fielding, but nevertheless as among the best practitioners of the kind. The *Critical*'s account of Sarah Fielding's *Countess of Dellwyn* is worth quoting at some length as a particularly good example of praise for an imitation for in some respects improving upon the original:

As Poussin the painter has been said to have excelled himself whenever he had Raphael in his eye, so the writer of the present romance may be asserted to succeed best when she assumes the humble task of an imitator, rather than the more arduous employment of being original. Nor is this a small degree of praise. The humour of Mr. Fielding, who may be stiled the father of our comic romance, has been often attempted by others without success; and indeed, without a very large portion of native fire, it is vain endeavouring to adopt the sallies of another.

The present history, as it is called, it must be owned, has fewer of those flights of fancy, less of that strong sense, and that thorough acquaintance with the vitious parts of human nature, for which the author of Tom Jones is justly famous; these defects, however, are compensated by an easy familiar stile, an agreeable uninterrupted vivacity, and a pleasing insight into scenes of domestic tranquillity, or distress.[14]

As these examples indicate, and as the treatment of Kimber's and the Minifies' work will show by contrast, comparison to such writers as Cervantes, Fielding, and Richardson can be as much a mode of elevation as a means of devaluing a work. Similarly, if connections are drawn backward to such earlier works as *David Simple* and *The Female Quixote*, notice taken of a falling-off from an established standard of expectation makes the backhanded compliment of coalescing the author's assorted writings into an oeuvre to be treated seriously. Lennox's 1762 *Sophia*, for example, is explicitly criticized because, though "not uninteresting in point of incident, nor inelegantly written," it "wants, nevertheless, much of that spirit and variety" which are found in "the *female Quixote*, *Henrietta*, and some other of her pieces," and so does not meet the public's expectation "of a writer, who hath acquired any portion of literary fame, that every new work he produces should be superior to the last."[15]

The place of Kimber and the Minifies, on the other hand, is similar to that assigned to them by Talbot: they are consistently categorized below Fielding and Lennox, though never in the lowest group of "vicious" fiction. Typical praise of the Kimber novels, for example, is by negative formulation as "not the worst of the works of this kind that we have seen" (regarding *Captain Neville Frowde*). Such praise therefore keeps this work above the lowest ranks: the reader is assured that *The Life and Adventures of James Ramble, Esq.* (1755) is not at all like "low," "obscene," "bombast[ic]," "inconsistent" recent publications such as the 1754 *History of Will Ramble, A Libertine.* Interestingly, once the "Monthly Catalogues" of both review journals begin to classify novels as a distinct category, Kimber's work several times appears first among this secondary group of publications, as a point of reference for the briefer subsequent notices. Thus Kimber's *Maria* is recommended for its virtuous and amiable heroine in a brief note which concludes, "That praise which is given to a writer who thus lifts our passions under the banners of duty, can never be too often repeated, since the feeblest efforts may thus be excited to usefulness; and while they contribute something to our happiness will, we hope, add much to that of the author." The following publication, *Family Pictures*, sometimes attributed to Susannah Minifie, is simply "another of those decent performances which are calculated to insinuate virtue under the masque of entertainment," whose "stile . . . is rather less inflated than that of the preceding, but [whose] subject is less interesting." As the *Monthly* puts it rather bluntly in a 1769 review of the Minifie novel *The Cottage*, since "novels may now be considered as a staple commodity," "the artists have, in general, learned to turn out tolerable work, of uniform texture, though the pieces seldom rise above mediocrity," and therefore it is "not easy to give separate characters to performances which have such a general resemblance." In this commodified context, the reviewer "can only say, that if *The Cottage* is not distinguished by peculiar merit, it is not debased by gross faults."[16]

Kimber's penchant for plots constructed as a series of adventures befalling a likable but gullible and sexually irresponsible hero has led twentieth-century readers to note his reliance on Smollett, Henry Fielding, and Eliza Haywood.[17] Yet their first reviewers did not draw such connections, except occasionally to emphasize an unbridgeable gap between Kimber and the leaders in the field: the *Monthly Review* sneeringly accepts *Joe Thompson*'s claim to be founded on fact because it is "not stamped with the least mark of imagination, or invention, or any of those fanciful embellishments with which *Cervantes, Fielding, Marivaux*" and other writers of fiction have made their work so entertaining. Lost in the steady stream of "life and adventures" stories issuing from the press in the 1750s, Kimber's tales appear not to have earned the same right to elevation by comparison as did those of Fielding and Lennox. Only for his last novel, *The Generous Briton*, is it noted that the title character, Mr. Goldsmith, is "the copy of Allworthy in *Tom Jones*"; one feels that Kimber has at last been accepted into the fringes of good company.

On the other hand, the case of *The Happy Orphans*, which is a translation of a 1754 French imitation of Haywood's 1744 *Fortunate Foundlings*, is revealing. The fact that the *Monthly Review* angrily accuses Kimber of copying Haywood, while the *Critical* professes itself at some pains to examine the evidence and clear Kimber of the charge, shows how much less respected the work of Kimber would have been if he had been successfully branded a mere plagiarist, or what the *Monthly* splutteringly terms "the pirate, or the copiest, or the cobler, or . . . whatever title the honest editor chuses." By the same token, Kimber's "originality" is defended as late as 1786 by the *Critical*'s reviewer of a new novel, *The Adventures of George Maitland, Esq.*, which he claims is an exact copy of the story of *James Ramble*, suggesting that one reviewer, at least in retrospect, felt Kimber had written a story worth defending.[18]

The *Monthly*'s notice of the Minifies' first novel, the 1763 *The Histories of Lady Frances S ——— and Lady Caroline S ———*, strikes an optimistic note of comparison, calling this work "Another imitation of Richardson's manner," and "a sober, moral tale," whose authors "have not *yet* eclipsed the merit of Clarissa, Roderic Random, or Tom Jones." The *Critical*'s reviewer similarly hopes that the sisters will improve their style and characterization, but concludes that "Upon the whole, we think the Miss Minifies have acquitted themselves very well in their first performance, and will venture to foretell that they will one day rank amongst the first authoresses of this authoress-creating age." These hopes go unrealized, as the *Critical* is forced to modify its enthusiasm in its account of the final volume of *Lady Frances and Lady Caroline*, issued the following year: "We have already given a character of this work, and should have been extremely glad for our own sakes, had the volume before us confirmed the character we then gave of the fair authoresses, who we think are far from improving either in invention or stile." Here authorial gender, even when noted, would appear to be neither an advantage nor an impediment with the reviewers, whose model is rather one of apprenticeship in a craft that requires the honing of two distinct skills, the invention of plots and characters, and the deployment of a correct and pleasing style.[19]

The Minifies are much more specifically imitative of Richardson's fictional mode in their earliest work than is Kimber, and we have already seen that this is not considered a fault in the reviews of their first novel. Plot devices include an estranged mother's distrust of a heroine's eloquence and elaborate abduction schemes staged by aristocratic rakes, in the manner of *Clarissa*, and detailed descriptions of wedding celebrations in the style of *Sir Charles Grandison*.[20] All five of their known novels, from the 1763 *Histories of Lady Frances S ——— and Lady Caroline S ———* to the 1783 *Coombe Wood*, are epistolary in form; the first self-consciously explains how such lengthy letters and such perfect recall are possible, but by the 1780s, the narrative device is essentially a first-person retrospective, with the letters so long and so removed from the moment as to become a virtually transparent medium. Thus, though the epistolary surface of the novels is maintained, and even emphasized in three of the last four novels through the title tag "A Novel. In a Series of Letters," the narratives themselves explore other devices, such as beginning in midstream with characters of mysterious identities and pasts, or the use of sentimental characters in pathetic circumstances in combination with worldly, cynical narrators, or the introduction of flighty, badly married heroines who learn from their mistakes, or a mixture of gloomy desolation and sentimental rurality of setting – all fictional developments of these decades.[21]

This flaunting of imitation, or at least identification of a feminized subgenre of the novel, even to the point of false advertising, suggests a strategic appeal. Indeed, the Minifies succeeded very well in targeting a market niche of "interesting," morally improving reading that was viewed as suitable for the ignorant and impressionable female reader. This shift from a general to a particular reader is reflected in the sisters' first appearance in the *Critical Review*: "The taste for novel-writing and novel-reading is grown so universal amongst us, that it might be deemed a *crimen lesae majestatis* against the public, to call it in question; more especially as it would be encroaching on the privileges and pleasures of the fair sex, who have an indisputable right to amuse themselves in what manner they please: we cannot, therefore, but be of opinion that the Miss Minifies, of Fairwater, in Somersetshire, were, at least, very innocently, if not usefully, employed, in writing the Histories of Lady Frances and Lady Caroline S ———." The *Critical*'s tendency to generous quotation from their novels appears to be motivated by the same audience profile, since the passages chosen as "best" are almost always extremely pathetic scenes of wronged young women on their deathbeds; where "humour" is favored, it is of the sort that exposes the social faults of the card-playing widow, or the selfish bachelor.[22]

Kimber, despite his sex, also succeeds in his later works in targeting that element of the fiction market focusing on the sufferings of the innocent. Critics select for quotation such sentimental passages as the description of young Neville Frowde's uncle's "struggle of nature and conscience with interest and villainy" as he is about to sell his trusting and affectionate young nephew in order to gain his inheritance, and, as an admonishment to "our gallant male readers," the speech of the Countess of Suffolk in *The Happy Orphans* lamenting the double standard applied to seduced women and their seducers. In the latter case, the *Critical*'s reviewer much prefers *The Happy Orphans* to Eliza Haywood's *The History of Jemmy and Jenny*

Jessamy (which it had been accused by the *Monthly Review* of plagiarizing), finding that Kimber's story clearly differentiates between its virtuous and vicious characters and stays away from "the *improbable* or *absurd*," unlike Haywood's "*farrago* of adventures." Kimber's first novels were not reviewed in gender-specific terms; rather, they were almost invariably criticized sharply for being full of improbable adventures, with the 1754 *History of the Life and Adventures of Mr. Anderson*, in particular, being dismissed as "probably the work of a professed *adventure-maker*."

Thus the increase in praise appears to correspond to a late 1750s shift in Kimber's emphasis toward more markedly sentimental and feminized plots; though the improbability of the adventures in *Maria* and *The Generous Briton* is still remarked upon by some of the reviewers, they subordinate this feature to the novels' promotion of virtue and goodness. A more explicit signal of this shift toward a gendering of the sentimental is the fact that *The Generous Briton*, Kimber's final novel, was published in its 1808 French translation as "Par Miss B******." Thus we see the Minifies being responded to with a gendering of their work that, if it does not actively help, certainly does not harm their careers; Kimber, while he cannot use his sex as a guarantee of his work's feminized qualities, nevertheless adopts similar plot effects, and is similarly rewarded by the reviewers for this.[23]

These distinctions therefore raise the matter of anonymity as it is related to authorial gender in the middle of the century. Kimber seems to have taken professional pride in his extensive output, since he indexed his *London Magazine* contributions under his own name, and recorded his works and the money he received for their sale in a notebook.[24] Thus it is not clear why neither he nor his booksellers chose to associate his first five novels with one another in some manner, since the "literary signature" was a device increasingly common for ostensibly anonymous work, as the previous chapter has shown, and since each of these narratives follows the "Life and Adventures" model. Whether to support the claim of factuality for his hero's narratives or to hide his involvement in so many projects as to risk charges of haste and hackwork, anonymity did allow Kimber to shift with the tides of novelistic taste, and it perhaps prevented his easy dismissal as a male writer when he did begin to write works such as *The Happy Orphans*, *The Ladies Complete Letter-Writer*, and *Maria*. Once *Maria* was successful enough to warrant a second edition in 1765, the booksellers Richard Baldwin and Thomas Lowndes (Kimber's most prestigious, at least for a novel, to date), issued it with the identifying mark, "By the Author of The Life and Adventures of Joe Thompson," drawing the connection to a novel of which Hinton had recently published a third edition. Only belatedly for Kimber was being associated with a novelistic oeuvre a positive professional move.[25]

The case seems to have been different for the more consistent specialization of the Minifies. As I have already noted, the *Monthly* is initially skeptical of their proclaimed identity – "the *Miss Minifies* of *Fairwater*, if there are such names" – implying not only their obscurity, but also that the tag might have been chosen to help sell the novel. The Minifies' practice consistently fits Margaret Ezell's suggestion that various modes of signalling female authorship might serve "as a costume rather than as a disguise, a means to signify to the reader that a certain type of role was being performed, a type of personality was being staged."[26] Clearly, it was to the Minifies' advantage to establish a "brand name" associated with the positive markers of female sex, youth, and country residence, which could be attached to each new product as a guarantee of safe amusement. One should not underestimate their entrepreneurial acuity in recognizing this, since they initiated the practice in 1763 with their first publication, even though, according to James Raven, it was not until the 1780s that the indication of authorship "by a lady," let alone the naming of the author, became all the rage.[27] Like the emphasis on epistolarity, each of the Minifies' later fictions is issued with authorial labeling that leaves little to chance: their works are presented as "by the Miss Minifies, of Fairwater in Somersetshire; Authors of the History of Lady Frances S ——, and Lady Caroline S ——" (*The Picture*, 1766), or "by Miss Minifie, Author of Barford-Abbey" (*The Cottage*, 1769), or "by Miss M. Minifie, one of the authors of Lady Frances and Lady Caroline S ——" (*The Count de Poland*, 1780), or "by the Author of Barford-Abbey and The Cottage" (*Coombe Wood*, 1783).

Outside confirmation of the success of this enterprise, in despite of, or perhaps aided by, the sisters' original obscurity and their provincial context, is indicated by the *Monthly Review*'s introduction to its account of *The Cottage*: "In an age when the passion for reading memoirs is so general, it is no wonder if the ladies, who are the principal students in this species of literature, should sometimes become professors of it: and Miss Minifie is one of two ladies, who, dating their productions from Fairwater in Somersetshire, have distinguished themselves, and taken their degrees, as novellists."[28] Cheryl Turner has noted the frequency with which the Minifies are named, along with the other mid-century women writers Haywood, Fielding, Lennox, Scott, Sheridan, and Brooke, in the catalogues of circulating libraries, suggesting again the effectiveness of their self-presentation.[29] Significantly, when Susannah became a very public player in a 1791 forgery scandal that saw her daughter falsely claiming an offer of marriage from the heir of the Marlborough family, the coherence of this persona was shattered; as Horace Walpole put it, "The Gunninghiad is completed – not by a marriage, like other novels of the Minifies."[30] Undaunted, Mrs. Gunning, wife of the general, sister-in-law to the famous and very well-married Gunning sisters, and mother of the perjured (or injured) young beauty, relaunched her authorial career under her married name, and on the strength of autobiographical echoes of her family scandal.[31] Once again, self-identification was an asset deployed effectively to raise her profile and promote her professional career.[32]

When compared to reviews of Fielding and Lennox publications, however, the limitations of the Minifies' well-defined but narrow specialization become clear. While the work of the former two authors is generally assumed to appeal to a broad audience of male and female readers, the best the Minifies can achieve is that of effective genre work. The highest praise the sisters' combined efforts receive is exemplified by that for *Barford Abbey*: "We cannot help making an exception of this novel from the common run of such publications. Few or none of the incidents are, indeed, new; but they are well wrought up." Although the characters of the Minifies' works are indeed frequently praised as well drawn and their scenes as "well wrought up," their plots also tend to be criticized either as confusing or as excessively simple.[33] The *Dictionary of National Biography*'s generalization about the works of Susannah Minifie Gunning epitomizes contemporary critics' views: "Mrs. Gunning's novels, many of which passed through several editions, are exceedingly harmless; an absence of plot forming their most original characteristic."[34]

Kimber's plots are often described as improbable or clichéd or both; in the case of *The Generous Briton*, for example, when the hero relieves a couple fallen from affluence into poverty, "The reader who is acquainted with novel-writing, begins by this time more than to suspect that this worthy couple are no more than the foundling's father and mother, which they actually prove to be."[35] Yet they are also consistently viewed by the critics as "interesting," in the eighteenth-century sense of engaging the reader's attention and emotions on behalf of the hero or heroine – in other words, like the narratives of the Minifies, they are relatively expert manipulations of generic formulae.

With respect to style, the Minifies are criticized more often than not for a lack of differentiation between characters' modes of writing and for a general faultiness, whereas Kimber's work is often described as natural and correct, though with the caveat of carelessness noted below. Since it has sometimes been argued that the female writer tended to be praised for a "natural" or "easy" style,[36] it is worth noting the superiority attributed to Kimber in these respects (as well as the frequency with which Lennox and Brooke, as I have shown in previous chapters, are recognized for their elegant and refined prose). For both Kimber and the Minifies, however, there is frequent criticism of sloppiness, and ultimately, an implication of reader exploitation. In 1766, *The Picture*'s prefatory connection of this novel with "the success of their first attempt" is turned against the sisters by the *Monthly*'s reviewer, who refuses to go beyond a recommendation for innocence, morality, and touches of nature: "Higher praise than this we cannot, with all our partiality for the sex, allow this performance; which, in truth, is not a finished piece, but is rather to be considered as an hasty, incorrect sketch: such as, we doubt not, these ingenious ladies could have greatly improved, had they allowed themselves due time for revising and retouching it"; the *Critical* insinuates of the same work that "the miss Minifies (or their bookseller) seem to have particularly studied" what will satisfy those who read primarily to boast of the number of a book's pages. In 1769 the *Monthly*'s review of *The Cottage* concludes drily, "The division of so small a work into three *minikin* volumes, is a matter more immediately between buyer and seller."[37]

As with the Minifies, the motive of Kimber's habit of extensive quotation is suspect: "He [the hero, Neville Frowde] also makes too free an use of his poetical reading; for there are so many quotations from our British Bards, that we cannot help concluding, they were brought in chiefly for the sake of increasing the number of his pages." Even for one of his latter novels, the 1764 *Maria*, praised by the *Monthly* for "sentiments . . . friendly to virtue and goodness, . . . language [that] is easy, though unequal, and . . . style elevated above the common rank of modern novels," the writer concludes, "we conjecture that the Author has been in a hurry to finish the work; and that he is capable of a better production, if allowed more time to finish it."[38] In short, the reviewers consistently respond to the Minifies' and to Kimber's work, but just as consistently treat it as a commodity whose value is to be appraised warily by the purchaser. Such connotations are notably absent from even the most critical of Fielding and Lennox reviews in the same journals. Significantly, on the one occasion when Fielding is faulted for excessive quotation, the reviewer's warning is couched in terms of the potential for diminishing her writerly status to that of a Kimber or Minifie: she ought to avoid "larding" her work "with bits and scraps of unnecessary quotations . . .

since, however they may enrich the pages of a poor writer, they ought to be very pertinent and striking indeed, when abruptly breaking into the sentiments of a good one."[39]

In this feature, the desire to appeal to targeted readers may be seen to diverge from the critical standards of reviewers as well as from notions of the best literature as transcending its context: both Kimber and the Minifies offer their readers contemporaneity and a flattering self-image in their references to fashionable amusements, familiar reading, and national celebrities. Although Kimber is criticized for inserting quotations merely to extend his novels' lengths, they do function in characterization: his heroes and heroines are always conspicuous for having read "the best authors" and boast a distinguishing knowledge of the classics despite their middling origins. Yet those authors and texts most often remain carefully unnamed, avoiding intimidating the novels' actual readers, whom the *Critical Review* characterizes for *Juvenile Adventures of David Ranger, Esq.*, Kimber's most damned performance, as "idle templars, raw prentices, and green girls" who will be impressed by such "bad poetry by the author; with scraps of plays, ballads, &c."[40] Similarly, such teasers as his promise of offering secret Jacobite memoirs in *James Ramble* and his allusion to David Garrick in the title and epigraph of his *David Ranger*, though roundly condemned by the reviewers, may well have achieved precisely their suspected purpose of boosting sales.

The Minifies' admirable characters are placed from the start in a more genteel social sphere but like Kimber's they are still busy displaying their refinement. Inserted original poetry seems calculated to heighten the elegant effect of the whole, as in their first novel's concluding hymn to Hymen sung by peasants enacting a pastoral scene on a country estate, or to increase the pathos of a heroine's grief at her parents' neglect, for example.[41] Quotations from Addison, Swift, Dryden, Milton, and Edward Young similarly signal the genteel educations of the letter-writers. Their accomplishments again set a high standard for readerly imitation, whether by fashionable or more traditional measures: one aristocratic heroine has "a perfect knowledge" of Greek and Latin, a deceased young lady is revealed to have been the author of the poetry printed in *The Spectator* No. 424, another heroine "knows more [of divinity, history, and geography] than half the great men who have wrote for ages past" and finds "the Roman History" so fascinating that it keeps her awake until three o'clock in the morning, and one Lady Mary Sutton is an artist whose portraits have been "even allowed by Reynolds to be masterly" on his visits to her home.[42]

In more direct appeals to fashion, when not writing letters or struggling through intensely emotional scenes with their lovers or parents, the young ladies also occupy themselves in working out "the conundrums set forth in the Ladies Diary for the year," attending masquerades, performances of *King Lear* or "Bach's concert," and being ultimately rewarded by introductions at Court, where "the great example of conjugal happiness," that of George III and Queen Charlotte, promises to diminish this very love of fashionable dissipation.[43] Such comments as "Is the nation in debt? – So much is Darcey in love," as well as a general idealization of the traditional ways of the country gentleman, are reminiscent of Frances Brooke's political stance, discussed in chapter 2, but the insertion is so awkward, and the treatment so unelaborated and unconsciously ironic in these stories devoting lengthy passages to descriptions of lavish amusements, that the appeal is surely clichéd rather than polemical.[44]

KIMBER AND THE MINIFIES IN LITERARY HISTORY

If readers contemporary with these authors were preoccupied with classifying the rapidly increasing quantity of printed materials vying for their attention, the urgency and regularization of such classifying activity only increased as the century progressed. Critics of the second half of the eighteenth century responded to the deluge of print by grouping and ranking these materials, according to objectively measurable categories such as genre, but also according to qualitative criteria, through evaluative processes related to a particular genre's perceived strengths, social functions, and readership. Euphrasia, Clara Reeve's principal speaker in her 1785 *The Progress of Romance*, nicely illustrates this dual system when she moves into a discussion of novels with the announcement that "I mean to take notice only of the most eminent works of this kind: – to pass over others slightly and leave the worst in the depths of Oblivion." Euphrasia immediately proceeds with an outline of the distinction between novels and romances, an effort which her principal interlocutor, Hortensius, receives with the redundantly emphatic "You have well distinguished, and it is necessary to make this distinction. – I clearly perceive the difference between the Romance and Novel, and am surprized they should be confounded together." Within the novel category, Euphrasia's plan is to sort the individual works she discusses according to a binary set of aesthetic and moral criteria – "wisdom and folly," "wit and stupidity," "religion and profaneness," and "morality and licentiousness" – so as to create a hierarchical order out of the "vast, unexplored regions of fancy" that comprise the genre. "Perfection" for the genre is defined as an ability "to represent every scene, in so easy and natural a manner, and to make them appear so probable, as to deceive us into a persuasion (at least while we are reading) that all is real, until we are affected by the joys or distresses, of the persons in the story, as if they were our own."[45]

Reeve's positioning of the Minifies and Kimber should therefore be of significance with respect to these evaluative criteria. In her system, Richardson's novels are of "capital merit," while Henry Fielding's are slightly inferior, though also "of the first eminence," because Euphrasia "consider[s] wit only as a secondary merit" to "morals and exemplary characters." Sarah Fielding's works, in this context, "are not unworthy next to be mentioned after her brother's, if they do not equal them in wit and learning, they excell in some other material merits, that are more beneficial to their readers," implying their rank among "capital" works. Similarly, Sheridan's *Sidney Bidulph* is discussed in detail as one of a third speaker Sophronia's favorite books, and as succeeding through its realism in making the reader "los[e] sight of the Author," while the advisability of its refusal to reward virtue is debated at some length. Frances Brooke and Sarah Scott (as unnamed author of *Millenium Hall*), are included in Euphrasia's "class of eminence" as well. In the same vein, the works of male and female writers alike (Samuel Croxall and Penelope Aubin) are eligible for classification in "the rank of mediocrity" and therefore do not merit discussion. Although Reeve's male speaker, Hortensius, starts from a gendered approach to genre as an assumed measure of value (for him, it is self-evident that male-associated genres such as history are superior to both the novel and the romance, particularly if these are authored by women), Reeve polemically neither accepts this evaluation nor makes the author's gender a distinguishing characteristic in the qualitative ranking of novelists.[46]

Reeve mentions neither Kimber nor any of his works; his best-received novels of the mid-1760s are presumably buried among those which, at that time, "seem to have over-run the press" to furnish an "Annual Supply for the Circulating Library," with the result that "the manufacturers of Novels were constantly at work for them, and were very poorly paid for their labours" – in contrast to rare standouts like Scott's *Sir George Ellison*, Thomas Amory's *John Buncle, Esq.*, and Oliver Goldsmith's *The Vicar of Wakefield.* Once Euphrasia has run through her shortlist of 1760s novels that have risen above the generally contemptible circulating library class, however, the exchange of my second epigraph takes place. Sophronia interjects the question, "Pray what is your opinion of Miss *Minifie*'s

Novels?" and Euphrasia replies, "They are in the class of mediocrity, if I were to mention such, it would make our task too long and tedious, I must therefore pass over these, and hundreds beside that are very innocent and moral books." Unnamed and unworthy of Euphrasia's notice though they may be, the Minifies' novels have nevertheless been distinguished ever so slightly from their peers in this "class of mediocrity" by the very question and answer, a distinction that, given Reeve's determination to integrate female writers into the tradition of admirable novels, one can with justification speculate is gained by these writers' sex, combined with their successful maintenance of a reputation for morally harmless entertainment.[47]

With the exception of Reeve's list, the Minifies are absent from contemporary "canons" of worthy female writers, indicating again that, if harmless, their fiction is not seen as equalling the intellectual or aesthetic achievement of a Fielding, Lennox, Sheridan, Scott, or Brooke. Kimber, not surprisingly, never appears in the latter part of the century's frequent all-male lists of those novelists who have rendered the genre respectable: those places are reserved invariably for Richardson and Henry Fielding, often for Marivaux, Johnson, Rousseau, and Smollett.[48] Indeed, since the merely informal, insider attribution of Kimber's work in his own time also resembles the case of Sarah Scott, it is not surprising that the sense of both authors as having produced a significant body of work is quickly lost.[49]

What are the implications of this relatively elaborated literary hierarchy for literary history and literary studies today? First, it appears that these distinctions, consistent as they were across contemporary and immediately subsequent commentary, were largely lost to literary history, and remain so to a significant extent. In 1935, for example, Black places Kimber on a par with a large, undifferentiated group of other "lesser novelists" writing between 1750 and 1765, which he identifies as "the period of Richardson, Fielding, Smollett, and Sterne"; Black's group comprises "Mrs. Haywood, Cleland, Coventry, Sarah Fielding, Sarah Scott, Lennox, Kidgell, Amory, Bannac, Woodfin, Charles Johnstone, Frances Sheridan, Frances Brooke, Johnson, Leland, Hawkesworth, Goldsmith (*The Citizen of the World* only), Horace Walpole, and Susannah Gunning."[50] Fifty years later, Janet Todd, focusing on the women writers of this time, discusses Brooke and the Minifies interchangeably as "popular writers of the mid-eighteenth century," whose novels are "Tissues of clichés and influences, artificial in language and characterisation, [that] purvey a common fantasy" of the power of passive femininity, "primarily for a female audience" – though she does acknowledge Brooke's stature in the eyes of Johnson, Richardson, the *Monthly Review*, and John Duncombe.[51]

Whether finely tuned or not, feminist discussions have at least re-inserted the Minifies into literary history by virtue of their sex. What might their place be, and where might Edward Kimber be resituated, in a general history of eighteenth-century writers? The earliest readers and reviewers of their work, whose comments I have summarized, offer some guidelines that remain useful. To recapitulate: I have shown that the critics suggest that both Kimber and the Minifies are run-of-the-mill imitators of the latest in generic trends, neither innovators nor even the best imitators, but also not unskilled or unscrupulous copyists. At no point are they seen as setting a trend or as improving upon a precursor, but they are relatively effective practitioners of an increasingly recognizable set of genre conventions. Although the fictions of Kimber and the Minifies are regularly commented on in the reviews and, to a lesser extent, by contemporary lay readers such as Catherine Talbot, no commentator speaks of the fictions of Kimber or the Minifies as making a contribution to the republic of letters.

In short, early readers and reviewers of fiction by Kimber and the Minifies appear to have employed criteria of judgment rather similar to those in general use today, despite intervening shifts in preferred modes or definitions of the genre, or in political stances with respect to gender, class, and the literary. Thus, while the *Critical*, especially, likes to quote morally improving or pathetic passages from these authors at some length, this feature would seem to serve ends distinct from that of critical evaluation, whereby these authors are consistently ranked as third-class "professors" in the genre hierarchy according to firmly established, genre-specific criteria recognizable at least since the mid-eighteenth century: consistent, appealing, and varied characters; original, plausible, and engaging plots; a fluent, varied, and correct style; and the ability to please a broad range of readers. Moral imperatives, if anything, led to their placement above what their artistic accomplishments alone would warrant.

This suggests, further, that when Spencer speaks of women writers of the mid-century as needing to abide by the "terms of acceptance" established by their male peers – the standards of modesty and propriety which allowed them access to the reading public – she is in fact identifying the terms which applied as well to someone like Kimber, who as a third-ranked novelist could not hope to dictate or even influence those terms.[52]

With the establishment of novels as "a staple commodity," the reviews, as an institution of an increasingly broad-based print culture, were able to bring to bear a set of evaluative criteria reflecting that commodity's social function as sanctioned entertainment. In this context, the author's gender played a role in determining a review's rhetoric, but it was not the determining factor in its ranking. Where the latter is concerned, contemporary readers, reviewers, and literary historians are agreed: the ingenious Mrs. Fielding and the spirited Mrs. Lennox, while not of the calibre of the penetrating Mr. Richardson and the witty Mr. Fielding, rise above the nonetheless-interesting Mr. Kimber and the harmless Miss Minifies. In reopening questions of value from the perspective of a recovery of so much of women's published writing in the eighteenth century, we could do worse than begin with these contemporary assessments.

CHAPTER 6

From propensity to profession in the early career of Frances Burney

> So early was I impressed myself with ideas that fastened degradation to this class of composition [the novel], that at the age of adolescence, I struggled against the propensity which, even in childhood, even from the moment I could hold a pen, had impelled me into its toils.
>
> (Frances Burney, *The Wanderer*, 1814)[1]

> my dear Fanny, for God's sake dont talk of *hard Fagging*! It was not *hard Fagging*, that produced such a Work as Evelina! – – – it was the Ebullition of true Sterling Genius! you wrote it, because you could not help it! – it came, & so you put it down on Paper! – leave *Fagging*, & Labour, to him
>
> – – – – – – – – – who high in Drury Lane,
> Lull'd by soft Zephyrs thro the broken pane,
> Rhymes ere he wakes, & prints before Term Ends,
> *Compell'd by Hunger & request of Friends.*
>
> Tis not sitting down to a Desk with Pen, Ink & Paper, that will command Inspiration.
>
> (Samuel Crisp to Frances Burney, 1779)[2]

There are two reasons why a treatment of Frances Burney may appear out of place in this study. First, she launched into print in 1778, a decade after the deaths of Sarah Fielding and Frances Sheridan, after Charlotte Lennox and Sarah Scott had produced most or all of their published work, and when only Frances Brooke continued in the public eye as a respected, if sometimes controversial, literary professional. But it is precisely this historical position which is of interest, for Burney's journals and letters register her consciousness of Fielding, Lennox, and Brooke, at least, as having achieved public recognition for some form of literary "career." She knew also that for many of her contemporaries, women's place in the public sphere of letters and the arts was a given; as she quotes Edmund Burke writing to her in 1782 in praise of her novel *Cecilia*, this was "an age distinguished by producing extraordinary women."[3] Burney's early career thus represents how one woman writer responded to the patterns of literary professionalization available to her in a rapidly developing print culture.

A second argument against examining Burney's emergence into the public eye as an author might be that, unlike the other authors of my study group, her career and the nature of her claim to literary authority have already been subject to a great deal of critical scrutiny over the past several decades. Indeed, this scrutiny was initiated by Burney's own self-conscious analyses recorded in the voluminous journals, and by her subsequent editorial rewritings of them. While this situation complicates the task, I suggest that it makes it all the more necessary. The overwhelming mass of particulars provided by Burney in her own accounts of her authorship encouraged early feminist critics to map both her private writings and her texts against the grid of the separate-spheres ideology to which it was assumed all eighteenth-century women writers were subject. The influential studies here were Kristina Straub's analysis of the doubleness of Burney's early fictions, Margaret Anne Doody's reading of Burney's writings through her family life, and Julia Epstein's exploration of what she called Burney's "anger" at being caught between late eighteenth-century prescriptions for the domestic woman's behavior and a desire to engage in public discussions of social issues.[4] In other words, a common strategy of early feminist treatments was to understand Burney's practice as typical of the woman writer for whom propriety and the doctrine that a woman's place is in the private sphere are considerations overriding all others, including different models of identity proceeding from individual and class situations. According to the terms of this model, outlined by Mary Poovey in her influential 1984 study of *The Proper Lady and the Woman Writer*, Burney's psychic and professional survival necessitated splitting off her identity as female writer from the models of female propriety which she endorsed in her writing.[5]

The result was what both Epstein and Doody themselves, in the foreword and afterword framing a number of the journal *Eighteenth-Century Fiction* devoted to *Evelina*, later identified as a psychobiographical habit of Burney criticism (particularly with respect to the ingenue Evelina, the eponymous heroine of Burney's first published novel) which has been hard to break.[6] In the past decade, there have been several important readings of Burney's career and writings that have answered the call to complicate the paradigm of domestic ideology as particularly enacted by the Burney family and represented in the fictions of its most famous daughter. Straub's and Doody's studies themselves emphasized social class as a consideration inseparable from that of gender in the formation of Burney's authorial identity; Straub, in particular, argued that a middle-class ideology of aspiration and self-improvement is as important as "the ideology of female powerlessness" in arriving at an understanding of Burney's "life expectations."[7] One productive line of inquiry has been that highlighting Burney's analyses of the emerging public sphere, exemplified by Helen Thompson's discussion of *Evelina* as problematizing the split between an abstractly universal public practitioner of letters and the embodied, spectacular female self. Such work is informed by that which illuminates Burney's examinations of the economic shifts of her day, represented by Sandra Sherman's discussion of *The Witlings* as "elaborat[ing] an encounter between emergent industrial discourse in which time, production, and money are imbricated, and a leisure class which appropriates this discourse but produces nothing." Most specifically relevant to my purposes, Catherine Gallagher's 1994 analysis of patterns of naming, namelessness, and debt in *Evelina* and *Cecilia* conveys a Burney "raised to the trade" of authorship in a family making its own place in an emerging literary-professional class; "the writings of other families might have been imagined as second-order realities, as accomplishments indicating a (past or present) economic independence, but the writings of the Burneys were the business of their lives."[8]

Implying Frances Burney's alertness to a multiplicity of pressures molding and obstructing late eighteenth-century female subjectivity, such studies have broadened the terms of reference for reading her work; they also suggest new approaches to Burney's own record of her early publishing life, approaches which acknowledge the options available to her and her agency in making career choices. Recently, Janice Farrar Thaddeus, in *Frances Burney: A Literary Life*, has set out to provide a corrective account of Burney as self-conscious professional: "I wish to stress at the start that Frances Burney at the age of 60 was – at least in some predicaments, and especially in her professional capacity as writer – very strong and confident . . . This point must be made – and made firmly – because Burney has so often been depicted as self-deprecating, even fearful." While not denying Burney's "fearfulness" and her "complex nature as a writer," Thaddeus provides an overview of her career which climaxes in the assertiveness and professional freedom she gained through her 1793 marriage and subsequent family life.[9] My argument is very compatible with Thaddeus's teleological narrative, but I focus on Burney's earlier period of authorship as equally formative in her professionalization. I will suggest that, as a writer emerging in the later 1770s, she deliberately chose the developing model of the literary professional as a means of fashioning a coherent public identity that could be continuous with, and complementary to, the life of deep domestic attachments that was also her choice. I propose to trace in this chapter Burney's use of a print-culture model of professionalism to establish an authorial identity that freed her, to a significant extent, from the limitations of an essentialized feminine identity while allowing her to adopt tenets of female propriety in her private life.

Clearly, Burney's notions of authorship cannot simply be collapsed with those of her gentry heroines Evelina and the two Cecilias of *The Witlings* and *Cecilia*, whose virtue is partly defined by their horror of publicity, and who inhabit texts peopled primarily by characters whose model of publication is one of epistolary or coterie circulation, rather than appearance in print.[10] George Justice has argued that this was in Burney a gradual divergence along an uncharted pathway: "Professional authorship . . . provides [for Burney] a way out of the restrictions of class and gender illustrated in her writings. Thus, her class and gender politics in her literary works can by themselves remain relatively conventional, relatively conservative, while her own life and career blazed new trails."[11] The timing of Burney's realization aside, Justice overstates the pioneering nature of Burney's enterprise, as this study has shown. Indeed, Burney's friends responded to her early anxieties about public naming as somewhat unusual; Burney's correspondent Samuel "Daddy" Crisp notes in this respect that she is one of the "Prudes," and Hester Thrale scolds her for "over-delicacy" (*EJL*, vol. III, pp. 187, 116). Burney's fictions and plays should thus no more be read as unmediated representations of late eighteenth-century views about women in the republic of letters than should Frances Brooke's 1777 novel *The Excursion*, which was published virtually simultaneously with *Evelina*, and whose well-born heroine's entrance into the world includes attempting to get a brilliantly written tragedy staged in London while cherishing manuscripts of an epic poem and a novel in her trunk. The older and much-published Brooke evidently found it strategic to draw attention to, and to assume the legitimacy of, women's authorial activities.

Although I make no claim to arrive at a definitive explanation for Burney's disguises and identifications over the three and a half years from *Evelina* to *Cecilia*, I hope to contribute a fresh perspective on this fascinating crux in her professional life by reading it in terms of the *kind* of public identity Burney was fashioning for herself, an identity enabled by the structures of a developing print culture. My argument will outline the significance of Burney's self-fashioning both as a reflection of, and an intervention in, late eighteenth-century shifts in the profession of letters and in the position of women writers within the profession. As my phrasing suggests, I contend that Burney did not simply insert herself into a mold labeled "female author" or "woman novelist" which by definition forced her to transgress a gendered private-public divide. Rather, her authorial self-construction was both particularly hers and determined by her historical position, both reactive to current conditions and influential in determining subsequent conditions of authorship for female novelists. In elaborating this self-construction, I will begin with Burney's accounts of the Streatham literary-professional circle of which she became a member during this period, and then discuss the texts of *The Witlings* and *Cecilia*, to reveal her acute analysis of Britain's rapidly elaborating print culture, in its implications for a woman with a propensity for writing who chose to pursue authorship as a profession.

CONSTRUCTING A PROFESSIONAL IDENTITY

As I have established in previous chapters, the 1770s and early 1780s were not predominantly hostile to women's literary and dramatic activity as such. Indeed, there is considerable evidence for arguing the contrary: that there existed from the middle of the century a climate of encouragement of, even fascination with, women's writing. One already cited instance of public encouragement was Mary Scott's 1774 poem *The Female Advocate*, which names numerous female authors who have "of late, . . . appeared with honour, in almost every walk of literature," with the result that "the sentiments of all men of sense relative to female education are now more enlarged than they formerly were." Other cases are Hannah More's 1774 epilogue to the third edition of *The Search after Happiness: A Pastoral Drama*, which praises Elizabeth Carter, Anna Laetitia Aikin (later Barbauld), Elizabeth Montagu, Frances Brooke, and Catharine Macaulay by name; and Richard Samuel's *circa* 1779 group portrait of Carter, Barbauld, Macaulay, Montagu, and More, as well as Charlotte Lennox, Angelica Kauffman, Elizabeth Sheridan, and Elizabeth Griffith as the *Nine Living Muses of Great Britain*. Successful female dramatists of this period or the recent past included More, Griffith, Brooke, Frances Sheridan, and Hannah Cowley.[12]

That Burney herself quickly attained the height of respectable fashion at this time is facetiously recorded in a 1784 letter from Aikin to her brother ("Next to the [hot-air] balloon, Miss B. is the object of public curiosity: I had the pleasure of meeting her yesterday. She is a very unaffected, modest, sweet and pleasing young lady: – but you, now I think of it, are a Goth, and have not read Cecilia. Read, read it, for shame!") and echoed more earnestly by a correspondent to the *Gentleman's Magazine* in 1785, who endorses "Miss Burney's *Cecilia*" as his example of "a particular exception" to a new subscription library's ban on romances because it is "a work of superior excellence." She was named, among other wise women, in Samuel Hoole's 1783 poem *Aurelia: or the Contest* and in the epilogue to Thomas Holcroft's 1787 play *Seduction.*[13] Thus the question was not whether a respectable woman author might have a public identity. Rather, it was a matter of what sort of identity she should pursue, and how she would negotiate those ascribed to her, whether that of the genderless, disembodied "author of *Evelina*"; of "little Burney," Dr. Burney's daughter; of the "domesticated" companion of Mrs. Thrale;[14] of the protégée of Mrs. Montagu; or of a lion of the *ton.*

For Burney, the most formative influence in this pursuit and negotiation was that of the literary circle centered on the Streatham house of Henry Thrale, presided over by Hester Thrale as hostess and Samuel Johnson as intellectual head. As William McCarthy has put it, during this time "An introduction to Streatham came to be a *badge of success in one's line.* So Charles Burney thought it . . . And so his daughter Frances thought it when her first novel, *Evelina*, earned her an invitation."[15] Under these circumstances, it is not surprising that Burney's accounts of this group paint a portrait of emergent professionalism – specifically, professional authorship. As in my previous chapters, my analysis of the Streatham circle's structure as similar to that of an occupational group draws primarily on sociological models which include, but are not limited to, the goal of economic remuneration for the practice of certain skills. When Johnson reports dining with Elizabeth Carter, Hannah More, and Frances Burney, adding, "Three such women are not to be found: I know not where I could find a fourth, except Mrs. Lennox, who is superiour to them all," Boswell suggests, "Might not Mrs. Montagu have been a fourth?," to which Johnson replies, "Sir, Mrs. Montagu does not make a trade of her wit; but Mrs. Montagu is a very extraordinary woman; she has a constant stream of conversation, and it is always impregnated; it has always meaning."[16] I am thus following Johnson's own explicitly drawn dichotomy, as recorded by Boswell, in emphasizing professional authorship as a defining, if not *the* defining, quality of the Streatham literary circle that Burney sets in contrast to rival circles such as that of Elizabeth Montagu's bluestockings.

Burney and her friends did, indeed, unabashedly subscribe to the most narrow sense of the professional as working for financial gain, seeing the publication of a novel or the production of a play as a means of economic self-support and accompanying social autonomy. In this view, seemingly self-evident to us, the group was in fact endorsing emergent views of the skilled author as worthy of her hire, as entitled to remuneration for intellectual labor despite the moral principle that knowledge should be publicly shared for the benefit of all humankind.[17] Thus Samuel Crisp's first comments upon learning that Burney is the author of *Evelina* include the statement that the bookseller Lowndes "would have *made an Estate* had he given [Burney] 1100 pounds for it, & . . . ought not to have given less!" (*EJL*, vol. III, p. 65), drawing on the parallel of author and landowner which Mark Rose, among others, has noted as fundamental to arguments in favor of authorial copyright privileges in the eighteenth century.[18] A frequently quoted proposal by Johnson that he and Burney visit Grub Street together illustrates this appropriation of the socially authoritative figure of the patrimonial estate. Burney writes:

> he offered to take me with him to Grub Street, to see the ruins of the House demolished there in the late Riots, by a mob that, as he observed, could be no Friend to the Muses! . . . "You and I Burney will go together, we have a very good *right* to go, so we'll visit the mansions of our Progenitors, & take up our own Freedom!"
> 'There's for You, Madam! *what can be grander*?'[19]

The trope makes explicit what is at stake: in the professional ethos, one's mode of making a living is fundamental to one's sense of identity and social place. And, significantly, both Crisp and Johnson assume that this identity is available to Burney as a woman.

Fundamental to this model of proprietary authorship is the acknowledgment of one's publications in order to establish ownership. And so Burney is put through a rigorous process of acclimatization to publicity, warned by Thrale that, "indeed you must blunt a little of this delicacy, – for the Book [*Evelina*] has such success, that if *you* don't own it – somebody else will!" (*EJL*, vol. III, p. 117). From such logic it is but a short step to the further principle that one must produce more as a means of taking up one's rightful property; Thrale next urges Burney to write a stage comedy with the words, "a *play* will be something *worth* your Time, it is the Road both to Honour & Profit, – & *why* should you have it in your power to gain these rewards & not do it?" (*EJL*, vol. III, p. 133).

The terms Burney uses to recount her publication of *Evelina*, while disingenuously denying ambition, are clear in their equation of authorship with print: "I had written my little Book simply for my amusement, I printed it . . . merely for a frolic, to see how a production of my own would figure *in that Author like form* . . . [But I] destined [*Evelina*] to no nobler habitation than a circulating library" (*EJL* vol. III, p. 32; my italics). That such a narrowly print-based view of the author is in formation in Burney's time has been thoroughly illustrated by Margaret Ezell's examinations of an earlier, but also to some extent coexistent, scribal culture's notion of manuscript authorship.[20] Once the link between true authorship and print has been established, as the above citations make clear, publication can be the source not only of profit, but also of honor. And so Burney gives pride of place in her journals and letters to the published members of the Streatham group, and makes it clear that her publication of *Evelina* was the basis of her own admission to the inner circle. McCarthy has noted that Hester Thrale, though functioning as hostess-patron of this circle at the time, had been generally named as contributing author of a poem and translation to Anna Williams's 1766 *Miscellanies in Prose and Verse*, and argues that her writing career was at this point merely "interrupted" and "stifled" by her first marriage.[21] Nevertheless, from Burney's perspective, the hostess's place was a subordinate one in this circle; she notes in some surprise Thrale's "most respectful silence" at Johnson's "astonishing" "freedom" and "intollerable" forcefulness in speaking critically of her and others (*EJL*, vol. III, p. 86).[22]

Beyond the mere fact of writing for publication and remuneration, professionalization for this group, as Burney describes it, included establishing an exclusive claim to literary expertise; doing so seems to have required establishing distinctions, albeit sometimes artificial ones, between its own members as authors, and others as mere hacks, at one extreme, or mere conversational wits, at the other. Thus George Huddesford, who dares to name Burney "*irreverently*" in his pamphlet *Warley*, is dismissed by Thrale as a nameless "Wretch," "God knows who, – in the Garret" (*EJL*, vol. III, pp. 206–7). Yet true authorship requires the approbation of a wide reading public as well as of a discriminating body of fellow-wits.

Thus Burney early disdains the "conceited" Mr. Keate who solicits praise from a sycophantic circle of female relations for his ode "upon Building," while crying "affectedly," "Why surely . . . you would not have me *Publish* it"; she directly juxtaposes this coy poet with the portrait: "My Father, – who thank Heaven, is an author of a different stamp, pursues his Work at all the leisure moments he can snatch from Business or from sleep" (*EJL*, vol. II, p. 36).

Nor does the potential for a sisterhood of female authors induce Burney to abandon distinctions between her own acclaimed work and that of a derivative and sentimental amateur. On the contrary, in one extended and highly shaped account in her journal, Burney struggles to disentangle herself from an encounter with the all-dismal Lady Hawke, thrust upon her as a "sister authoress" by that lady's zealous flesh-and-blood sister Lady Saye and Sele. Indeed, the term "authoress" is used insistently by this enthusiast, appearing eight times in a six-page account. Burney is obviously uncomfortable with the assumption of a common bond as a female author with the "extremely languishing, delicate, and pathetic" Lady Hawke, who writes because "I really can't help writing. One has great pleasure in writing the things; has not one, Miss Burney?" but has "never printed yet" – though she intends to print her epistolary novel, *The Mausoleum of Julia*, "just for her own friends and acquaintances" (*DL*, vol. II, pp. 60–66).

The informal structural principles of the Streatham circle as Burney records them thus included a hierarchy of cultural prestige based on literary accomplishments rather than social status; as she enters the group, Burney describes herself as "a poor mere *Worm* in Literature, . . . the identical Grub he [Johnson] has obliged" by his praise of *Evelina*, proof that "the greatest minds are ever the most candid to the inferior set!" (*EJL*, vol. III, p. 61). Johnson, at the apex of this hierarchy, is in Burney's view "the acknowledged Head of Literature in this kingdom, & . . . has the most extensive knowledge, the clearest understanding, & the greatest abilities of any Living Author"; the initiate author therefore sets herself to be instructed and entertained by his surpassing "Conversation," "Wit," and "Language" (*EJL*, vol. III, pp. 73–74). Wit employed in authorial projects (Johnson was at the time completing his prefatory "lives" of the poets) is by implication more admirable than the conversational "flash" of a *salonnière*.

Perhaps in compensation for her own sense of unease in large conversational circles, Burney repeatedly mingles disdain with evident fascination when discussing such conversational "flashers" as Elizabeth

Montagu (joined, at times, by Thrale), who holds herself up for mockery as well as flattering attention, and who cares "not a fig" to hear the views of others, "as long as she [speaks] *herself*" (*EJL*, vol. IV, pp. 33, 38, 99). In this context, Johnson's famous challenge to Burney to attack Montagu – "*Down* with her, Burney! – *down* with her! – spare her not! attack her, fight her, & *down* with her at once! – *You* are a *rising* Wit, – *she* is at the *Top*" (*EJL*, vol. III, p. 151) – might be read to evoke, not so much a single and internally competitive literary sphere, as the attack of a rising professional system on an earlier hierarchical structure, one built primarily upon the leisured cultivation of conversational skill and embodied in the literary salon rather than in the disembodied authorial production judged by widespread public approbation.[23]

The essentially middle-class professional ethos of this Johnson-centered circle is evidenced as well by its conscious pride in the social power wielded by its most established members. For example, a conversation on the set topic of "*The Respect due from the lower Class of the people*" evolves significantly from a concern about distinctions of social rank into a discussion of the respect accorded to Johnson, of whom Thrale says, "I believe there is no man in the World so *greatly* respected" (*EJL*, vol. III, p. 132). Similarly, the success of the painter George Romney is attributed to the patronage of the playwright Richard Cumberland, upon which Johnson says, "See, Madam, what it is to have the favour of a *Literary* man!" (*EJL*, vol. III, p. 168). As I have already indicated, this group buttressed its own cultural prestige by holding all manner of patrons, amateurs, inferior authors, and undiscriminating admirers at a distance; even Charles Burney, as too sycophantic, and Hester Thrale, as too shallowly outspoken and facetious, are marginalized at points in the accounts of Thrale and Frances Burney, respectively.[24] As an initiate to the profession, Burney proudly records moments when members of the Streatham circle signal acceptance of her as a fellow intellectual laborer, across the divides of gender, age, and social status. Thus in recording a conversation with Sir Joshua Reynolds which she has been dreading, Burney uses pointedly horizontal, egalitarian terms to describe the relieving of her anxiety: they discuss "Dr. Johnson's Lives of the Poets; – we had *both* Read the *same*, & therefore could praise them with *equal* warmth, – & we *both* love & reverence the Writer, & therefore could mix observations on the *Book* with the *Author* with *equal* readiness" (*EJL*, vol. III, p. 201; my italics).

I believe that, in this formative stage of professionalism, Burney found the individualistic, merit-based authorial identity offered by such conversations preferable to Mrs. Montagu's version of advocacy, which insistently embodied her as female, accomplished, and therefore worthy of patronage, but simultaneously invoked the subordinate social status of the same authorial body in her disgust at the vulgarity of *Evelina*'s Branghtons and Captain Mirvan.[25] Even Burney's oft-quoted assertion "I would a thousand Times rather forfeit my character as a *Writer*, than risk ridicule or censure as a Female" (*EJL*, vol. III, p. 212), it should be noted, maintains, if in some tension, the existence of two distinct identity categories, and therefore the potential for balancing the claims of both. Thus Burney is particularly impressed by a three-way conversation with Thrale and Johnson in which the latter distinguishes between love, flattery, and his own great admiration of herself. She comments that "I have long enough had reason to think myself *loved*, – but *admiration* is perfectly new to me!," leading Johnson to elaborate to Thrale: "I admire [Burney] for her observations, – for her humour, – for her Discernment, – for her manner of expressing them, – & for *all* her *Writing* Talents" (*EJL*, vol. III, p. 155). While Burney clearly worried about the high expectations being established for her future work, the possibility of such an advance in authorial prestige on her own merits must have made the literary-professional model a powerfully attractive one. Certainly it offered an autonomy more appealing than the thought of having her current project, the manuscript *The Witlings*, subject to "the interference of the various Macaenas's who would expect to be consulted, – of these I could not confide in *one*, without disobliging all the rest; – & I could not confide in *all*, without having the play read all over the Town before it is acted. Mrs. Montagu, Mrs. Greville, Mrs. Crewe, Sir Joshua Reynolds, Mrs. Cholmondeley, & many inferior &cs, think they have an *equal* claim, one with the other, to my confidence." (*EJL*, vol. III, p. 264).[26]

AMATEUR LITERARY CULTURE IN THE WITLINGS

Burney's accounts of the literary circle she enters after *Evelina*'s publication thus fit the sociological notion of the professions as exclusive, self-regulating, and socially prestigious bodies organized hierarchically on the basis of a common body of knowledge and a specialized set of skills. In this light, the signature "By A Sister of the Order" on the manuscript title page of *The Witlings*, though it has generally been read as Burney's self-deprecating placement of herself among the would-be wits the play satirizes, is quite possibly much more ambiguous. If her journals and letters make clear the value she places upon the publicly acclaimed author, the satiric focus of this play is on the threat posed to print-based professionalism by the amateur reader and writer, against whose pretensions and foibles it is held as an implied standard.[27] Barbara Darby has noted that the innovative first act, set in a milliner's shop, establishes the play's focus on various economies and their systems of value: "everyone has something for sale, the price varies with availability, and the ability to pay monopolizes others' attention." While varying the terms, Thaddeus makes the parallel observation that the play is ultimately about "competing kinds of authority, intellectual, financial, and familial."[28]

Within such a commodified framework, the amateur author and critic is in competition with the professional, exploiting the resources of flattery, social connections, and propertied leisure to monopolize influential readers' attention. Thus an incestuous and exclusive coterie circle based on manuscript exchange obstructs the free circulation of texts and the resultant determination of value through public opinion; the needy and, by implication, genuinely gifted author lacks the mediation of the influential reader-patron in reaching a public and gaining the just rewards of her or his labors. Hence the skepticism of Miss Jenny, the milliner's apprentice, upon being assured that the smartly dressed Mr. Dabler is "one of the first Wits of the age," who "can make Verses as fast as [his landlady, Mrs. Voluble] can talk." When Miss Jenny exclaims, "Dear me! why he's quite a fine Gentleman; I thought Poets were always as poor as Job," Mrs. Voluble explains, "Why so they are, my dear, in common; your *real* Poet is all rags & atoms; but Mr. Dabler is quite another thing; he's what you may call a Poet of Fashion."[29] Mr. Dabler is usurping the rightful place of the "real Poet," who never appears in this play.

If there is no living "real Poet" in this world of Witlings, Censor, the eccentric moralist who brings about the resolution of the play's plot, comes close on several counts, despite his financial independence and elevated social status. Although he need not live by the pen, he does not disdain publication; he speaks casually in the closing scene of "my Printer" (5.824), and indeed, appears to have the necessary connections in the trade to have lampoons and ballads printed or suppressed instantaneously and at whim. Unlike Dabler, who initially claims to view printed lampoons as "poor Stuff" and "mere impotent efforts of Envy" (5.666–67), Censor understands the use of publication to control public opinion: he threatens to deploy the daily papers, the coffee houses, and the ballad-singers either to "prejudice the World against [Lady Smatter]" (5.719–20), or to have "the liberality of [her] Soul, and the depth of [her] knowledge . . .

recorded by the Muses, and echoed by the whole Nation!" (5.846–48). The parallel fears of Lady Smatter and William Congreve's earlier Lady Wishfort, successfully blackmailed by her fear of having her name dragged before the courts, make it clear that the "Way of the World" has changed since the turn of the century: when Lady Smatter threatens to "have [Censor] prosecuted with the utmost severity of the Law" for libel, he replies knowingly, "You will have the thanks of my Printer for your reward" (5.822–24). In an optimistic mirror image to Frances Brooke's tirade against the print trade's abuse of truth in the form of scandal papers (see chapter 2), publicity through print here functions as society's moral guarantor.

Censor embodies an institutional function in the play like the print culture role of the critic, making and preserving a tradition of great English poets, and thereby enforcing the laws of taste. In this he resembles Burney's mentor Johnson, currently engrossed in his accounts of English poets for the mutual benefit of booksellers asserting claims to publishing rights and a reading public asserting its cultivation. Thus it is Censor who corrects the false attributions to Pope and Swift that Lady Smatter, head of the Esprit Party, is continually making; in the process, as well as in his own constant allusions, he identifies Spenser, Shakespeare, Waller, Prior, Pope, Swift, Addison and Steele, Gay, and Thomson as the authors whose beauties every educated reader should know.[30] And he protects the reputations of Great Authors from dishonor in his detection of Dabler's attempt to put off one of his own feeble productions as a posthumous work of Gay, thereby affirming the principle of canonical purity.

In short, though Doody has coupled the amateur Dabler with the play's heroine Cecilia as her "male counterpart,"[31] I take Burney, when writing to her sister Susan of her own temptation to turn "censor*ess*" (*EJL*, vol. III, p. 205), to be deliberately identifying herself with this alert subject in a print economy who knows how to employ the "*power*" of the press to make good his threat "either to establish [Lady Smatter's] Fame upon the firmest foundation, or to consign [her] for life to Irony and Contempt" (5.827, 820–21). Nevertheless, in keeping with Darby's observation that "the figures with unchallenged power and authority [in Burney's plays] tend to be patriarchal Englishmen, heads of households and of communities who uphold exacting communal standards for behavior, choice, contrition, and resolution of conflict," print's moral force is embodied, for the purposes of the stage, in the socially privileged male character Censor. Darby emphasizes, drawing on Hélène Cixous, the body and its sex as an inescapable material presence in the theatre. I would extend this principle to suggest that theatrical representation led Burney to satirize the embodied structures of the conversational salon, including its gendered role-playing, while the disembodied relations of print culture are gestured to offstage as the desirable alternative.[32]

If the figure of Censor seems a fantasy projection of the cultural power denied the play's heroine Cecilia and sought by the playwright Burney, the members of Lady Smatter's Esprit Party provide a revealing, though hyperbolic, anatomy of the pressures of contemporary print culture on those who aspire to recognition as authors and wits. Dabler, for one, is obsessed with and oppressed by the demand for originality arising from the ready availability of print editions of previous authors. Thus his verse lament "Ye gentle Gods, O hear me plead, / And Kindly grant this little loan; / Make me forget whate'er I read / That what I write may be my own" (2.196–99), reductively parodies Edward Young's 1759 *Conjectures on Original Composition* in its complaint that "illustrious Examples *engross*, *prejudice*, and *intimidate*."[33] On the spectrum of readers, Lady Sapient at one extreme is a plagiarist who endlessly trots out the most commonplace of clichés as her unique opinions, while at the other, Lady Smatter authorizes her every word and action by reference to a Great Author (though, as we have seen, her attributions are generally mistaken). Indeed, Lady Smatter idolizes Books and Authors; when Beaufort exclaims that the names of "Pope, Swift, Shakespeare himself" are "hateful to my Ear, & detestable to my remembrance" while he is in agony over the fate of his beloved Cecilia, Lady Smatter accuses him of "downright blasphemy" (3.18–21). Similarly, his frustrated wish that there were "not one [Book] in the World" is the sure sign that he is "plunging" into "Ignorance & Depravity," and meets with cries of "Monstrous, shocking, and horrible!" (4.625–32).

In Lady Smatter, this cult of Author and Book has come to stand in for genuine learning. She boasts to Cecilia, "I am never at rest till I have discovered the authors of every thing that comes out," and when Cecilia comments that Lady Smatter "devotes . . . much Time to these researches," the latter is quick to defend her investment: "I do indeed devote my Time to them; I own it without blushing, for how, as a certain author Says, can Time be better employed than in cultivating intellectual accomplishments?" (2.6–15). As David Kaufer and Kathleen Carley have noted in their analysis of the interdependence of print and oral media, the "reverse vicariousness" of talking about books before, or even rather than, actually reading them is an integral feature of print culture. This feature in theory enables the wide circulation of information about books, and thereby an expanded readership.[34] The desire to participate in such circulation is satirized in both Lady Smatter, who declares that "if my pursuits were not made public, I should not have any at all, for where can be the pleasure of reading Books, & studying authors, if one is not to have the credit of talking of them?" (2.23–25), and Dabler, who confides that, despite his wish of forgetfulness, "one must read; one's reputation requires it; for it would be cruelly confusing to be asked after such or such an author, and never have looked into him. especially to a person who passes for having some little knowledge in these matters" (2.203–5). The problem, though, and what makes the Esprit Party the object of satire, is the fact that its members talk only to each other and merely echo one another's views; when Codger dares to express a dissenting interpretation, he is driven out of the circle. Furthermore, the currency they exchange consists entirely in degenerate replicas of the works of authors long dead and their own inferior productions. Such self-enclosed reflexivity, superficial adulation of past writers, and mutual puffery hold out no hope for the struggling contemporary professional who needs to have her publications talked about.

Instead, this nest of amateurs, far removed from the test of genuine success with a reading public, provides the ideal venue for Dabler the Poet of Fashion, whose rhyming dictionary and social suppleness allow him to indulge the illusion that his having "from infancy . . . devoted all [his] Time to the practice of Poetry" gives him the best "Title" to being a judge of it (4.156–59). Clearly, he is no more qualified to write and judge "new Authors or productions" than the Elizabeth Montagu whom Burney has Johnson classify as one of "those who *know,* & *judge* by *rules,*" and whose opinions must therefore be "ever despise[d]" by the new author (*EJL,* vol. III, p. 222). Yet the obsession that draws these amateurs to devote all of their time to literature is the common ground they share with the newly minted professional, and therefore what she must define herself against. Dabler's lifelong devotion comes perilously close to the young Burney's own incessant scribbling as precursor to authorship; so, too, does Lady Smatter's coy fear that her own "enthusiasm for poetry" is a "propensity" which she may possibly "indulge . . . too much" (2.110–12). As Clayton Delery notes in his edition of *The Witlings,* this term is used by Burney herself to describe her early and lifelong urge to write fiction, when in her preface to the 1814 *The Wanderer,* quoted at the head of this chapter, she confesses that "at the age of adolescence, I struggled against the propensity [to write novels] which, even in childhood, even from the moment I could hold a pen, had impelled me into its toils."[35]

PROPENSITY VS. PROFESSION

It is therefore of note that, when Burney does finally create a professional author figure, Belfield in her novel *Cecilia*, "propensity" is the term he employs to describe the curse and blessing of literature as vocation. The overeducated and gifted son of a tradesman, Belfield is, in Doody's view, the eighteenth century's most effective "picture of the economic, social, and mental confusion that rising by the talents can involve." Doody adds that "the problems of Belfield are the problems of the displaced risers Charles Burney and Frances Burney, ungentle geniuses who did not quite belong anywhere."[36] After languishing in hopes of preferment through the patronage of his socially privileged schoolfriends, Belfield is at last engaged as a tutor, but he finds he cannot support the dependence and subservience inherent in the patronage system. Swinging to the opposite extreme of independence through physical labor, Belfield concludes this scheme to be impracticable because the "general tenor of education" is as powerful as "Nature herself" in limiting the kinds of employment for which he is suited.[37] Determined to maintain his independence, he turns as his only resource to the very studies which have made him unfit for other physical labors. In describing this resource, however, Belfield submerges nurture in nature, and authorship becomes an undeniable impulse, almost a pathological condition. I will quote the relevant passage at some length:

> "From my earliest youth to the present hour," continued Belfield, "literature has been the favourite object of my pursuit, my recreation in leisure, and my hope in employment. My propensity to it, indeed, has been so ungovernable, that I may properly call it the source of my several miscarriages throughout life. It was the bar to my preferment, for it gave me a distaste to other studies; it was the cause of my unsteadiness in all my undertakings, because to all I preferred it. It has sunk me to distress, it has involved me in difficulties; it has brought me to the brink of ruin by making me neglect the means of living, yet never, till now, did I discern it might itself be my support" (p. 737).

Belfield, as Burney conceived him, illustrates Clifford Siskin's hypothesis of the interrelated appearance in the later eighteenth century of a model of "the deep, developmental self" and of the professional who has "the authority to convert knowledge of the deep self into prescriptive expertise."[38]

Unlike the treatment of Dabler's and Lady Smatter's romanticization of their literary impulses, Belfield's turn to authorship is respected by Cecilia, who tellingly has herself just gained her majority and hence her long-awaited financial independence. She inquires if he has "written anything that [is] published with his name," and his bookseller assures her that this author is "a very great genius," who will soon produce "something considerable," "something extraordinary" (p. 723). Belfield's economic prospects appear to match his hopes, since the bookseller continues, "he has taken a very good road to bring himself home again [i.e. into cash], for we pay very handsomely for things of any merit, especially if they deal smartly in a few touches of the times" (pp. 723–24). Although Straub initially suggests that Belfield can be seen as a deliberate effort to broaden the representation of the literary profession beyond the experience of the woman writer alone, she ultimately returns to the notion that he is masking Burney's fundamentally feminocentric concerns:

> Burney's doubling of Cecilia's course-of-life plot in Belfield's search for employment may serve a dual function: while it draws attention away from the gender-linked specifics of social problems – perhaps strategically – it also allows her to treat seriously a difficulty that might otherwise be dismissed as merely female, a dismissal perhaps all too likely in a society that rationalized a plethora of social abuses as women's religion- and tradition-determined lot to bear.

Belfield is more than "a sort of mirror for the ideological position specific to femininity in eighteenth-century culture," however;[39] the doubleness he experiences, one which dogged Burney as well, is that of the professional author caught between economic realities and the developing discourse of genius. He insists initially to the bookseller that writing is for him a disinterested calling rather than a matter of economic exchange: "To terms I am indifferent, for writing is no labour to me; on the contrary, it is the first delight of my life, and therefore, and not for dirty pelf, I wish to make it my profession" (p. 722). This idealism meets with defeat in the face of the economic exchange logic upon which literary professionalism depends; Belfield turns from book-writing to book-keeping when he realizes that to live by the pen is "to write by rule, to compose by necessity, to make the understanding, nature's first gift, subservient to interest, that meanest offspring of art! – when weary, listless, spiritless, to rack the head for invention, the memory for images, and the fancy for ornament and allusion; and when the mind is wholly occupied by its own affections and affairs, to call forth its faculties for foreign subjects, uninteresting discussions, or fictitious incidents! (p. 883). Straub parallels this passage with Burney's complaints about the "rule" and "necessity" imposed by the others to whom she was "subservient,"[40] but to do so skews Belfield's sense: he feels the necessity of his own financial constraints, not those artificially imposed by others. It is this need to succeed in the marketplace by making a trade of his wit that makes him broadly representative of the literary professional's situation.

Belfield reappears frequently through the novel as Cecilia's male, middle-class double; by Cecilia he is taken seriously as a worthy friend, by others, as one of her suitors. Within a few pages of the novel's opening, he serves as spokesman for the plot's central focus on Cecilia's struggle to reconcile her individual genius and her convictions about conduct and taste with the need to conform to the world. At its conclusion, he has returned to a more established profession, the army; Cecilia, meanwhile, has married into a family whose head believes that it would be the height of impropriety for "a young lady of rank" to pursue her "desire to be known . . . by studying like an artist or professor" (p. 935). Belfield's ultimate inability to reconcile propensity with the demands of professional life, despite his generally deserving character, together with the senior Delvile's dismissal of young ladies' aspirations to be known for their practice of a profession, leaves the reader of *Cecilia* with a vision of professional authorship as unviably divided, whether for a woman or a man. The bleakness of Belfield's experience is reminiscent of the exchanges recorded in Burney's journal and letters following the decision to suppress *The Witlings*. Burney complains to her father of her "mortification . . . at throwing away the *Time* [on *The Witlings*], – which I with difficulty stole, & which I have Buried in the mere trouble of *writing*" (*EJL*, vol. III, p. 347), and worries that it is only through "hard fagging" that she will manage to publish anything that same winter. In a romanticization of Burney's writing process that defies all realities, Samuel Crisp then writes:

> my dear Fanny, for God's sake dont talk of *hard Fagging*! It was not *hard Fagging*, that produced such a Work as Evelina! – – – it was the Ebullition of true Sterling Genius! you wrote it, because you could not help it! – it came, & so you put it down on Paper! – leave *Fagging*, & Labour, to him
>
> – – – – – – – – – who high in Drury Lane,
> Lull'd by soft Zephyrs thro the broken pane,
> Rhymes ere he wakes, & prints before Term Ends,
> *Compell'd by Hunger & request of Friends.*
>
> Tis not sitting down to a Desk with Pen, Ink & Paper, that will command Inspiration. (*EJL*, vol. III, p. 352)

Crisp's quotation of Alexander Pope's *Epistle to Dr. Arbuthnot* here is a telling throwback to that poet's insistent separation of the true author from Grub Street, a separation which we know was artificial even for Pope, and which Burney's apprenticeship in the Streatham circle, not to mention her previous initiation to the print trade as her father's amanuensis and copyist, had shown her to be so.[41]

BURNEY'S PROFESSIONAL PRACTICE

Cecilia does conclude in a middle-class professional place for Belfield, and with his hopes of satisfying his personal "ambition" through his own efforts to win "future honour" (p. 940). And Cecilia will ultimately regain, through a legacy left specifically to her by a woman, "part of that power and independence of which her generous and pure regard for [her husband] has deprived her" (p. 937). Professionalism and economic independence are thus affirmed as legitimate aspirations and as important components of self-realization, itself implied as the individual's ultimate goal. Similarly, the same correspondence which can be read as a record of defeat and silencing shows Burney taking increasing ownership of the suppression of *The Witlings*, of the composition of *Cecilia*, and of her relations with the various literary and social circles vying for her membership. Once she has to abandon her play, she is the one who holds firmly to the decision, insisting to Richard Brinsley Sheridan that she is "not *Coqueting*" in refusing to show him the play (*EJL*, vol. III, p. 390), and resisting when her father, "ever easy to be worked upon, [begins] to waver," and when Crisp inclines from one course to another (*EJL*, vol. IV, pp. 8, 18). Not long after this, she refuses to change Mrs. Delvile's character or *Cecilia*'s ending at Crisp's behest (*DL*, vol. II, pp. 71–73, 80–81).

From the start of Burney's friendship with Hester Thrale, the latter complains in her journal of her friend's insistence upon "the Dignity of a Wit, or of what She values more – the Dignity of *Doctor Burney's Daughter*."[42] The very fact that different critics have seen the greatest pressure and greatest support at opposing ends of the Charles Burney-Hester Thrale tug-of-war for Frances's company from 1778 to 1782 indicates that Frances was able to use each to balance and set limits to the claims of the other.[43] While reported praise from Hester Chapone in 1780 leads her to comment, "There's for you, – who would not be a blue stocking*er* at this rate?" (*EJL*, vol. IV, p. 93), she is even then cynical about her lionization by the more superficial, "sickening Heartless *ton*-led people" at Bath (*EJL*, vol. IV, p. 168), and by 1782 she is recording in her journal:

I begin to grow most heartily sick and fatigued of this continual round of visiting, and these eternal new acquaintances. I am now arranging matters in my mind for a better plan; and I mean, henceforward, never to go out more than three days in the week; and, as I am now situated, with Mrs. Thrale to seize every moment I do not hide from her, it will require all the management I can possibly make use of to limit my visits to only half the week's days. But yet, I am fixed in resolving to put it in practice . . . I will restore my own spirit and pleasure by getting more courage in making refusals (*DL*, vol. II, pp. 155–56).

In Betty Rizzo's view, Burney had by this point "all but originated the role in fashionable society of a respectable and entirely acceptable professional woman."[44] The truest sign of such acceptance is the confidence to deny one's presence, something which Burney's father never achieved, judging from his daughter's subsequent report that "I have now a little broke my father into permitting my sending excuses" (*DL*, vol. II, p. 253).

Thus it is in her private writing that Burney most fully articulates the location of the professional writer *as woman* within contemporary print culture, even if she worked toward this in several of her dramatic and fictional characters. In her novels, her determination to separate her intelligent, socially elevated, and readerly heroines from her writerly, middle-class male characters is reinforced by the fact that she consistently aligns these works, in their prefaces, with a masculine tradition of literary authority, naming such figures as Johnson, Richardson, Marivaux, and Burke, but never any female authors. This fact suggests to me that Burney herself contributed to what Clifford Siskin has called "The Great Forgetting – a Great Forgetting that became . . . The Great Tradition." The mechanism of how this occurred, Siskin argues, "was a matter of whose texts, read or *even unread*, did get talked about and reproduced and whose texts, unread or *even read*, slipped into silence and out of production."[45] Burney read women writers herself, but the names of male authors figure far more prominently in the conversations she records. Like her *The Witlings* character Censor, she knew how to lend authority to her own voice: by invoking a literary tradition, specifically a fictional and aesthetic tradition, through what Thaddeus for *Evelina* has called "a canny transvestism [assumed] in order to control and extend her audience."[46]

And she chose to pursue that authority for herself – not cowed by the patent absurdities of Mr. Seward giving her Anna Laetitia Aikin's poetry to read and hinting that Aikin's brother helped her write it (*EJL*, vol. III, pp. 72–73), or Samuel Crisp urging her to write without labor, or *Cecilia*'s Delvile Senior asserting that a gentlewoman must never study like a professor, but pragmatically going where the surest path to professional status lay. Rizzo and Thaddeus have both argued that Burney's father figures, specifically Charles Burney and Samuel Crisp, should not simply be read as paternalistic oppressors of her creative impulses; rather, both to some extent encouraged and enabled her self-construction as professional author rather than middle-class wife.[47] Thus they provided her initially with something she wanted, but which she moved beyond through the *Witlings* episode and in her resistance to some of their specific pressures regarding *Cecilia.* Similarly, to "get [herself] talked about" in Siskin's terms, she aligned herself with the largely masculine Streatham circle of literary professionals, in the process writing her numerous female colleagues out of the canon while earning a prestigious rank for herself in the developing literary hierarchy. Commentators and reviewers made very clear the value of association with Richardson and Fielding: among many instances are Mrs. Thrale's insistence to a skeptical male acquaintance that "Dr. Johnson . . . says Richardson would have been *proud* to have written [*Evelina*]," followed by Johnson's avowal of "things & Characters in it *more* than worthy of Fielding" (*EJL*, vol. III, pp. 114–15), and the *Monthly Review*'s praise of *Cecilia* as exhibiting "much of the dignity and pathos of Richardson; and much of the acuteness and ingenuity of Fielding," as well as a style that "appears to have been formed on the best model of Dr. Johnson's."[48]

In short, though speculating about Frances Burney's public silence on the subject of the professional woman writer may not provide simple or satisfying answers, the question remains worth asking. Most immediately, we may gain a greater understanding of Burney's own negotiation of a professional identity at a crucial moment in the establishment of the print-based author function, whose mixed messages of authorship pitted patronage against self-determination, amateur disinterest against professional association, embodied gender and status against disembodied merit, original genius against economic enterprise. Her early career illustrates just how much space a woman writer could create for herself in this formative moment. At the same time, a fuller picture of how and why Burney wrote women writers out of her stories may help us understand the complex and fateful turns of late eighteenth-century women's literary history. It is to such acts of obliteration on the part of women writers, as well as to their acts of naming and remembering, that I turn in my final chapter.

CHAPTER 7

Women writers and "the Great Forgetting"

> and if a rainy morning deprived [Catherine and Isabella] of other enjoyments, they were still resolute in meeting in defiance of wet and dirt, and shut themselves up, to read novels together. Yes, novels; – for I will not adopt that ungenerous and impolitic custom so common with novel writers, of degrading by their contemptuous censure the very performances, to the number of which they are themselves adding – joining with their greatest enemies in bestowing the harshest epithets on such works, and scarcely ever permitting them to be read by their own heroine, who, if she accidentally take up a novel, is sure to turn over its insipid pages with disgust. Alas! If the heroine of one novel be not patronized by the heroine of another, from whom can she expect protection and regard? I cannot approve of it. Let us leave it to the Reviewers to abuse such effusions of fancy at their leisure, and over every new novel to talk in threadbare strains of the trash with which the press now groans. Let us not desert one another; we are an injured body. . . . "And what are you reading, Miss———?" "Oh! it is only a novel!" replies the young lady; while she lays down her book with affected indifference, or momentary shame. – "It is only Cecilia, or Camilla, or Belinda;" or, in short, only some work in which the greatest powers of the mind are displayed, in which the most thorough knowledge of human nature, the happiest delineation of its varieties, the liveliest effusions of wit and humour, are conveyed to the world in the best chosen language.
>
> (Jane Austen, *Northanger Abbey*, 1817)[1]

Jane Austen's enumeration in *Northanger Abbey* of the qualities shared by the best novels – knowledge of human nature, an entertaining variety of character and wit, and an appropriate, aesthetically pleasing style – echoes those valued by the eighteenth-century private readers, reviewers, and literary historians of the novel whose commentary I have cited in this study. Indeed, Austen's list appears, upon first reading, a mere collection of banal clichés. Yet it is prefaced by her critique of how novel readers and novel writers are themselves portraying the genre, suggesting that the recognition of these supposedly crowning achievements of the form is somehow threatened from within.

I will therefore conclude this study by turning to women writers as readers, readers who contributed to determining the place of novels (and to some extent, other works) published by eighteenth-century women in literary history. In *British Women Writers and the Writing of History*, Devoney Looser has suggested that Jane Austen, when she so insistently reappropriates Frances Burney's *Cecilia* and *Camilla* for a tradition that leads to and authorizes her own *Northanger Abbey*, shows an early suspicion of the motives behind Burney's own hesitation to identify herself explicitly as a novelist.[2] That suspicion is no doubt the more acute because of Austen's own alertness to the importance of strategic placement within competing generic traditions. Austen's statement clearly formulates the issue as one of women writers' power *as readers* to influence the status of both the novel and its practitioners – and therefore to participate in the very creation of a generic tradition through their textual acknowledgments – or their suppression of them.

The feminist literary histories of the 1980s and early 1990s carried out and pointed the way to invaluable work in the recovery of women's writing. However, the assumptions of these literary histories often, as I indicated in the introduction to this study, inadvertently reinforced some of the trends and assumptions of literary history which Austen identifies and condemns so forcefully almost two centuries earlier, including the relegation of proper women writers and readers to a literary form presumed to be domestic, derivative, and inferior. While identifying how such feminist histories have replicated the historiographical models and biases of the late eighteenth and early nineteenth centuries, Margaret Ezell in turn retold in 1993 a story of women writers being "marginaliz[ed] or even eras[ed]" by the all-powerful male makers of literary history in that historical crux. In the same year, Paula McDowell's critique of the mid-eighteenth-century origin of "a distinct literary history of women" as working "to contain and control what was by the eighteenth century recognized as a genuine threat to the existing social order: the unprecedented opportunities inherent in the new literary marketplace for women's public political and social critique," similarly sounded the theme of the victimization of women writers. While acknowledging that those late eighteenth- and nineteenth-century women who acted as literary life-writers and anthologists sometimes engaged in "violent repudiation of earlier women writers for transgressing the boundaries of their *own* historical periods," McDowell explained this as "a necessary strategy; a way of forestalling male criticism by repudiating the female 'other.' . . . [Early] feminist literary historians were forced to construct a 'pure' past."[3] As I suggested in the introduction to this study, I believe our efforts in writing eighteenth-century women's literary history are now hampered less by a lack of awareness of the problem than by our resistance to rethinking women writers' and readers' positions toward, and implication in, this defining moment in women's literary history, wherein they were purportedly being relegated to the footnotes and margins of the central narrative, soon to be erased from it altogether.

Let me illustrate the problem by quoting the moment in Clifford Siskin's 1998 book *The Work of Writing: Literature and Social Change in Britain, 1770–1830* from which I take my chapter's title phrase "the Great Forgetting."[4] In the final movement of this study of the formation of literature as one discipline within a newly professionalized system of intellectual labor, Siskin tells this story of dispossession:

> Let me paint the problem with broad brushstrokes. As we have seen, during the late eighteenth and early nineteenth centuries many women wrote in many different genres with a considerable degree of popular and often critical success. On the other hand, we have also examined the narrowing of the notion of *literature* in Britain, showing how a term that had once embraced all kinds of writing came, during this same period of time, to refer more narrowly to only certain texts within certain genres. This means that these acts of narrowing were also acts of gendering; . . . they took writing out of the "hands" of women. The discipline that, during the next century, took this newly restricted category of literature as its field of knowledge was thus founded in an extraordinary act – in scope and in speed – of gendered exclusion and forgetting.[5]

This account, in which many small "acts" are concerted as one "extraordinary [super]act," encapsulates the suturing of feminist literary history with a historicism that focuses on institutions and discourses as the determinants of the individual subject's actions. Siskin's discussion, literally creating a capital-letter event out of an erasure trope that has become so conventional as to be almost itself invisible, carefully takes the responsibility for initiating, supporting, and executing this purge out of individual hands, even though its effect was to take writing out of the hands of women. Indeed, he notes that the term "forgetting" is not intended to "naturalize the loss [of women writers] as simply a psychological lapse," but rather "to specify some of the key socio-economic and institutional ways in which the exclusion worked." Yet this caveat exposes the slippage in the explanations Siskin offers for the disappearance of women writers from the tradition. Ranging from a nonvolitional "psychological lapse," through the depersonalized mechanisms of the print market and a fragmenting readership, these mechanisms are ultimately exploited, it is revealed, by the "old-boys network" of *The Edinburgh Review*, in a return to the favored model of female victims and male perpetrators.

Although Siskin uses Jane Austen, whom my epigraph shows to be a highly self-conscious practitioner and advocate of the novel genre, to mark the moment of disappearance, he goes out of his way to clarify that his Austen is simply "a source of important models" for a male-controlled, professionalized "discipline" in "subsuming" her contemporaries, rather than "an ambitious and/or mean-spirited Austen [who] deliberately managed to depose her rivals."[6] I share Siskin's reluctance to accuse any woman writer of "mean-spirited" (read "catty") rivalry, but I also question the implication that an Austen who is a passive and unconscious pawn of literary history is somehow preferable to an ambitious Austen. I am interested, indeed, in examining the nature and situation of the ambition that would lead a woman writer either to name, or "forget" to name, another woman writer.

And here it is Jane Austen herself, in her *Northanger Abbey* analysis of the situation, who points the way. She does so by identifying the influential role in constructing literary history played by professional women readers – that is, women readers who are themselves publishing writers – who name or deny the texts they read. In an explicit challenge to Frances Burney and Maria Edgeworth as "forgetters" of the tradition that has shaped them, Austen positions herself as a "namer" – even more, she couches her acts of naming in terms of a tradition that includes not only Richardson's *Sir Charles Grandison* and Matthew Lewis's *The Monk*, but also Lennox's *The Female Quixote*, Burney's *Evelina*, *Camilla*, and *Cecilia*, and Ann Radcliffe's *The Mysteries of Udolpho* and *The Italian*.[7] In this way, her literary historical agency is exercised differently not only from that of a Lennox and a Burney, who in the pursuit of their own career objectives aligned themselves deliberately with male founders,[8] but also from that suggested by Siskin when he implies that Austen was complicit, though not instrumental, in subsuming her female predecessors. Like Lennox and Burney in their use of Richardson and Johnson, Austen, in Looser's words, "co-opted [Burney and Edgeworth] to advance her own classificatory cause"; her own ambitions for a "place in the literary market, and ultimately in the history of letters," led her, unlike them, to "[invoke] a women's literary tradition" to suit her own definition of the genre she was working in – one that claimed importance through its incorporation of both "masculine" and "feminine" generic features.[9]

This study has drawn repeatedly on the *Monthly* and *Critical Reviews* as setting the terms by which new works would be read, and occasionally, elevated as reference points for later works. For the period in question, the reviewers were presumably all male. In this chapter, I will turn to influential female readers of my group of eighteenth-century writers, all of them writers themselves, to examine their agency in relation to "the Great Forgetting" of their female colleagues and immediate forerunners. In tracing their reception of mid-eighteenth-century women writers, I have indeed found myself confronted with variations upon, and complications within, our dominant narrative of erasure. Focusing on the namers and forgetters, rather than the named or forgotten, I will first recount how two avid reader-writers, Catherine Talbot and Elizabeth Carter, created influential career narratives and reputations through their repeated naming of their contemporaries Sarah Fielding and Charlotte Lennox. Then I will discuss briefly cases from the second half of the eighteenth century involving Sarah Scott and Frances Burney, as well as Clara Reeve's 1785 *Progress of Romance*, Frances Brooke's preface to the second edition of *The Excursion* in the same year, and finally, the memorializing of such writers in the early nineteenth century. Together, these instances exemplify a spectrum of acts ranging from naming, through partial naming, to silence, over which can be laid another spectrum of position-taking within a rapidly organizing print universe, from ordering bodies of printed material, to resisting amnesia, to advancing a career through self-presentation, to professionalizing as an author. In all, the pattern that emerges, if there is such a pattern at all, is one of contingency and accident, enabled as much by these literary professional women as by their male counterparts.

TALBOT AND CARTER INTERPRET FIELDING AND LENNOX

In chapter 4 of this book, I compared the professional careers of Sarah Fielding and Charlotte Lennox. Here I will briefly retrace the story of those careers, this time as "narrated" by readers who helped construct their divergent literary reputations as modest and improper, respectively: Catherine Talbot and Elizabeth Carter, writing between 1741 and 1770. In doing so, I will illustrate Frank Donoghue's assertion that a career is "a product of interpretation . . . a narrative that cannot be authored entirely by its own subject." While Donoghue focuses on the contest between authorial self-representation and "the institution of critical reading" – in other words, the reviews – in constructing a career, his claim that "Out of this very struggle, which is also, paradoxically, an uneasy collaboration, emerge the literary history, literary biography, and established canons that are the hallmarks of later-eighteenth-century letters"[10] can be extended as well to the kind of collaborative reading recorded by influential women readers in their private correspondence.

Talbot and Carter between them represent significant segments of the book-buying public of the time: Carter, the well-educated, middle-class intellectual actively participating in the republic of letters, and Talbot, the well-connected, though not personally wealthy, urban-based woman with the leisure, education, and tastes to support socially worthy writing projects. As women readers, moreover, they were unabashedly and particularly interested in the work of women writers. Their correspondence reveals their wide reading, the careful eye they kept out for new books, and their habit of working through a critical response by means of epistolary dialogue.[11] They acted on their judgments as readers through recommendations of reading to a wide network of social contacts, support of the work of authors they admired in the form of subscriptions, advocacy, and contributions, and published interventions in discussions of taste and conduct. Here is where this private reading has implications for the historical record; Talbot's and Carter's strong preference for Fielding over Lennox is quite distinct from such assessments as that of Mary Scott in her 1774 *The Female Advocate*, published five years after Fielding's death and after the most productive period of Lennox's career, where Scott praises both authors in similar terms as advocates of virtue and fine observers of human nature. Lennox is described as "virtue's friend" for, among other things, role-playing coquetry to dramatize its faults; as I will show below, Carter and Talbot disagreed strongly with Scott on the moral tendency of such role-playing.[12] And yet I will suggest below that by the turn of the century Carter's and Talbot's was more influential than Scott's publicly voiced position.

Fielding's anonymous "epistle of Ann Boleyn," from her brother's *Miscellanies*, appears first in the correspondence, in 1743, as a work Talbot is sure Carter will be "charmed with"; Talbot's special notice of this piece may well arise from Henry's footnote broadly hinting that it was written by a woman.[13] The opinions of the hero of the 1744 *Adventures of David Simple* on friendship and marriage appear next in their discussion of those subjects, implying an easy and well-disposed familiarity with the recently published book. By the time Talbot writes in 1753 of the *Familiar Letters between the Principal Characters in David Simple* as her group's amusement during a coach outing, "Mrs. Fielding" is known to Carter, whom Talbot envies as "happy in her acquaintance." One effect of this personal knowledge appears to be an ability to see good qualities ("where she writes naturally" and "a goodness of heart and a delicacy of sentiment") even in a work that is seriously flawed: "'Tis vexatious . . . to find such a mixture of refinement *a perte de vue* proceeding from her inclination to support, I fancy, a false system, and deduce every variety of action from the sources of pride and vanity."[14] Since Talbot and Fielding were both close to Richardson at this time, it may be supposed that Talbot was hearing much about this writer from several sources, if they had somehow not yet met each other. From the mid-1750s, Elizabeth Montagu was a close friend of Elizabeth Carter, and references to Fielding begin to reflect information about her projects gained from Montagu. The complaint about refinements reasserts itself for *The Cry* in 1754, though Carter also finds this trait in the work of Tacitus, and adds, "But is she not in general a most excellent writer?" while Talbot insists that "On the whole, Mrs. Fielding is a favourite with us all."

Just how much the person of the writer has become identified with the published author is revealed when in 1757 Talbot and her mother name two hens Cleopatra and Octavia, an announcement which takes Talbot directly into the question of how "Mrs. Fielding who is so good a woman" could "make Octavia self-sufficient under sufferings and trials" rather than pious, and let Cleopatra remain unpunished in the afterlife, though the story of Octavia is "enchantingly told" and made her "cry very heartily." Among the final references to Fielding are Talbot's playful threat to bring Carter before "Mrs. Fielding" as a Justice of the Peace superior to her brother "in points of delicacy and feeling," and her speculation that the anonymous 1759 *Histories of Some of the Penitents in the Magdalen-House* "is at least a very good likeness of Mrs. Fielding," both comments reflecting her sense of a consistency and coherence to the body of Fielding's publication. It is equally clear that this "author-function" is influenced in part by what is known about the writer herself, and in part by the elevating effect of comparisons to the morally serious and significant Tacitus and to Henry Fielding, Justice of the Peace.[15]

Lennox appears at least as often as Fielding, and with reference to an extended series of publications, indicating a parallel sense of this author as building a reputation over time. Indeed, references back to earlier works, the poem "The Art of Coquetry"(part of *Poems on Several Occasions*) and

The Female Quixote, are more prominent for Lennox than for Fielding, suggesting that her publications made a stronger affective impression on these two readers. The poem is of interest because of the writers' mixed response to it. They disapprove of its speaker's advocacy of female artfulness, including the art of pretending to understand intellectual conversation (Carter: "For the edification of some of my young friends, we read one of [Charlotte Lennox's poems] on the art of coquetry, at which they were much scandalized. The poetry is uncommonly correct, but the doctrine indeed by no means to be admired. It is intolerably provoking to see people who really appear to have a genius, apply it to such idle unprofitable purposes"), while finding the argument a definitive point of reference for years afterward, as in Talbot's 1753 "But do now write me an essay upon this sort of vanity [of boasting of one's many admirers], and its too frequent consequence coquetry. Not the art of coquetry like Mrs. Lenox, but an edifying essay proper to be put into the hands of Misses" and in Carter's 1757 "In walking about the rooms we were joined by one of the most celebrated beauties in the assembly, the study of whose life, as far as can be judged by appearances, has been Mrs. Lenox's sort of coquetry."[16]

The Female Quixote is well received by Talbot; she writes, "I have begun reading a book which promises to be some laughing amusement, "The Female Quixote;" the few chapters I read to my mother last night while we were undressing were whimsical enough and not at all low." A few weeks later, "Arabella too, as a little book, is mighty diverting, and much in fashion." The suggestion of grudging praise here arguably stems from more than the genre, since Talbot enjoyed reading novels for amusement; her close connection with Richardson at this time would justify the conclusion that she knew who its author was, and was prepared to disapprove, notwithstanding Richardson's support of the novel.[17] By 1758, despite Lennox's intervening well-known and well-received translations of French political memoirs, the sort of works Talbot, again, loved to read,[18] the new novel *Henrietta* was jointly discredited by these correspondents; in Talbot's words, despite the fact that it "has been useful to us here [in the country], . . . there are many things in it that I dislike, and that tally with my opinion of the writer."

This picture of Fielding's and Lennox's careers as conveyed by two avid female readers of the 1740s to 1760s illustrates their exposure as consumers to a wide range of publications; supplemented by a degree of inside knowledge of the London publishing world,[19] this enables them to build a coherent sense of a writer's oeuvre through magazines, novels, and other genres, a project they are clearly interested in. In constructing such narratives, however, their literary tastes and social networks come into combined play, leading them to emphasize the works they disapprove of in categorizing Lennox's writing, despite their apparently finding both her poetry and her fiction well-crafted and highly readable, and correspondingly to downplay their consistent and fundamental criticisms of Fielding works. Juxtaposing these two "narratives," one is tempted to conclude with Kate Levin that "Because of the negative reception of her former publications, Lennox needed Arabella's cure, not only for her novel and its female readers, but also for herself,"[20] but also that the cure had only limited success. Even though this correspondence was not published until 1809, Talbot's and Carter's highly selective, dichotomous categorization of these two writers might ultimately have been more influential on an influential writer like Burney than were the more evenly distributed and public accolades of Richardson, Mary Scott, or the reviewers in determining the long-term dichotomous fate of these writers' reputations.

SCOTT AND BURNEY SILENCE WOMEN WRITERS

Carter's dismissal of *Henrietta* implies a blurring of work and author in a manner that may have been inevitable in the literary world of the mid-eighteenth century, where for all the ostensible anonymity of many publications, a separation of the professional and the private was difficult to achieve. I have shown, indeed, how Fielding was able to benefit from this linkage in my discussion of her career, but for Lennox it appears to have worked to her long-term detriment. Sarah Scott's changing response to the historian Catharine Macaulay similarly illustrates how intellectual tolerance could be overwhelmed by personal notoriety. Having recently published two works of history herself, Scott writes generously in 1763 about her fellow-historian, a childhood acquaintance, though she disagrees with her republican politics. Apparently, Scott has no quarrel with Macaulay's authorial activity or choice of genre. But fifteen years later, Macaulay became the scandal of Bath with her marriage to a man twenty-two years her junior; the scandal was significantly exacerbated for Scott by the circulation of a private letter, ostensibly by Macaulay, describing her need to marry in order to satisfy her sexual appetites. In response, Scott calls for an extreme act of obliteration, writing to her sister Elizabeth Montagu that "If there is any zeal still remaining in the World for Virtues cause the grave Virgins & virtuous

Matrons who reside in the place, will unite & drown her in the Avon, & try if she can be purified by water."[21]

Scott's reaction to Macaulay's second marriage appears to support McDowell's suggestion that in such cases of transgression against the norms of feminine propriety, some form of "violent repudiation" was a necessary strategy for women writers, as a means of forestalling male criticism. While I do not entirely dispute the existence of such a motive here, I note that Scott's views are those of a woman who wielded much less social influence than did Talbot or Carter and are articulated in a private letter to a sister. Furthermore, far from seeking a favorable male response for herself, Scott appears to have carried out repeated acts of self-obliteration as well. I have argued earlier that she consistently obscured the relation between her private identity and the public sphere of letters, publishing her first history, *Gustavus Ericson*, as "by Henry Augustus Raymond" and her other works anonymously, and thus contributing actively to her paradoxical status as, in Gary Kelly's words, "the most published yet one of the least known of the first-generation bluestocking writers in their time."[22] Scott's constant change of booksellers and the apparent collusion of her contemporaries, whether friends and relations, booksellers, or reviewers, also helped maintain a split between private person and public author. The price of such invisibility was that the name of "Mrs. Scott" the author disappeared from even limited public awareness within a year or two of her final publication – even though she exploited current interests effectively enough to reap financial and critical rewards upon their first appearance. It might be argued, then, that Scott's repudiation of Macaulay was of a piece with her model of citizenship in a republic of letters based on print culture as ideally disembodied, even nameless.

If drowning is indeed an extreme trope for the desire to obliterate a writer's gendered body, there are other means of obliterating or distorting memory as well. Frances Burney, for example, uses naming, not in the negative sense of openly repudiating female colleagues, but positively as a means of identification with the male professionals who could best authorize her work and thereby further her aspirations. In the space between, however, lie a significant number of unnamed women writers. The young, private Burney refers admiringly to Elizabeth Griffith, Frances Brooke, and Charlotte Lennox, for example. But she chooses to lend authority to her writer's voice by invoking an all-male novelistic and aesthetic tradition in her novel prefaces, in what Janice Thaddeus has called "a canny transvestism [assumed] in order to control and extend her audience."[23] Jane Spencer's recent analysis of the profound influence of "ancient metaphors of literary genealogy" on eighteenth-century constructions of "a national literary tradition" provides us with insight into the symbolic significance of Burney's choices: Spencer points out that since the generative function in the tradition was understood as male, the relation of daughter to a male writer was more easily imagined than that of daughter to a mother figure.[24] In Burney's case, her following in the footsteps of her biological author-father makes such an imaginative connection all the more likely with respect to other forefathers. More pragmatically, Burney is obviously concerned to cultivate her contacts with professional or leading intellectuals and artists of both sexes, whether Samuel Johnson, Richard Sheridan, and Joshua Reynolds, or Elizabeth Carter, Hester Chapone, and Hannah More.

Repudiation appears more pointed, however, in the extended scene of the early journals noted in the previous chapter, in which Burney distances herself from Lady Hawke, introduced to her as a "sister authoress." It is surely no accident that this doubly gendered term is used so insistently by the foolish Lady Say and Sele in this scene, while Burney, as both actor in the farce and its author, uses her discomfort as a means of implicit commentary. I suggest that Burney is here rejecting the restrictive authorial model of the "extremely languishing, delicate, and pathetic" woman writer who writes only for a coterie of family and friends, and the women who patronize her – the model that Ezell, McDowell, and other late twentieth-century feminist historians have also found distasteful. Significantly, it is in this context that Burney reports that Lady Say and Sele "mentioned to me a hundred novels that I had never heard of, asking my opinion of them, and whether I knew the authors."[25] As she resists the label of amateur authoress, Burney here repudiates the assumption of a generic determinism of reading and authorship embedded within the gendered model, sensing, perhaps, that "constructing a separate, entirely female tradition threatened to lock women writers into a literary-historical ghetto."[26] Just as naming Johnson, Richardson, Marivaux, Burke, and her own father in her novel prefaces furthers Burney's claim to a place in literary history, the two aristocratic women, in their patently fictionalized presentation, allow Burney to resist the feminization of the novel genre and of her own authorship without explicitly rejecting recognizable women writers or intellectuals.

But traces of Burney's more uncollegial repudiations remain as well. For example, in the account of her first meeting with Frances Brooke cited in chapter 2, Burney writes that the elder author "is very short & fat, &

squints, but has the art of shewing Agreeable Ugliness."[27] She is alluding here to Sarah Scott's 1754 novel translation *Agreeable Ugliness,* though Scott is never named in the journals. But given Scott's own choice of obscurity, a more revealing erasure can be found in the shift between an early and a belated response to Charlotte Lennox. In 1778, as a novitiate in the Streatham circle, Burney comments, "[Dr. Johnson] gave us an account of *Mrs. Lenox*: her Female Quixote is very justly admired here; indeed, *I* think *all* her Novels far the best of any *Living* Author, – but Mrs. Thrale says that though her *Books* are generally approved, Nobody likes *her.*" Significantly, this conversation as recorded in Burney's journal immediately moves to discussion of two pieces by "our Mr. Harris," Sarah Fielding's collaborator James Harris; the two pieces were both published anonymously in Fielding's *Familiar Letters,* but the textual context is not in any way identified by Burney. And next, Johnson questions Burney, " 'what sort of Reading do you delight in? – History? – Travels? – Poetry? – or Romances?' " and she resolutely refuses to answer the question, certain that "the examination which would have followed, had I made any direct answer, would have turned out sorely to my discredit."[28]

As I have shown in chapter 6, Burney's journal of this time, just after the publication of her first novel, is very much about learning the protocols of successful authorship. This sequence seems to record her struggle to integrate her admiration of a woman's writing with the unexpected revelation that that writer is a social outsider, followed by an immediate textual submersion not only of the names of women writers, but even of the identification of preferred genres. It is worth noting here that Burney is *not* in fact mocked by Johnson for reading Lennox's novels, or romances; she appears to believe she must forestall such mockery, but the gap between her self-conscious anxieties and their provocation is wide enough in her early journals to prevent any easy application of McDowell's assertion that she acted out of the "necess[ity]" of "forestalling male criticism by repudiating the female 'other.' "

Years later, this struggle is well over, having ended in Lennox's total defeat: Burney responds to an inquiry from Charles de Guiffardière about Boswell's *Life of Johnson,* wherein the Doctor's "preference there expressed of Mrs. Lenox to all other females had filled him with astonishment, as he had never even heard her name," with the comment "These occasional sallies of Dr. Johnson, uttered from local causes and circumstances, but all retailed verbatim by Mr. Boswell, are filling all sorts of readers with amaze, except the small party to whom Dr. Johnson was known, and who, by acquaintance with the power of the moment over his unguarded conversation, know how little of his solid opinion was to be gathered from his accidental assertions."[29] Faced with a male reader's amnesia about the still-living Lennox, Burney shows no concern to revive her memory, indeed implying that silence represents a more accurate public judgment than did Johnson's "accidental" statement of preference. She here seems to have forgotten not only her own "just" admiration of Lennox's novels above those of all living authors, but also Hester Thrale's recognition of artistic merit as separable from writerly personality.

Burney's refusal to name women writers, then, while it initially seems less harsh than Scott's active figure of drowning, is arguably the more calculated and categorical – and, as Austen implies, certainly the more influential. Moreover, it follows the direction plotted by Talbot's and Carter's dichotomous judgments, in operating most actively against Lennox, suggesting a direct line of descent through Thrale and an incremental influence of such judgments. If, as Harriet Guest argues, the period of the 1750s to 1770s was one of a temporary instability and openness in the "definition of differences of social structure and gender," a condition superseded by more rigidly restrictive role definitions in the latter decades of the century, Burney's practice with respect to other women writers, in contrast to her own aspirations, appears to have contributed to that rigidity.[30]

REEVE REMEMBERS (WHILE BROOKE PROTESTS)

It is in relation to this complex and variously motivated array of naming, repudiation, and forgetting that Clara Reeve's 1785 *The Progress of Romance through Times, Countries, and Manners* again becomes interesting. This two-volume history of the romance and novel genres, written in dialogue form, was published when Reeve's reputation as a translator and novelist was well established. The *Progress* has figured in feminist histories of women's writing primarily as a didactic text concerned to distance itself from the amorous fictions of that notorious trio of women in the early print marketplace, Aphra Behn, Delarivier Manley, and Eliza Haywood.[31] Yet an examination of the method, rather than the judgments, of the notorious passage reveals an overriding concern with deploying acts of naming and obliteration to construct an accurate and value-based, rather than purely arbitrary, literary history in the newly ephemeral world of market-driven publication. In introducing Behn, Reeve's principal mouthpiece Euphrasia insists on her desire to "do justice to [Behn's] merits" as well as to "cast the veil of compassion over her faults." Behn's novella *Oroonoko* is singled out to ensure that its author's name "will not be forgotten," while with respect to the rest, Euphrasia's male interlocutor Hortensius concludes, "Peace be to her *manes*! – I shall not disturb her, or her works."

This careful sorting in itself enacts a memorial, unlike the ensuing very brief dismissal of Manley's "still more exceptionable" scandal fiction, which, we are told, includes "a work too well known in the last age, though almost forgotten in the present; . . . I forbear the name, and further observations on it, as Mrs. *Manley*'s works are sinking gradually into oblivion." When Hortensius "help[s her] memory" by referring to Eliza Haywood's early amorous fictions, Euphrasia admits reluctantly to them, "all of which I hope are forgotten," while saying that she had intended to name *Betsy Thoughtless*, *The Female Spectator*, and *The Invisible Spy* as Haywood's reformed writing of the mid-century. It is the last two of these "by which she is most likely to be known to posterity"; the discussion concludes with "May her first writings be forgotten, and the last survive to do her honour."[32]

Thus Reeve's overview of the work of these three women writers at once asserts that a natural selection process is at work in literary history, by which unworthy productions will sink into oblivion and merit will be rewarded by posterity,[33] and recognizes the need to help history along by strategic naming and forgetting. She illustrates her method in the negative by condemning Alexander Pope's conferring of "infamous immortality" on Haywood through his attack on her scandal novels in *The Dunciad*. Unlike Pope, who not only named where he should have remained silent, but was also "too severe in his treatment of this lady" because of "some private offence," Euphrasia claims to model a less gender-driven, impartial severity, asserting that she "would be the last to vindicate [Haywood's] faults, but the first to celebrate her return to virtue, and her atonement for them."[34] In effect, the lengthy discussion of these three writers does exactly this – it carefully distributes its textual weight according to its relative judgment of the writers and aspects of their oeuvre, thereby doing spatial, as well as substantive, justice where Reeve believes it is due.

In general, as I suggested in chapter 5, Reeve's study works to undermine perceived gender distinctions of moral and aesthetic value, whether distributed between authors, genres, or readers. Euphrasia devotes considerable attention to Charlotte Lennox, Sarah Fielding, Frances Sheridan, and Frances Brooke as "capital writers" of the romance/novel form. She presents these writers as versatile and accomplished, taking time to name their translations, children's books, and oriental tales. At the same time, she condemns the fictions of Voltaire on the same grounds as those of Behn, refusing despite Hortensius's provocations to do more than quote the *Monthly Review*'s condemnation of *Candide*, saying, "you have led me to speak of *Voltaire*'s works, which I would rather have avoided," and when asked if she will indeed "say nothing more of his Novels," replying flatly, "Nothing." Reeve later uses Hortensius to insist that Euphrasia comment on Sterne's *Tristram Shandy*, even though "it is not a woman's book" in her view; as he points out, "You have spoken freely enough of many other writers, and if you are a competent judge of them, why not of *Sterne*?" In other words, while reading patterns appear to be gendered, aesthetic value is not. Euphrasia affirms the educational value of modern imaginative reading as well as of historical or classical studies, while placing equal emphasis on the dangers of unsupervised reading for the young in either of these traditionally gendered curricula.[35]

Reeve makes it clear that one consequence of the gendering of genre is a kind of forgetting which is already underway. Thus Euphrasia introduces Sarah Fielding immediately after extended discussion of Samuel Richardson and Henry Fielding with the words "Miss *Sarah Fielding*'s works are not unworthy next to be mentioned after her brother's . . . They well deserve the protection of your sex *Hortensius*, and the plaudit of ours," to which Hortensius replies, "You must bring me acquainted with this lady's works, pray what are their titles?" Only by attacking the assumption that novels written by women are unworthy of the notice of men can the memory of a writer like Sarah Fielding be preserved. In another case, obscurity appears to have defeated even Reeve: when Euphrasia and Sophronia speak approvingly of Sarah Scott's *Millenium Hall*, it is without naming its author, and when *Sir George Ellison*, its sequel, is cited later, it is again without attribution, simply as one of the few worthy novels of 1766, and no link is drawn between the two texts.[36] It can therefore be concluded that, scarcely twenty years after publication of the sequel, Reeve does not know either the identity of the author or that the two works are products of the same pen. Her silence reminds us that in this early period of widespread print production, Reeve was working without the *English Short Title Catalogue* or any number of the institutions of print, literally creating through her naming a generic category and tradition, in defiance of an ephemerality that threatened more than women's fictional writing with oblivion.

Throughout the *Progress*, Reeve insists upon her own authority as critic in a manner that not only draws on male critics but also asserts her own professional expertise and that of other women. In her text's introduction, she names "*Hurd, Beattie, Warton, Percy*, and *Mallet*" as learned men whose attention to the romance proves that the subject "cannot be undeserving the notice and protection of the public." Unlike Burney, however, she continues, "It is with sincere pleasure I add a name that will not disgrace the list, a writer of my own sex, Mrs. *Dobson* the elegant writer of the *History of the Troubadours* and the *Memoirs of Ancient Chivalry*." While Reeve may put much of the material on "immodest" works like the novels of Fielding and Sterne into the mouth of Hortensius, yet she also uses his skepticism to expose gender bias and ignorance, and has him concede frequently to Euphrasia as a means of heightening her authority as primary speaker. Finally, here there is no need for a conversion from novel-reading, no coy disclaimer about not having read a hundred novels known to her sisters; rather, Reeve redefines such readerly knowledge as professional expertise. Thus when Hortensius taunts Euphrasia "that from your part in our past conversations, any person who did not know you well, would conclude that your principal, if not only study, had been Romances and Novels," she replies, "If like the industrious bee I have cull'd from various flowers my share of Honey, and stored it in the common Hive, I shall have performed the duties of a good citizen of the Republic of letters, and I shall not have lived in vain."[37]

Reeve's text, in its use of a dialectic between male and female readers' notions of the memorable, and in its carefully weighted discussion both of texts that Reeve would like to have forgotten and of texts she wishes to memorialize, attempts to intervene in the construction of a literary tradition. At the same time, it makes explicit the competing principles by which selective forgettings may be justified. Laura Runge suggests that one of Reeve's criteria for remembering, "the moral and didactic function of literature," is "what the discourse [of literary values] eventually simplifies and represses."[38] Indeed, in Hortensius's less nuanced disdain for all novels by (and in his view, solely for) women, unlike Euphrasia's distinctions between memorable moral fiction and forgettable immoral fiction, the *Progress* also exposes and resists the gendered assumptions upon which the developing discourse of literary values will rest. The temporary space within which Reeve holds these competing notions of literary value in play is that of the dialogue, soon to be displaced by a more monologic and unitary narrative of literary history within which there is simply room for fewer writers. Thus many of those Reeve strenuously remembers fade from view despite her efforts.

If an increasingly dominant stream of literary tradition was submerging authors as it rolled forward through the latter part of the century, some of this chapter's examples certainly suggest that such submergences were in part enabled by the blank spaces left by women writers pursuing public recognition for themselves. In the same year as Reeve's *Progress* appeared, in fact, Frances Brooke, in the guise of a claim that women writers were being driven out of the field of the novel, presented just such a narrative as her preface to the 1785 second edition of *The Excursion.* As we have seen, Brooke here implies that her work has been criticized because of a move afoot "to exclude from the road to literary fame, even by the flowery paths of romance, a sex which from quick sensibility, native delicacy of mind, facility of expression, and a style at once animated and natural, is perhaps, when possessed of real genius, most peculiarly qualified to excel in this species of moral painting." This assertion is at odds with the evidence, compiled by James Raven, that women were in fact finally surging in the late 1780s into a majority position as novel-writers.[39]

To support her claim of discrimination, Brooke quotes the misogynist phrasing of a somewhat irrelevant source, John Pinkerton's preface to his 1783 *Select Scottish Ballads*; then in defence of women novelists she names Richardson, Johnson, Mackenzie, and Goldsmith as examples of "the brightest ornaments of literature amongst the other sex" who have legitimized the novel form. Brooke claims in the conditional mode that "if the female sex have not been undistinguished" in this elevation of the genre, their work is to be applauded – but she carries off her entire critique without naming a single one of these admirable women writers.[40] I have already suggested that in this case, as in others when Brooke plays the gender card, she is using the conspiracy accusation strategically, to deflect attention from the attack on David Garrick that was in fact the focus of criticism of the novel's first edition. If so, the cry of gender discrimination was presumably one Brooke felt would be responded to sympathetically by her contemporary readers. A side effect of this momentary diversionary tactic, unfortunate in the long term, is the suppression of the very names of the writers for whom she claims to be an advocate. Ironically, Frances Burney's concurrent distancing of herself from other women writers would soon in its turn help obscure Brooke's career achievements: while in 1774 Burney's journal records her first meeting with the fifty-year-old Brooke in terms which display admiration of her professional reputation – "Mrs Brooke . . . is very well bred, & expresses herself with much modesty, upon all subjects. – which in an *Authoress*, and Woman of *known* understanding, is extremely pleasing"[41] – Burney avoided professional association with her, as I have shown in chapter 2, and never mentions Brooke in print.

THE GREAT DEFORMATION

At least one of the writers in my study group colluded against herself in the simplifying and repressive work of a monologic literary history. Sarah Scott arranged that her private papers be burned after her death, effectively completing the self-obliteration I have already attributed to her. We do have Scott letters, however – those preserved by her sister, the bluestocking leader Elizabeth Montagu, through principles of selection we can only guess at. Elizabeth also collated her own correspondence, initiating a process which culminated in her nephew Matthew Montagu's publication of a four-volume edition of Montagu's letters in 1809.[42] This editor was guided, he said, by "the wish of producing nothing which may cast a less favourable light upon her disposition." At precisely the moment in which Siskin locates "the Great Forgetting," the moment of *Northanger Abbey*, literary biographers were in fact busily engaged in "a great remembering" of the lives of eighteenth-century intellectual women: nephews, friends, and grandchildren were publishing the correspondence of, or writing memoirs of, Elizabeth Montagu, Elizabeth Carter, Frances Sheridan, Hester Chapone, Catherine Talbot, Frances Burney, and others. Gary Kelly has noted the significance of the dating of these publications, coming after the discrediting of the sentimental and revolutionary feminisms of the last decades of the eighteenth century. But we may go beyond Kelly's suggestion that "bluestocking letters could be used to sustain a kind of feminism less threatening than those that had followed," to note the effect of this spirit on the earlier writers' stories themselves.[43] As Matthew Montagu's comment illustrates, these productions are highly selective, silently edited, hagiographical accounts. To some extent, my own study has been a systematic exercise in circumventing these stories.

Herein, of course, lies another position on the spectrum of forgetting, one that might be termed "the great deformation." Elizabeth's edited letters erase portions of her life – those of the young dependent lady's companion and the vastly wealthy coal magnate, for example – leaving precisely the learned lady of the private salon, whose "witty conversation [was] supported by the reading of the finest authors" – once again, George Ballard's 1752 ideal as Ezell describes it and as Frances Burney tried to repudiate it.[44] Again in the case of Frances Sheridan, as I have shown, the anecdotal accounts of her contemporary and cousin, Samuel Whyte, published in 1800 but containing correspondence and diverse, loosely associated materials accumulated over many decades, differ significantly from the edited versions of these incorporated by Sheridan's granddaughter

Alicia Lefanu in her 1824 memoir. Whyte's concern is to defend the Sheridan family from the aspersions cast upon it by Boswell's *Life of Johnson*, while Lefanu's is to present a woman whose authorial ambitions were firmly subordinated to her domestic roles as wife and mother. Such "deformations," while elevating their subject and preserving her memory, paradoxically distort the record of an earlier, broader openness to women's professional activity, an openness that Frances Sheridan, as well as Sarah Fielding, Charlotte Lennox, Frances Brooke, and Sarah Scott took advantage of to the extent of their wishes. One might generalize that this distortion was the effect of reading their career narratives through a presumptive governing framework of gendered separate spheres.

To bring the focus full circle to the aims of this study: like the great deformers of the early nineteenth century, we too can benefit from a more self-conscious understanding of our investments in narrating (women's) literary history. The historiography of "the Great Forgetting" has perhaps served its function; it is now time to remember how invested and various were the acts of naming, forgetting, and obliteration of 1780 to 1820, and how many of them were carried out by women. Further, an understanding of the dynamics of eighteenth-century print culture, one that takes into account modes of production of careers as well as of texts, the placement of an individual publication by its writer, the power of readers, and how the developing institutions of literature were manipulated by those hoping to be named in literary history, can help us appreciate the complexity of those acts, and the provenance of our own print-culture politics. Once we have grappled with that complexity, and with our own relation to it, we can begin to determine where we go from here.

Coda

I have insisted throughout this book on the general interpretive principle of writerly agency in explaining generic choices, publication modes, and plot structures. In other words, while not divorcing these authors from their material or discursive contexts, we must consider more seriously the potential in reading them as professionalized subjects, as agents in the public sphere of letters. Such an approach, at its simplest, merely recognizes what their closest contemporaries took as a given. As Charlotte Lennox prepared *The Female Quixote* for publication, for example, she received a letter from Samuel Richardson which encouraged her to think professionally: "You are a young Lady have therefore much time before you, and I am sure, will think that a good Fame will be your Interest. Make therefore, your present work as complete as you can, in two Volumes; and it will give Consequence to your future writings, and of course to your Name as a Writer."[1] Richardson's argument here clearly suggests that Lennox consider herself primarily as a young writer rather than as a "Lady" author. As my chapter epigraphs have demonstrated, extant correspondence, paratexts, and reviews support my claim that Charlotte Lennox, as well as Sarah Fielding, Frances Brooke, Sarah Scott, and Frances Sheridan were directly engaged as actors in the public sphere of letters and its material medium, the literary marketplace.

Thus this project is above all a plea for more detailed scrutiny, for closer attention paid to everything we can possibly discover about these eighteenth-century women and their literary and social culture. As Paula Backscheider once expressed it in a talk which made a number of similar points, we must "Doubt Everything," most especially all "familiar answers" about women writers.[2] In the end, I believe, the effort of such a reimagining will result in a sharper understanding of how gender figured in an individual writer's experience. Such an analysis, while not denying these women's need to negotiate the interdependent conditions of social status and gender expectations, has the potential to produce a fresh reading of their ambitions and achievements. It allows us to consider the possibility that Scott, in writing historical biography, or Brooke, in expressing her political opinions, or Sheridan, in invoking Home's *Douglas*, might have had something besides, or beyond, her own gender position in mind. It is only when we are prepared to let go of gender as our fundamental interpretive category, it is only when we self-consciously rethink the frameworks through which we currently see and do not see mid-eighteenth-century women writers, it is only as we begin to consider women writers and their texts as the participants in literary and publishing networks that they were, that we will be freed of the constraining picture of their working in the shadow of the dominant male writers of their day, condemned to having their literary aspirations shipwrecked on the rocks either of modest acquiescence or of marginalized transgression.

In my introduction I invoked the analogy of wine and wineskins – more accurately and polemically, I have offered no one new and improved wineskin (or picture frame) which will correct our critical tastes (or perspectives). Rather, my study has sought to demonstrate, through its series of case studies, that the wine we now have to savor is a heady new blend of rediscovered writers, newly discovered texts, and long-established contexts. But unless we allow this new mixture to burst the old wineskins, to challenge our established categories, we will not fully explore the subtle and broad range of variations in its flavors, and from there be able to reconstruct interpretive "wineskins" for eighteenth-century writing that will be less narrowly determined by taxonomies of gender and genre than those of the two ensuing centuries have been. As a study on the way to such revised interpretive categories, this book has many limitations. I have felt most dissatisfied with its divided focus on a group of writers and a series of approaches, any one of which arguably merits a full-length examination.[3] But such work, I believe, will come, and I trust that this book's limitation will also prove its strength, in its modeling of how we might take second looks at a category of writers we have created in our first recovery work, but have as yet revisited only in piecemeal ways. If I have succeeded at all, we may find new ways to talk about mid-eighteenth-century women writers – as variously ambitious, variously professionalized, variously influential – even, as interesting.

Notes

INTRODUCTION: "BUILDING ON PUBLIC APPROBATION"

1 Frances Brooke to James Dodsley, British Library Additional Manuscript 29747, ff. 68–69.
2 Janet Todd, *The Sign of Angellica: Women, Writing and Fiction, 1660–1800* (New York: Columbia University Press, 1989), p. 125, quoting Samuel Johnson, *The Adventurer* 115 (December 11, 1753). The other "ladies" named by Todd in this passage are Charlotte Lennox, Frances Sheridan, and Hester Mulso Chapone.
3 Todd, *Sign of Angellica*, chapter 7.
4 Patricia Meyer Spacks, review in *Eighteenth-Century Fiction* 2 (1990), p. 364.
5 For a full outline of the model, see Jane Spencer, *The Rise of the Woman Novelist: From Aphra Behn to Jane Austen* (Oxford: Blackwell, 1986), especially chapter 1's section on "The New Ideology of Femininity" and chapter 3, "The Terms of Acceptance," and Todd, *Sign of Angellica*, Part Two, especially chapters 6 to 8.
6 Kathryn Shevelow, *Women and Print Culture: The Construction of Femininity in the Early Periodical* (London: Routledge, 1989), p. 5; Todd, *Sign of Angellica*, p. 4.
7 Spencer, for example, in identifying three strands of "response" to the ideological climate for women writers – the novel of protest, the novel of conformity, and the novel of escape – acknowledges overlap between her categories, and traces manifestations of each throughout the long eighteenth century (*Rise of the Woman Novelist*, pp. ix-x, chapters 4–6).
8 Todd, *Sign of Angellica*, p. 2.
9 Spencer, *Rise of the Woman Novelist*, p. 95.
10 Spacks review, p. 365.
11 See especially the essay collection *Aphra Behn Studies*, edited by Todd (Cambridge: Cambridge University Press, 1996); Spencer's *Aphra Behn's Afterlife* (Oxford: Oxford University Press, 2000); Ros Ballaster, *Seductive Forms: Women's Amatory Fiction from 1684 to 1740* (Oxford: Clarendon, 1992); Catherine Ingrassia, *Authorship, Commerce, and Gender in Early Eighteenth-Century England: A Culture of Paper Credit* (Cambridge: Cambridge University Press, 1998); Kirsten T. Saxton and Rebecca

P. Bocchicchio (eds.), *The Passionate Fictions of Eliza Haywood: Essays on Her Life and Work* (Lexington: University Press of Kentucky, 2000).

12 Paula McDowell, *The Women of Grub Street: Press, Politics and Gender in the London Literary Marketplace 1678–1730* (Oxford: Clarendon, 1998).

13 Kathryn R. King, *Jane Barker, Exile: A Literary Career, 1675–1725* (Oxford: Clarendon, 2000), pp. 7–20.

14 Amanda Vickery, "Golden Age to Separate Spheres? A Review of the Categories and Chronology of English Women's History," *The Historical Journal* 36 (1993), p. 413. See also Vickery's own "attempt to map the breadth and boundaries of female experience," in *The Gentleman's Daughter: Women's Lives in Georgian England* (New Haven: Yale University Press, 1998).

15 Lawrence E. Klein, "Gender and the Public/Private Distinction in the Eighteenth Century: Some Questions about Evidence and Analytic Procedure," *Eighteenth-Century Studies* 29 (1995), p. 97, 102; see also Kathleen Wilson, "Citizenship, Empire, and Modernity in the English Provinces, c. 1720–1790," pp. 69–96 in the same journal issue.

16 Jürgen Habermas, *The Structural Transformation of the Public Sphere: An Inquiry into a Category of Bourgeois Society*, trans. Thomas Burger with the assistance of Frederick Lawrence (Cambridge, MA: MIT Press, 1989), pp. 51–56.

17 Todd, *Sign of Angellica*, p. 161.

18 McDowell, *Women of Grub Street*, p. 5 and n8. McDowell is here returning to the claims of her earlier article, discussed below.

19 Frank Donoghue, *The Fame Machine: Book Reviewing and Eighteenth-Century Literary Careers* (Stanford: Stanford University Press, 1996), p. 6.

20 Ibid., pp. 7, 160–61.

21 Todd, *Sign of Angellica*, p. 125.

22 Margaret J. M. Ezell, *Writing Women's Literary History* (Baltimore: Johns Hopkins University Press, 1993), pp. 88–89.

23 Paula McDowell, "Consuming Women: The Life of the 'Literary Lady' as Popular Culture in Eighteenth-Century England," *Genre* 26 (1993), p. 222.

24 See especially chapter 2, "The Myth of Judith Shakespeare: Creating the Canon of Women's Literature in the Twentieth Century."

25 McDowell, "Consuming Women," p. 222.

26 As I will elaborate in my final chapter, McDowell's article hints at the collusion of women in the erasure of other women, and Spencer's notion of "terms of acceptance," of course, suggests a bargain struck, if not between equals, then between active participants.

27 Harriet Guest, *Small Change: Women, Learning, Patriotism, 1750–1810* (Chicago: University of Chicago Press, 2000), p. 15.

28 Elizabeth Eger, "Representing Culture: 'The Nine Living Muses of Great Britain' (1779)," pp. 75–103, and Charlotte Grant, "The Choice of Hercules: The Polite Arts and 'Female Excellence' in Eighteenth-Century London," pp. 104–32, in Elizabeth Eger, Charlotte Grant, Cliona O Gallchoir, and

Penny Warburton (eds.), *Women, Writing and the Public Sphere, 1700–1830* (Cambridge: Cambridge University Press, 2001).

29 Eger, "Representing Culture," p. 125.

30 Patricia Howell Michaelson, *Speaking Volumes: Women, Reading and Speech in the Age of Johnson* (Stanford: Stanford University Press, 2002), p. 1. See further Gary Kelly's essay, "Bluestocking Feminism," in Eger et al. (eds.), *Women*, pp. 163–80, as well as Nicole Pohl and Betty A. Schellenberg (eds.), *Reconsidering the Bluestockings* (San Marino, CA: The Huntington Library, 2003). However, although Kelly consistently argues for a bluestocking feminism that played a significant role in the "complex cultural revolution that would eventually, among other things, found the modern state" based on capitalism, consumerism, and the civil society embodied in a bourgeois professional class (p. 164), his model for this feminism is firmly based on distinct, if dialectically related, private and public spheres as "foundational for the modern state" (p. 163).

31 Sylvana Tomaselli, "The Enlightenment Debate on Women," *History Workshop Journal* 20 (1985), pp. 101–24.

32 Laurie Langbauer, *Women and Romance: The Consolations of Gender in the English Novel* (Ithaca: Cornell University Press, 1990), pp. 62, 81.

33 Charlotte Lennox, *The Female Quixote*, ed. Margaret Dalziel (Oxford: Oxford University Press, 1989), pp. 366, 377.

34 These terms are respectively those of Catherine A. Craft, in "Reworking Male Models: Aphra Behn's *Fair Vow-Breaker*, Eliza Haywood's *Fantomina*, and Charlotte Lennox's *Female Quixote*," *Modern Language Review* 86 (1991), p. 822, and David Marshall, in "Writing Masters and 'Masculine Exercises' in *The Female Quixote*," *Eighteenth-Century Fiction* 5 (1993), p. 117. Langbauer says something very similar in arguing that Arabella is "inaugurated into man's realm and becomes indistinguishable from the men in it" by "participating in the patriarchal discourse of moral law" (p. 81).

35 Duncan Isles, among others, has rejected this supposition, which was first put forward in the mid-nineteenth century; see "The Lennox Collection," ed. Duncan Isles, *Harvard Library Bulletin* 18 (1970), p. 341 n31.

36 Elizabeth Kraft, *Character and Consciousness in Eighteenth-Century Comic Fiction* (Athens: University of Georgia Press, 1992), p. 99.

37 Todd, *Sign of Angellica*, p. 176; Spencer, *Rise of the Woman Novelist*, p. 94.

38 See the evidence provided by James Raven's *British Fiction 1750–1770: A Chronological Check-List of Prose Fiction Printed in Britain and Ireland* (Cranbury, NJ: Associated University Press, 1987).

39 Samuel Johnson, *The Letters of Samuel Johnson*, 3 vols., ed. Bruce Redford (Princeton: Princeton University Press, 1992), vol. I, p. 137.

40 Alicia Lefanu, *Memoirs of the Life and Writings of Mrs. Frances Sheridan* (London: Whittaker, 1824), pp. 93–96.

41 Richardson to Lennox, in "Lennox Collection," 18, p. 337; NB Isles's revision of this letter's dating in *Harvard Library Quarterly* 19 (1971),

pp. 433–34; Richardson to Fielding, in *The Correspondence of Samuel Richardson*, 6 vols., ed. Anna Laetitia Barbauld (London, 1804), vol. II, p. 102.

42 Walter Harte to Lennox, "Lennox Collection," 19, p. 416. Isles identifies this "Mrs. Scot" tentatively as "the novelist Sarah Scott," but the likelihood is strong when one takes into account Scott's authorship of the 1761 *The Life of Gustavus Ericson*, of which Isles does not seem to have been aware, Harte's own 1759 *History of the Life of Gustavus Adolphus, King of Sweden*, and the fact that the greeting is part of a short response to Lennox's request to borrow from Harte the French historian Bougeant's history of the Thirty Years' War.

43 I grant here the important distinction drawn by Isobel Grundy between Johnson and some other male figures (and I would place Richardson in the same category as Johnson, though not to the same degree): "Johnson liked to grant not only whatever goods might lie in his power – shelter, money, food – but also the power to gain. This he offered by nourishing talent, by fostering confidence, and by insisting on professional standards. Most of his male contemporaries were chary of offering women this second kind of help; willing to grant goods, they were possessively retentive of the power to gain. Today the second kind of gift or patronage looks the more valuable of the two" ("Samuel Johnson as Patron of Women," *The Age of Johnson* 1 [1987], p. 61).

44 Lefanu, *Memoirs*, pp. 86, 95–96.

45 Cheryl Turner's *Living by the Pen: Women Writers in the Eighteenth Century* (London and New York: Routledge, 1992), for example, despite its broad title, deals only with prose fiction.

46 Judith Phillips Stanton, "Statistical Profile of Women Writing in English from 1660 to 1800," in Frederick M. Keener and Susan E. Lorsch (eds.), *Eighteenth-Century Women and the Arts* (New York: Greenwood, 1988), pp. 247–54.

47 Guest, *Small Change*, p. 15.

48 Alvin B. Kernan, *Printing Technology, Letters, and Samuel Johnson* (Princeton: Princeton University Press, 1987).

49 See Magali Sarfatti Larson, *The Rise of Professionalism: A Sociological Analysis* (Berkeley and Los Angeles: University of California Press, 1977), for an overview; Geoffrey Holmes, *Augustan England: Professions, State and Society, 1680–1730* (London: Allen and Unwin, 1982), and Penelope J. Corfield, *Power and the Professions in Britain, 1700–1850* (London: Routledge, 1995), examine the early development of modern professionalism in the eighteenth century.

50 Susanne Janssen uses the terms "reputational" or "incomplete" to describe the artistic professions, in "The Empirical Study of Careers in Literature and the Arts," in Dick Schram and Gerard Steen (eds.), *The Psychology and Sociology of Literature. In Honor of Elrud Ibsch* (Amsterdam: John Benjamins, 2001), pp. 323–57; see chapter 4 for a fuller discussion of the application of this model to Lennox's career.

51 Dustin Griffin, *Literary Patronage in England, 1650–1800* (Cambridge: Cambridge University Press, 1996).

52 Michel Foucault, "What is an Author?," in Donald F. Bouchard (ed.), *Language, Counter-Memory, Practice*, trans. Donald F. Bouchard and Sherry Simon (Ithaca: Cornell University Press, 1977), pp. 113–38.

53 Mark Rose, *Authors and Owners: The Invention of Copyright* (Cambridge, MA: Harvard University Press, 1993), and Martha Woodmansee, "Genius and the Copyright," in Martha Woodmansee, *The Author, Art, and the Market: Rereading the History of Aesthetics* (New York: Columbia University Press, 1994), pp. 35–55, 157–63. A key text, of course, is Edward Young's 1759 *Conjectures on Original Composition*, but the increasing emphasis on originality can be traced in reviews of the period as well; see my article "'The Measured Lines of the Copyist': Sequels, Reviews, and the Discourse of Authorship in England, 1749–1800," in Debra Bourdeau and Elizabeth Kraft (eds.), *And Now for the Sequel: Examining Updates of Eighteenth-Century Works* (forthcoming).

54 Turner, *Living by the Pen*, p. 100.

55 See Clifford Siskin, *The Work of Writing: Literature and Social Change in Britain, 1700–1830* (Baltimore: Johns Hopkins University Press, 1998), for an analysis of the emergence of authorial professionalization within eighteenth-century British print culture, and the related "forgetting" of women writers; I address the latter aspect of this argument in chapter 7 below.

56 An important attempt to circumvent the ghettoization of female authorship which results from such treatments is Catherine Gallagher's *Nobody's Story: The Vanishing Acts of Women Writers in the Marketplace, 1670–1820* (Berkeley and Los Angeles: University of California Press, 1994), which sets out to find in the discourse of authorship itself an explanation other than gender for longstanding generalizations about women authors' exclusion from full authorial agency. Gallagher notes "the universality of the theme of dispossession in the rhetoric of authorship generally," so that "the rhetoric of female authorship differs, in this regard, from that of authorship in general [merely] by exaggerating and sexualizing the common theme" (pp. xiv–xv, xx–xxi). Despite this encouraging start, however, in her discussion of the mid-century Lennox, Gallagher's reliance on readings of mid-century women writers as wearing a modest domestic aspect prefashioned for them (p. 147) results in a collapse of rhetoric and authorial gender. In discussing "how Charlotte Lennox became the center of a remarkable circle of (mostly male) collaborators and promoters" (p. 200), Gallagher separates the conditions of Lennox's authorship, which she has used to illustrate those under which all mid-century authors labored, from Lennox's remarkable professional achievements, thereby personalizing and gendering these colleagues' support as a response to Lennox's "dispossession" as an unhappily married woman (p. 202). See chapter 4 below.

57 Jerome Christensen, *Practicing Enlightenment: Hume and the Formation of a Literary Career* (Madison: University of Wisconsin Press, 1987), pp. 4, 18.

58 See Kernan, *Printing Technology*, pp. 59–62, for an overview of this trend, and Siskin, *Work of Writing*, pp. 160–61, for a theory of its import in the creation of authors.

59 Christensen, *Practicing Enlightenment*, p. 125. Christensen's claim that for Hume, "The disinterested propagation of ideas, which was the aim of the republic of letters, was never separate from the individual's ambition for the success of his own writings" (p. 127) is a refreshing corrective to the common critical assumption that disinterest and ambition are incompatible. See chapters 2 and 4 below.

60 Seán Burke, *The Death and Return of the Author: Criticism and Subjectivity in Barthes, Foucault and Derrida* (Edinburgh: Edinburgh University Press, 1998), pp. 202–4.

61 See James Raven's introductions to his *British Fiction 1750–1770: A Chronological Check-List of Prose Fiction Printed in Britain and Ireland* (Cranburry, NJ Associated University Press, 1987) and James Raven and Antonia Forster, with Stephen Bending (eds.), *The English Novel 1770–1829: A Bibliographical Survey of Prose Fiction Published in the British Isles, Volume I: 1770–1799* (Oxford: Oxford University Press, 2000), as well as his essay "The Anonymous Novel in Britain and Ireland, 1750–1830," in Robert J. Griffin (ed.), *The Faces of Anonymity: Anonymous and Pseudonymous Publication from the Sixteenth to the Twentieth Century* (New York and Houndmills: Palgrave Macmillan, 2003), pp. 141–66.

62 Turner, *Living by the Pen*, p. 114. In a study of the end of the period, Jan Fergus and Janice Farrar Thaddeus arrive at a set of thought-provoking paradoxes: "women believed that they were working in an atmosphere that did not condone their money-making activities," and "Much of the current rhetoric supported this belief," yet the records of several women's dealings with two firms, Hookham and Carpenter, and Longman, suggest that they "do not actually seem to have discriminated against women writers," that "increasingly, women were negotiating for themselves," and in some cases, were "quite adroit in converting their publishers' patronizing impulses into financial support" ("Women, Publishers, and Money, 1790–1820," *Studies in Eighteenth-Century Culture* 17 [1987], p. 201). Such findings at the least point to the need to be aware of the rhetorical function of isolated prefatory complaints by women, or of journalistic comments on the inferiority of young lady novelists.

63 Martin C. Battestin and Clive T. Probyn (eds.), *The Correspondence of Henry and Sarah Fielding* (Oxford: Clarendon, 1993), p. xxx.

64 Donoghue, *Fame Machine*, pp. 3–4.

65 Battestin and Probyn (eds.), *Correspondence of Henry and Sarah Fielding*, p. xxvii; *MR* 39 (July 1757), p. 39. When Peter Sabor notes, for Fielding, that the Xenophon translation "is probably the [work] for which she would most wish to have been remembered" (Introduction to Sarah Fielding, *The Adventures of David Simple*, ed. Peter Sabor [Lexington: University Press of Kentucky, 1998], p. xxiii) one is struck by the fact that it is rather the

memory of Fielding's earlier novel-writing, and particularly of that first, self-deprecating effort, which has survived not only in traditional literary histories (because of interest in the Henry Fielding preface), but also in feminist retellings of the story. It would appear that the presumed link between modest women and the novel is so well served by Henry's notorious preface that the new histories have colluded with the old. See also chapter 4 below.

66 Margaret Ezell has recently provided examples to counter the predominant view that in the early eighteenth century anonymity served "to disguise the identity of the [female] author and to shield feminine modesty," in "'By a Lady': The Mask of the Feminine in Restoration, Early Eighteenth-Century Print Culture," in Griffin (ed.), *Faces of Anonymity*, p. 68.

67 Thus the hapless Skelton complains to Richardson: "I had a most honest intention in writing the Discourses now in your hands. I took infinite pains to finish them; all my friends approved of them, pressed for the publication of them, and do still press. Yet how unfortunate have I been in every step! Johnston kept them a month on the way [from Ireland to London]; Wilson kept them three, and does nothing, only hints a sort of contemptuous censure of them to you, and huffs them out of his hands. The booksellers despise them, and I am forced to print them, when the season for sale is over, or burn them. God's will be done" (Barbauld [ed.], *Correspondence of Richardson*, vol. V, p. 234).

68 These terms are taken from Susan Wiseman's discussion of "Catharine Macaulay: History, Republicanism and the Public Sphere," in Eger et al. (eds.), *Women*, p. 194.

FRANCES SHERIDAN, JOHN HOME, AND PUBLIC VIRTUE

1 Samuel Whyte, *Miscellanea Nova*, 2nd ed. (Dublin, 1800; rpt. New York: Garland, 1974), pp. 105–6.

2 Klein, "Gender," 102; Terry Lovell, "Subjective Powers? Consumption, the Reading Public, and the Early Eighteenth-Century Domestic Woman," in Ann Bermingham and John Brewer (eds.), *The Consumption of Culture 1600–1800: Image, Object, Text* (London and New York: Routledge, 1997), p. 30; Klein, "Gender," p. 102, italics in original; Shevelow, *Women and Print Culture*, p. 5.

3 Frances Sheridan, *Memoirs of Miss Sidney Bidulph*, ed. Patricia Koster and Jean Coates Cleary (Oxford: Oxford University Press, 1995). References are to this edition.

4 Barbauld (ed.), *Correspondence of Richardson*, vol. IV, pp. 143–44, 176. Barbauld identifies this novel as *Sidney Bidulph*, but the letters are written in 1756 and 1758, whereas Sheridan indicates to her cousin Samuel Whyte that the book had been written in the winter of 1759–60 (in Samuel Whyte, *Miscellanea Nova*, p. 102). The *Correspondence* references are therefore to the earlier *Eugenia and Adelaide*, which Richardson submitted to Robert Dodsley for consideration (Cleary, Introduction to *Sidney Bidulph*, p. x).

5 Todd, *Sign of Angellica*, p. 125; Cleary, Introduction to *Sidney Bidulph*, pp. xvi–xvii; Margaret Anne Doody, "Frances Sheridan: Morality and Annihilated Time," *Fetter'd or Free?: British Women Novelists, 1670–1815*, ed. Mary Anne Schofield and Cecilia Macheski (Athens: Ohio University Press, 1986), pp. 327, 343, 356.

6 Guest, *Small Change*, p. 15.

7 Whyte, *Miscellanea Nova*, pp. 89–127.

8 Alicia Lefanu, *Memoirs of the Life and Writings of Mrs. Frances Sheridan* (London, 1824), pp. 88, 97.

9 Whyte, *Miscellanea Nova*, pp. 105–6; Lefanu, *Memoirs*, p. 87.

10 Lefanu, *Memoirs*, pp. 87, 85–86, 218, 218, italics in original.

11 An early expression of this sense of rivalry comes from Thomas Sheridan, as a young actor writing to Garrick to suggest that they divide the London and Dublin audiences between them "like Castor and Pollux, appear[ing] always in different hemispheres" (April 21, 1743; quoted in Esther K. Sheldon, *Thomas Sheridan of Smock-Alley* [Princeton: Princeton University Press, 1967], p. 39). Although Sheldon's study provides a running account of the shifting tides of this relationship, she is not explicit about its nature during the first London stay; I am extrapolating from her quotation of Thomas Davies's description of Sheridan's 1760 agreement with Garrick to act on shares for Drury Lane: "It was, perhaps, the mutual interest of Mr. Garrick and Mr. Sheridan to come to a reasonable agreement; this was soon effected, notwithstanding a coldness had subsisted between them for some time" (quoted in Sheldon, *Thomas Sheridan*, p. 260).

12 Although Garrick initially rejected plays by Home and Smollett, his relations with the Scottish literati appear to have warmed after 1756, when he staged, first Home's *Agis* (1758) and then *The Siege of Aquileia* (1760), as well as Smollett's comedy *The Reprisal* (1757); see Richard B. Sher, "'The favourite of the favourite': John Home, Bute and the Politics of Patriotic Poetry," in K. W. Schweizer (ed.), *Lord Bute: Essays in Re-interpretation* (Leicester: Leicester University Press, 1988), pp. 184, 200–1, and James G. Basker, *Tobias Smollett: Critic and Journalist* (Newark: University of Delaware Press, 1988), pp. 100–01.

13 Sheldon, *Thomas Sheridan*, p. 228.

14 See Hume's Dedication of his *Four Dissertations*, published in 1757, to John Home as author of *Douglas* (*The Philosophical Works*, 4 vols., ed. Thomas Hill Green and Thomas Hodge Grose [London, 1882; rpt. Darmstadt: Scientia Verlag Aalen, 1964], vol. IV, pp. 439–41; *MR* 17 (May 1757), p. 426; *CR* 3 (March 1757), p. 258.

15 This according to James Boswell's report in *Journal of a Tour to the Hebrides*, vol. V of *Boswell's Life of Johnson*, ed. George Birkbeck Hill, rev. L. F. Powell, 6 vols. (Oxford: Clarendon, 1934), p. 360. See Garrick's letter to Home, in *The Letters of David Garrick*, 3 vols., ed. David M. Little and George M. Kahrl (Cambridge, MA: Belknap Press [Harvard University Press, 1963]), vol. I, pp. 269–71.

16 Sheldon cites Davies in describing the agreement that Sheridan "was to act a stipulated number of nights and receive a one-quarter share of the profits after £80 a night for expenses had been deducted" (*Thomas Sheridan*, p. 260).
17 K. J. H. Berland, "Frances Brooke and David Garrick," *Studies in Eighteenth-Century Culture* 20 (1990), p. 219.
18 Whyte, *Miscellanea Nova*, pp. 110–11. See also the Introduction to *The Plays of Frances Sheridan*, ed. Robert Hogan and Jerry C. Beasley (Newark: University of Delaware Press, 1984), pp. 21–22, 31–33, for a fuller account of the play's preparation, stage production, and publishing history.
19 While such conclusions must remain speculative, it is possible that the Sheridans had found Richardson's influence less powerful than they had hoped. Richardson's intervention on Thomas's behalf in the Dublin theater conflicts of spring 1758 was unsuccessful (see below), while it was in March of the same year that Dodsley rejected *Eugenia and Adelaide* in spite of Richardson's recommendation.
20 Boswell, *Life of Johnson*, vol. I, pp. 374, 385–86; vol. II, p. 320.
21 Boswell, *Life of Johnson*, vol. I, pp. 374, 386–87.
22 Quoted in Sheldon, *Thomas Sheridan*, p. 261.
23 My argument is greatly indebted to Sher's account of Home's moment in the political sun as "the favourite of the favourite." Sher disputes the contemporary view "that Garrick agreed to produce *Agis* solely because of Bute's influence" (p. 200), but an eye to political positioning should not be discounted; see Garrick's 1760 letter to George Colman, in which he writes, complaining of difficulty in preparing a number of new roles, "If Mr. Home will defer his performance to ye next Year to which purpose I shall write immediately to him, I can Master Oakly very well by ye time – but he is so connected with Ld Bute & a much greater personnage, that I must be a little delicate in that Business – " (Little and Kahrl [eds.], *Letters of Garrick*, vol. I, p. 333; Little and Kahrl identify the play as *Agis*, but the dating would rather indicate *The Siege of Aquileia*).
24 Whyte, *Miscellanea Nova*, pp. 18, 2n.
25 See Dustin Griffin, *Literary Patronage in England, 1650–1800* (Cambridge: Cambridge University Press, 1996), pp. 61–65, regarding the general climate of expectation at the new king's accession that learning and the arts would be patronized on a nonpartisan basis; the citation is from the *Critical Review* 5 (March 1758), p. 242, quoted p. 61.
26 Griffin, *Literary Patronage*, pp. 65–66.
27 Sher, "'The favourite,'" pp. 197–205.
28 See, for example, her admission, "Too well I love that valour which I warn" (John Home, "Home's *Douglas*," ed. Hubert J. Tunney, *Bulletin of the University of Kansas Humanistic Studies* 3 [1924], 5.173). References are to this edition.
29 Cleary, Introduction to *Sidney Bidulph*, p. xvi.
30 Sher, "'The favourite,'" p. 194.

31 Barbauld (ed.), *Correspondence of Richardson*, vol. IV, pp. 170–73.

32 Boswell's account of his own mollifying role in the disagreement is undermined by his own reasons for dissatisfaction with the Sheridans at this time; these are recounted in Hogan and Beasley, Introduction to *Plays of Sheridan*, p. 22. Certainly Whyte felt that Boswell's account of the quarrel in the *Life of Johnson* was highly partisan (see *Miscellanea Nova*, pp. 2, 15–16, 45–46).

33 Boswell, *Life of Johnson*, vol. I, p. 389.

34 Ibid., p. 390.

35 *CR* 2 (March 1757), pp. 260, 268. Susan Staves has given a detailed account of audience response to *Douglas*, and especially to the character of Lady Randolph, in "Douglas's Mother," in John Hazel Smith (ed.), *Brandeis Essays in Literature* (Waltham, MA: Brandeis University Press, 1983), pp. 51–67.

36 *MR* 24 (April 1761), p. 260.

37 See Richardson's Postscript to *Clarissa* for an attack on the current notion of "*poetical justice*" as contrary to the "dispensation . . . with which God by Revelation teaches us he has thought fit to exercise mankind; whom, placing here only in a state of *probation*, he hath so intermingled good and evil as to necessitate them to look forward for a more equal distribution of both" (*Clarissa*, ed. Angus Ross [Harmondsworth: Penguin, 1985], p. 1495).

38 Tunney, Introduction to *Douglas*, pp. 13–14.

39 David Wheeler, "The Pathetic and the Sublime: The Tragic Formula of John Home's *Douglas*," in Donald C. Mell, Jr., Theodore E. D. Braun, and Lucia M. Palmer (eds.), *Man, God, and Nature in the Enlightenment* (East Lansing, MI: Colleagues, 1988), pp. 176, 180.

40 Sher has commented on this feminization in a note to his discussion of Home, suggesting that Home shares his contemporaries' association of "heroic and sentimental virtue" with "masculine and feminine ideals," respectively, while making young Douglas embody both ideals ("'The favourite,'" pp. 208–9 n7). Staves also notes that "Home's talent lay partially in dispensing with the older forms of aristocratic masculine action . . . and in replacing them with the smaller, more domestic actions in which his bourgeois audience could realistically engage"; central to this appeal, she elaborates, is Lady Randolph as "the image of a wife and mother who exists only for [husband and children] and who will remain faithful to them forever" ("Douglas's Mother," pp. 54, 57). Staves's commentary thus implies that a deployment of the "feminine" as part of audience appeal merely appropriates sentiment to reify existing gender assumptions rather than entailing a rethinking of female heroism.

41 Lady Randolph's suicide was controversial in Scotland, fueling an attack on Home's play-writing as a minister of the Church. The high profile of this debate, carried on in numerous publications ranging from pamphlets to stage burlesques, supports my claim that Sheridan is self-consciously distinguishing her heroine from the Lady Randolph of the play; see Ernest

Campbell Mosner, *The Forgotten Hume: "Le bon David"* (New York: Columbia University Press, 1943; rpt. New York: AMS, 1967), pp. 49–55.

42 The more well-known case of a woman writer's denying a difference in rational and moral capacity between men and women is of course that of Mary Wollstonecraft, in her *Vindication of the Rights of Woman.* Janet Todd has described as "revolutionary" Wollstonecraft's "insistence that private and public are joined and . . . that personal and political are one" (Introduction to Mary Wollstonecraft, *Political Writings* [Oxford: Oxford University Press, 1994], p. xix). Sheridan thus provides evidence for Guest's claim in *Small Change* that apparently socially conservative women of these earlier decades prepared the way for feminist thinking such as that of Wollstonecraft.

43 See, for example, Robert Palfrey Utter and Gwendolyn Bridges Needham, *Pamela's Daughters* (New York: Russell and Russell, 1972); Gerard A. Barker, *Grandison's Heirs: The Paragon's Progress in the Late Eighteenth-Century English Novel* (Newark: University of Delaware Press, 1985); and Jerry C. Beasley, "*Clarissa* and Early Female Fiction," in Carol Houlihan Flynn and Edward Copeland (eds.), *Clarissa and Her Readers: New Essays for The "Clarissa" Project* (New York: AMS, 1999), pp. 69–96, which devotes a section to Richardson's "literary daughters" (p. 85). Beasley's carefully nuanced treatment of Richardson's complex appeal as at once empowering female characters through linguistic authority and idealizing a pure patriarchal model of culture is a valuable vantage point for his overview of precursors and followers, but the ultimate effect of his sweeping perspective is to flatten out the period's shifts both in the patriarchal culture and in women's responses to it. Isobel Grundy, "'A novel in a series of letters by a lady': Richardson and Some Richardsonian Novels," in Margaret Anne Doody and Peter Sabor (eds.), *Samuel Richardson: Tercentenary Essays* (Cambridge: Cambridge University Press, 1989), pp. 223–36, 288–90, and Ruth Perry, "Clarissa's Daughters: Or, The History of Innocence Betrayed," in Flynn and Copeland, pp. 119–41, offer more historically particularized readings of shifts in gender relations and fictional representations of them.

44 *MR* 29 (August 1763), p. 160, writing of Margaret and Susannah Minifie's *History of Lady Frances S ——— and Lady Caroline S ———*. As discussed in chapter 5, this labeling by the reviews is in fact neither as widespread nor as uniform in its import as we may think it to be.

45 Perry, "Clarissa's Daughters," p. 119.

46 A case in point is the sort of generalizations Beasley makes for all women novelists from Aphra Behn to Mary Wollstonecraft and Mary Hays; he argues that all fictions imagining "independence and freedom from subjection" for a female character ended either in "rejection or assimilation," and that "Whatever the resolution, the effect is the same: a loss of separate identity, a death of the self" ("*Clarissa*," p. 78).

47 Perry, "Clarissa's Daughters," p. 122; Grundy, "A novel," p. 223.

48 Ezell has referred to this as "the Clarissa model" of the woman writer: "a well-educated, middle-class girl, . . . [who] writes constantly in private, but

[whose] written texts have no effect since they are not 'published' until she is dead, when all who read them are moved" (*Writing*, pp. 10–11). See my introduction for a fuller discussion of Ezell's argument about the influence of this model. Spencer argues rather that Richardson's naive but unswervingly virtuous heroines are less influential as models than are such characters as Haywood's Betsy Thoughtless and Lennox's Arabella, who serve as prototypes of "the mistaken heroine who reforms" (*Rise of the Woman Novelist*, p. 141).

49 Jacqueline Pearson, *Women's Reading in Britain, 1750–1835: A Dangerous Recreation* (Cambridge: Cambridge University Press, 1999). Jodi L. Wyett's unpublished dissertation, "Reading Women: Female Novelists, Female Readers, 1751–1818" (Detroit, MI: Wayne State University Press, 1999), though it does not address the specific question of responses to *Clarissa* and although it differs from my interpretations of individual novels such as *The Female Quixote* and *Sidney Bidulph*, asks very similar questions about portrayals of women's reading in mid- to late eighteenth-century novels, concluding as well that women writers modeled, and offered their female readers, active, engaged reading practices.

50 Samuel Johnson, *Rambler* 4 (March 31, 1750), *The Yale Edition of the Works of Samuel Johnson*, 16 vols., ed. W. J. Bate and Albrecht B. Strauss (New Haven: Yale University Press, 1969), vol. III, pp. 19–22.

51 Johnson, *Rambler* 4, vol. III, p. 24.

52 Tom Keymer, *Richardson's "Clarissa" and the Eighteenth-Century Reader* (Cambridge: Cambridge University Press, 1992), p. 66. Although Keymer's consistent emphasis is on Richardson's active model of reading, which he argues never "carries the inescapable force of metalinguistic commentary," he does discuss the novel's third installment as a "riposte," designed to "reassert his authority over readers, and to intervene in the processes of interpretation" (pp. 196, 198). For an argument for Richardson's self-conscious and coherent management of reader engagement in the moral struggle at the heart of his novel, see Nicholas Hudson's "Arts of Seduction and the Rhetoric of *Clarissa*," *Modern Language Quarterly* 51 (1990), pp. 25–43.

53 Frances Sheridan, *Conclusion of the Memoirs of Miss Sidney Bidulph* (London: 1767), p. 402.

54 Lefanu, *Memoirs*, p. 108.

55 Margaret Anne Doody suggests the parody here ("Frances Sheridan," p. 327); Grandison's curls flow down to his back, and Harriet tends to describe him as the sun at the center of an admiring circle; Adam in *Paradise Lost* is also adorned with hyacinthine locks. One might, indeed, argue that Sheridan puts a Clarissa and a Sir Charles Grandison together in the same novel and makes them lovers. The result? Actuated by extreme selflessness, they destroy one another.

56 In this, I differ from the critical tradition beginning with the novel's first reviewers and continuing to Jane Spencer's argument that the stated moral is endorsed by the novel ("Women Writers and the Eighteenth-Century

Novel," in John Richetti (ed.), *The Cambridge Companion to the Eighteenth-Century Novel* [Cambridge: Cambridge University Press, 1996], pp. 223–24). I am more sympathetic to Doody's formulation of a reader's response: "What is Frances Sheridan doing? She seems perhaps to be betraying the cause of women, and even of morality – those causes that Richardson said were the same" ("Frances Sheridan," p. 343).

57 Spencer, "Women Writers," pp. 224–27.

58 I have similar difficulties with Wyett's reading, which parallels mine in its argument that the novel invites reading against the grain of its explicit moral and that Sidney is capable of a more critical response to experience than the one she enacts, but which lays the blame for Sidney's tragic fate in the limitations society places on women ("Reading Women," pp. 88–110).

59 Doody, "Frances Sheridan," p. 345. Barker similarly describes Sidney as "a woman for whom decorum is 'an inviolable law' . . . and whose conduct is marked by the rigidity of a casuist" (*Grandison's Heirs*, p. 63).

60 For a discussion of this effect in the sequel to *Pamela*, see my *The Conversational Circle: Rereading The English Novel, 1740-1775* (Lexington: University Press of Kentucky, 1996), pp. 42, 49.

61 See Elizabeth L. Eisenstein, *The Printing Press as an Agent of Change: Communications and Cultural Transformations in Early-Modern Europe*, 2 vols. (Cambridge: Cambridge University Press, 1979), vol. I, pp. 43–159, for a classic summary of the implications of print technology for the structure and dissemination of knowledge.

62 *CR* 11 (March 1761), pp. 197–98.

63 *CR* 2 (January 1757), pp. 258, 267.

THE POLITICIZED PASTORAL OF FRANCES BROOKE

1 Frances Brooke, *The Old Maid*, rev. ed. (London: Millar, 1764), p. 259.

2 Quoted in Lorraine McMullen, *An Odd Attempt in a Woman: The Literary Life of Frances Brooke* (Vancouver: University of British Columbia Press, 1983), p. 78. The biographical information in this chapter is drawn primarily from McMullen. I have relied especially on her painstaking accumulation of biographical materials from archival sources such as the United Society for the Propagation of the Gospel Archives, the Murray Papers in the Public Archives of Canada, and the Fulham Papers in the Lambeth Palace Library; where I quote from these materials, I cite the McMullen page numbers only.

3 H. T. Dickinson, *Liberty and Property: Political Ideology in Eighteenth-Century Britain* (London: Weidenfeld and Nicolson, 1977). Dickinson does not formally define the term as he uses it, but he introduces it in the context of his argument that, in order to understand the motives of political action in eighteenth-century England, one must look at what is said, not only by "great thinkers and philosophers," but also by "political activists, propagandists and commentators," even when these agents "often gave

expression to prejudices which were irrational and illogical and . . . only rarely subjected their deep-seated assumptions to careful analysis" (p. 1).

4 See my introductory discussion of separate-spheres theory and recent critiques of it.

5 Sarah Fielding, on the other hand, addresses contemporary social issues in a generalized and nonreferential way, and Charlotte Lennox appears primarily concerned with positioning herself strategically for the benefit of her own career, and with challenging literary and social hierarchies to that end (see chapter 4).

6 G. J. Barker-Benfield, *The Culture of Sensibility: Sex and Society in Eighteenth-Century Britain* (Chicago: University of Chicago Press, 1992), p. 228. As this example suggests, readings of Brooke as a sentimental novelist rely heavily on her first work of fiction.

7 McMullen, *An Odd Attempt*, p. 68.

8 Robert Merrett, "The Politics of Romance in *The History of Emily Montague*," *Canadian Literature* 133 (1992), pp. 100, 107, 93; it is not ultimately clear to me whether Merrett sees Brooke's work as "simple-minded" (p. 93) or "equivocal" (p. 96) or self-contradictory, perhaps because he tends to dissociate the character William Fermor's understanding of the political complexity of Canada, for example, from what he sees as Brooke's fanciful discussion of "female social power" and "the typically self-exposing contradictoriness of the tiny community which Mrs. Brooke celebrates" (pp. 93–94). In other words, Brooke is identified entirely with Arabella Fermor and her coterie, and the supposed provenance of analyses such as Fermor's is not identified.

9 See, for example, W. H. New, "*The Old Maid*: Frances Brooke's Apprentice Feminism," *Journal of Canadian Fiction* 2 (1973), pp. 9–12; Ann Edwards Boutelle, "Frances Brooke's *Emily Montague* (1769): Canada and Woman's Rights," *Women's Studies: An Interdisciplinary Journal* 12 (1986), pp. 7–16; and Jane Sellwood, "'A Little Acid Is Absolutely Necessary': Narrative as Coquette in Frances Brooke's 'The History of Emily Montague,'" *Canadian Literature* 136 (1993), pp. 60–79.

10 Paula R. Backscheider and Hope D. Cotton, Introduction to *The Excursion*, by Frances Brooke (Lexington: University Press of Kentucky, 1997), pp. xi–xii, xxxiv–xxxv. Min Wild, "'Prodigious Wisdom': Civic Humanism in Frances Brooke's *Old Maid*," *Women's Writing* 5 (1998), pp. 422–23. While I agree wholeheartedly with Wild's view that the discourse of civic humanism is employed constantly in the periodical, showing Brooke to be an example of women writers' "resourcefulness" in claiming "participation within the public sphere" (p. 431), I do not share her sense that "Mary Singleton," Brooke's persona, is a necessary disguise enabling Brooke to adopt a discourse and style entirely out of line with what she might have expressed in her own voice (p. 422) – one need only consult Ode IX, cited below, to see that Brooke was willing to adopt the public-spirited voice and subject matter of the bard. K. J. H. Berland, "The True Pleasurable Philosopher: Some

Influences on Frances Brooke's *History of Emily Montague*," *Dalhousie Review* 66 (1986), pp. 286–87. Berland complains further that a British genre tradition of criticism "has tended to place the novels of Frances Brooke firmly in the Richardsonian school, almost as if this classification took care of everything there is to say" (p. 286).

11 General James Murray to Robert Cholmondeley, 1764, quoted in McMullen, *An Odd Attempt*, p. 75.

12 See notes of extracts from Brooke's letter to Bishop Terrick of London, January 24, 1765; quoted in McMullen, *An Odd Attempt*, pp. 76–77.

13 See McMullen's chapter on "The Brookes in Canada." John Brooke is similarly feminized as a means of rebuke when Murray admonishes him for "engaging in the Idle, very Idle disputes of a Tea Table Conversation" between Frances's sister and a military officer (quoted in McMullen, *An Odd Attempt*, p. 75).

14 Brooke, *The Excursion*, p. 83. References are to this edition. For a detailed account of Brooke's conflict with Garrick, see Berland, "Frances Brooke and David Garrick," *Studies in Eighteenth-Century Culture* 20 (1990), pp. 217–30.

15 By Garrick's own account, in his anonymous review of *The Excursion*, Brooke's dramatization of the unencouraging theater manager is a "retailing [of] the dull and hackneyed jest of the awful monarch of the theatre giving haughty audience to a levee of hungry poets – a jest which has been imitated from *Smollet*, which, by the way, he was afterward very sorry for, by every pretender to humour, or ridicule, who, either having written a bad play themselves, or envying those who have written good ones, think to enliven their book by some trite insipid piece of pertness on the errors of theatrical management" (*MR* 57 [August 1777], p. 142). For a successful playwright's version of the experience, see chapter 1.

16 *OM* 18 (March 13, 1756), p. 149.

17 See Gwendolyn B. Needham, "Mrs. Frances Brooke: Dramatic Critic," *Theatre Notebook* 15 (1960–61), pp. 47–52.

18 Little and Kahrl (eds.), *Letters of Garrick*, vol. II, p. 461.

19 Garrick's side of the exchange, with excerpts of Brooke's letters, can be found in Little and Kahrl (eds.), *Letters of Garrick*, vol. III, pp. 1093–94.

20 *MR* 57 (August 1777), p. 144. In an earlier letter to Frances Cadogan, Garrick similarly turns Brooke's complaint into a display of his chivalrous success with women playwrights: "She has invented a Tale about a Tragedy, which is all a Lie, from beginning to ye End – she Even says, that I should reject a Play, if it should be a Woman's – there's brutal Malignity for You – have not ye Ladies – Mesdames, *Griffith*, *Cowley* & *Cilesia* spoke of me before their Plays with an Over-Enthusiastick Encomium? – what says divine Hannah More? – & more than all what Says the more divine Miss Cadogan?" Little and Kahrl (eds.), *Letters of Garrick*, vol. III, p. 1172.

21 *MR* 14 (June 1756), p. 560.

22 *MR* 29 (August 1763), p. 159.

23 Francis Maseres to Fowler Walker, September 14, 1766, *The Maseres Letters 1766–68*, ed. W. Steward Wallace (Toronto: University of Toronto Press, 1919), p. 46, quoted in McMullen, *An Odd Attempt*, p. 81; *Town and Country* 21 (March 1789), p. 115.

24 Frances Burney, *The Early Journals and Letters of Fanny Burney*, 4 vols., *Vol. II (1774–1777)*, ed. Lars E. Troide (Montreal and Kingston: McGill-Queen's University Press, 1990), pp. 4–5. As often, Frances Burney presents an illuminating perspective; this aspiring author, looking to a preceding generation of women writers, finds in Brooke, unlike Charlotte Lennox, an admirable personal character that accords with her fine writing. I discuss this comment further in my concluding chapter. The allusion to Sarah Scott's 1754 novel translation *Agreeable Ugliness* is of interest here as well.

25 Frances Brooke, *The History of Emily Montague*, ed. Mary Jane Edwards (Ottawa: Carleton University Press, 1991), p. 98. References are to this edition.

26 Todd, *Sign of Angellica*, p. 177. Todd, indeed, goes on to note that *Lady Julia Mandeville* in fact idealizes benevolent patriarchalism and celebrates social hierarchy as an "absolute" in the manner of earlier Tory writers, while sentimentalizing and domesticating it (p. 179).

27 For a review of early eighteenth-century theological conflicts within the established Church, see Frans DeBruyn, "Latidudinarianism and Its Importance as a Precursor of Sensibility," *Journal of English and Germanic Philology* 80 (1981), pp. 349–68; for a historical overview of the collaboration of landed gentry and Church of England clergy in Country ideology, but also of the tensions between "Tory" parish clergy and more religiously tolerant Country "Whigs," see Dickinson, *Liberty and Property*, especially chapter 5.

28 McMullen quotes several letters of the late 1750s from Brooke to her friend Richard Gifford indicating her need for money (*An Odd Attempt*, pp. 43–49). John Brooke's military chaplaincy did not always involve payment, and his various petitions during his military service generally included an appeal for an income appropriate to his station, though he held several livings in England simultaneously (see McMullen, *An Odd Attempt*, pp. 48, 67–83).

29 For examples of women engaging in such controversies, see Guest on Elizabeth Carter in *Small Change*, pp. 125–27, 136–39; and Susan Staves on Carter, Susanna Wesley, Hannah More, Mary Bosanquet, and others, in "Church of England Clergy and Women Writers," in Pohl and Schellenberg (eds.), *Reconsidering the Bluestockings*, pp. 81–103.

30 Quoted. in Mary Jane Edwards, "Frances Brooke's *The History of Emily Montague*: A Biographical Context," *English Studies in Canada* 7 (1981), p. 179.

31 Quoted in McMullen, *An Odd Attempt*, p. 76.

32 See ibid., pp. 46–48, 120–22.

33 Merrett, "Politics of Romance," p. 93.

34 See John Barrell and Harriet Guest on the long poem in "On the Use of Contradiction: Economics and Morality in the Eighteenth-Century Long Poem," in Felicity Nussbaum and Laura Brown (eds.), *The New Eighteenth Century: Theory, Politics, English Literature* (New York: Methuen, 1986), pp. 121–43; April London, *Women and Property in the Eighteenth-Century English Novel* (Cambridge: Cambridge University Press, 1999).

35 London, *Women and Property*, pp. 7–8, 65.

36 Self-assertion for Brooke was a claim to her rightful social position, rather than an ambitious attempt at social mobility, and her contemporaries seem not to have found her public activity threatening, as they perhaps did that of Charlotte Lennox.

37 This endorsement does not name Smollett, but the discussion is initiated by a letter signed "T. S.," at a time when the project was known only to Smollett's acquaintances. Basker also notes Smollett's reference in a 1754 letter "to a rejected Virginia becoming an 'old maid,'" suggesting plausibly that Smollett may have been one of Brooke's advisers and mentors as she attempted to launch her professional career (Basker, *Tobias Smollett*, pp. 23–24, 288 n42). He describes Smollett's criticism in his review of *Virginia* as unusually gentle and tactful (pp. 76, 98–99).

38 Robert Donald Spector, *English Literary Periodicals and the Climate of Public Opinion During the Seven Years' War* (The Hague: Mouton, 1966), pp. 19–20, and more generally, chapter 1, "Fighting the War."

39 Brooke to Richard Gifford, quoted in McMullen, *An Odd Attempt*, p. 28, who estimates the date of the letter as sometime around July 10, 1756. The *Old Maid* ceased publication several weeks after this; any contributions by Murphy were to remain secret and none has been identified.

40 Spector, *English Literary Periodicals*, pp. 99–100. As a successful actor and playwright, Murphy continued a friend; we know that the actress Mary Ann Yates was a close associate of both, and as a late mark of the friendship, almost at the close of Brooke's career, Murphy contributed the Epilogue, "Written by a Friend" and spoken by Yates, to Brooke's tragedy *The Siege of Sinope.*

41 Quoted in McMullen, *An Odd Attempt*, p. 47.

42 Redford (ed.), *Letters of Johnson*, vol. I, p. 137. Redford does not identify this "Mrs. Brookes," but Frances and the portrait artist Catherine Read were longtime friends (Burney first met them together); this association, together with Brooke's own references to Johnson in this period, justifies the identification.

43 *The European Magazine* introduces this story in its "Anecdotes of Mrs. Frances Brooke," which ends in Johnson calling Brooke out of the room to kiss her farewell, with the remark that it "has only newspaper authority for its truth" (15 [February 1789], p. 100). It is doubtful that the then eighteen-year-old Hannah More was present.

44 See *Letters of Anna Seward: Written between the Years 1784 and 1807*, 6 vols. (Edinburgh, 1811), vol. I, pp. 65–66; vol. II, p. 120; vol. IV, pp. 151–52,

170. In her February 4, 1796 letter to Lady Eleanor Butler, Seward expresses a preference for the novels of Brooke, Sheridan, and several others over those of Burney, while adding that "As to Richardson and Fielding, they sit exalted above all the novel tribe in approachless excellence" (vol. IV, pp. 151–52).

45 Guest, however, emphasizes Seward's development of a "distinctively female patriotism" in the early 1780s in response to the crisis of British confidence in its imperial power (*Small Change*, p. 254). Guest's discussion of Seward's 1781 *Monody on Major André* makes clear how close Seward's representations of heroism's domestic context, of Britain's dangerous luxury, and of the interference of the French in the conflict are to the views expressed in Brooke's *Siege of Sinope*.

46 Authors of course varied the pattern of dedications with claims of friendship and disclaimers of flattery, but the model remained that generalized by Dustin Griffin: the patron did not solely provide a gift of money or other tangible rewards, but lent his encouragement, protection, and authority to the work (*Literary Patronage*, pp. 18–29).

47 See Miriam Rossiter Small, *Charlotte Ramsay Lennox: An Eighteenth Century Lady of Letters* (New Haven: Yale University Press, 1935; rpt. Archon Books, 1969), pp. 5–6.

48 These were Samuel Crisp's *Virginia*, staged at the Drury Lane Theatre in February of 1754, and only very moderately successful, and John Moncrief's *Appius*, March 1755, at the Covent Garden Theatre, even less of a success.

49 Frances Brooke, *Virginia*, in *Virginia, A Tragedy, with Odes, Pastorals, and Translations* (London: Millar, 1756), 1.7, 1.2, 1.1, 1.7. Further citations from the play are indicated by act and scene numbers in parentheses. Crisp's interpretation, by contrast, makes the story a psychological drama, exploring the conflicting passions of love, jealousy, loyalty, pride, and lust in all the major characters, and thereby much deemphasizing the story's ideological dimension.

50 See Livy, *The Early History of Rome*, translated with Introduction by Aubrey de Selincourt (Baltimore: Penguin, 1960), pp. 215–22.

51 Such a representation can of course be viewed as the heroine's internalization of patriarchal values and as an exploitation of female suffering in the tradition of the she-tragedy, but it is noteworthy that the most potentially sensational elements of the story occur offstage – a feature for which the play was criticized. The *Critical Review* writes, "With all due deference to *Aristotle*, *Horace*, and the *French* critics, we should have been pleased to see that august, affecting, horrid scene, in which the father sacrifices his darling daughter" (*CR* 1 [April 1756], p. 279).

52 Dickinson, *Liberty and Property*, pp. 130–38.

53 See New, "*The Old Maid*"; New does discuss Brooke's persistent linking of "emotional and national liberty" and her "concern for political commentary" as subsets of this feminism (p. 11).

54 Spector, *English Literary Periodicals*, p. 23.
55 E. Phillips Poole, Introduction to *Lady Julia Mandeville*, by Frances Brooke (London: Scholartis, 1930), p. 28. References are to this edition.
56 The text may allude directly to Pitt when Lord Belmont, writing to convince Henry to stand candidate for election to parliament, deplores not only "mercenary or ambitious purposes," but also "the mean vanity" that might lead a "senator" into "opposing the just measures of his Prince from a too eager desire of popularity" (p. 81).
57 The observation is Wyett's ("Reading Women," p. 189), but curiously she simultaneously argues that Brooke undermines the idealization of Belmont (and of Rivers's country estate in *Emily Montague*) as excessively patriarchal – only in *The Excursion*, where one of the satiric targets is the corrupt city society's mistreatment of a literary young woman, does Wyett see the estate as relatively positive in Brooke's scheme of values.
58 London, *Women and Property*, p. 10; see also chapter 6. For a thought-provoking treatment of *Emily Montague* as one of three novels which combine sensibility and a transatlantic plot to valorize the concerns of "an underfunded intellectual upperclass (with intellectual status serving as a figure for class status and vice versa) distanced both from commercial speculation in England and from manual labor on the frontier" (p. 304), see Julie Ellison, "There and Back: Transatlantic Novels and Anglo-American Careers," in Carla H. Hay and Syndy M. Conger (eds.), *The Past as Prologue: Essays to Celebrate the Twenty-Fifth Anniversary of ASECS* (New York: AMS, 1995), pp. 303–24.
59 The novel's financially happy ending, enabled by the reappearance of Emily's long-lost and wealthy nabob father, Colonel Willmott, at first glance compromises the couple's insistence that they value domestic happiness over wealth and luxurious show. However, Willmott's infusion of capital is carefully prepared by prior expressions of limited, unselfish dissatisfaction on Rivers's part – for example, he "should wish for a very small addition only to my income, and that for the sake of others, not myself" (p. 350). When wealth comes, Rivers insists that nothing much will change; reinforcing the link of pastoralism with nonacquisitiveness, he explains, "I would not leave my native Dryads for an imperial palace: I have, however, agreed to let him build a wing to Bellfield, which it wants, to compleat the original plan, and to furnish it in whatever manner he thinks fit" (p. 407).
60 It is perhaps significant that the Brookes found their closest allies in the English merchants of Quebec, rather than in the military authorities.
61 BL Add. Ms. 29747 ff. 68.
62 Frances Brooke, *The Elements of the History of England, From the Invasion of the Romans to the Reign of George the Second. Translated from the French of Abbé Milot* (London: Dodsley, 1771), p. v.
63 The substance of Brooke's notes is frequently a quotation (with attribution) from another historian, particularly Hume.

64 Backscheider and Cotton hint at Garrick's possible behind-the-scenes obstruction (Introduction to *The Excursion*, p. xxxi). Other fresh sources of rancour on both sides included not only his refusal to stage various plays of hers, but also conflicting performance dates, the need to share various actresses' time, and more trivial matters such as the retrieval of borrowed books.

65 See Backscheider and Cotton, Introduction to *The Excursion*, p. xxviii.

66 Even Lord Melvile, the unworthy object of the heroine Maria Villiers's affections, when faced with his French mistress sitting in the seat formerly occupied by "his noble, his amiable, mother," experiences a sequence of affective responses: "He ate little, he was gloomy, he was silent; the sprightly sallies of Dorignon missed of their usual effect. He looked up, the picture of Lady Claremont met his eyes: the blood rushed to his heart, a tear of remorse started; he fancied he saw the picture glow with indignation; he rose from table, pretended illness, and retired" (p. 61). Since the novel generally begins a new paragraph with every sentence, paragraphing has been removed from quotations.

67 The second edition of *The Excursion*, published in 1785, reduces slightly the length and harshness of the Garrick episode and inserts a footnote praising "the various excellencies of his performance," but it nevertheless reiterates its disapproval of "his illiberal maxims of government" and "the errors of his management" (p. 85 n).

68 *Town and Country Magazine*, feeling the smart of this allusion to its "Tete-à-tete" scandal features (while claiming the attack was a "pointless arrow"), accused Brooke of hypocritically performing the same sort of literary assassination on Garrick: ". . . Mrs. Brook forgets that she seriously declares her characters are not imaginary, but in real life; if so, her book is the most scandalous chronicle we ever met with" (9 [August 1777], p. 434). *The Critical Review*, consistently sympathetic to Brooke, defended her portrait of the manager as truth rather than libel: "The dialogue on this occasion gives us a humorous representation of the illiberal maxims of government, adopted by his theatrical majesty, and a striking idea of those humiliations, those mortifying repulses, to which genius has been often obliged to submit" (*CR* 44 [July 1777], p. 63).

69 Burghley's current resident was Lady Elizabeth Cecil, Brooke's friend and the dedicatee of her first book (see *Excursion*, pp. 168–69 n5).

70 Brooke, *The Siege of Sinope: A Tragedy* (London: Cadell, 1781), p. iii. References to the play are by act number.

71 Guest, for example, has noted the representation of the American war in women's writing of the early 1780s as a violent rupture of family ties (*Small Change*, chapter 10, especially p. 266).

72 *European Magazine* 15 (February 1789), 100. As this description notes, the appeal of William Shields's musical setting was a major factor in the opera's lasting success.

73 Frances Brooke, *Rosina* (London: Cadell, 1783), Act 2. References to the opera are by act number.

74 See Edith Sedgwick Larson, "A Measure of Power: The Personal Charity of Elizabeth Montagu," *Studies in Eighteenth-Century Culture* 16 (1986), pp. 197–210.

75 I am not including here the 1791 posthumous publication by Brooke's son of *The History of Sir Charles Mandeville*, sequel to *Lady Julia Mandeville*. Critics are divided as to the authenticity of this attribution, and even if the work is Brooke's, there is no evidence that she wished to have it published, at least in its existing form.

76 Frances Brooke, *Marian* (London: Strahan, 1800), Act 2, Act 1.

77 Quoted in McMullen, *An Odd Attempt*, pp. 204–5.

78 It also represents a shift from Brooke's much more tentative and ambiguous suggestion, in the preface to her translation of Nicolas Framery's *Memoirs of the Marquis de St. Forlaix*, that "perhaps, but this idea is offered with diffidence, woman alone can paint with perfect exactness the sentiments of woman" (2 vols. [London, 1770], vol. I, p. xi).

SARAH SCOTT, HISTORIAN, IN THE REPUBLIC OF LETTERS

1 Henry St. John, Viscount Bolingbroke, *Letters on the Study and Use of History* (London: Millar, 1752), p. 28.

2 Elizabeth Montagu to Sarah Scott, [August] 29, [1759], The Huntington Library, Montagu Collection mo5777. All Montagu-Scott letters are from this collection unless otherwise indicated. I have used the library's dating of the letters in the collection; square brackets indicate tentative dates or portions thereof.

3 Scott to Montagu, December 10, [1790], mo5469.

4 See my Introduction. In an argument that is suggestive here, Margaret J. M. Ezell's *Social Authorship and the Advent of Print* (Baltimore: Johns Hopkins University Press, 1999) claims that alternate models of authorship to that privileged by a print marketplace continued to offer advantages to some writers, such as women writers and those living outside London, well into the eighteenth century.

5 See Betty Rizzo's *Companions without Vows: Relationships among Eighteenth-Century British Women* (Athens: University of Georgia Press, 1994), pp. 37–40, and chapter 13, for Scott's involvement in what she calls "the Bath community of women" and "the Hitcham experiment."

6 *The History of Gustavus Ericson, King of Sweden. With An Introductory History of Sweden, from the Middle of the Twelfth Century* (London: Millar, 1761); *The History of Mecklenburgh, from the First Settlement of the Vandals in that Country, to the Present Time; Including a Period of about Three Thousand Years*, 2nd ed. (London: Newbery, 1762); *The Life of Theodore Agrippa D'Aubigné, containing A Succinct Account of the Most Remarkable Occurrences during the Civil Wars of France in the Reigns of Charles IX. Henry III. Henry IV. and in the Minority of Lewis XIII.* (London:

Dilly, 1772). Further references to these texts will be indicated in parentheses.

Since Donald A. Stauffer's inclusion of *Gustavus Ericson* and *The Life of Theodore Agrippa D'Aubigné* in his comprehensive overview of *The Art of Biography in Eighteenth Century England* (Princeton: Princeton University Press, 1941 [facs. rpt. Ann Arbor, MI: University Microfilms, 1967]), important exceptions to this critical silence have included Gary Kelly's brief but suggestive discussion of the histories in his introduction to *A Description of Millenium Hall* (Peterborough, ON: Broadview, 1995), pp. 22–25, and Alessa Johns's linking of Scott's historiography with her "partial" utopian vision in "21st-Century Feminism and the Lure of an Enlightenment Utopian Paradigm," read at the Society for Utopian Studies conference in Vancouver, Canada, October 2000.

7 Scott to Montagu, [April 1763], mo5301; [January] 1754, mo5238.

8 Kelly, Introduction to *Millenium Hall*, p. 18.

9 Elizabeth Heckendorn Cook, "Going Public: The Letter and the Contract in 'Fanni Butlerd,'" *Epistolary Bodies: Gender and Genre in the Eighteenth-Century Republic of Letters* (Stanford, CA: Stanford University Press, 1996).

10 Wilson, "Citizenship, Empire, and Modernity," p. 76. In this view Wilson significantly qualifies the now-familiar claims of Jürgen Habermas, with respect to the eighteenth-century English literary public sphere (*Structural Transformation*, p. 56), and of Benedict Anderson, with respect to the "imagined community" of the print public sphere (*Imagined Communities: Reflections on the Origin and Spread of Nationalism*, rev. ed. [London: Verso, 1991], pp. 34–35).

11 See Rizzo's discussion of "the Bath Community," noted above, and Elizabeth Child, "'To Sing the Town': Women, Place, and Print Culture in Eighteenth-Century Bath," *Studies in Eighteenth-Century Culture* 28 (1999), pp. 155–72.

12 Kelly, Introduction to *Millenium Hall*, pp. 17, 15.

13 See Foucault, "What Is an Author?" pp. 113–38.

14 Mark Salber Phillips, *Society and Sentiment: Genres of Historical Writing in Britain, 1740–1820* (Princeton: Princeton University Press, 2000), p. 24.

15 D. R. Woolf, "A Feminine Past? Gender, Genre, and Historical Knowledge in England, 1500–1800," *American Historical Review* 102 (1997), pp. 645–56. Kathryn Temple makes a similar argument specific to Hume as a historian who "draws on both generic traditions [i.e. both history and romance or the 'secret history'], carving out a space for a history of the nation precisely by distinguishing it from what he defines as a disruptive counternational 'romance' – a form associated since the late seventeenth century with both a generalized femininity and a specific female readership"; see "'Manly Composition': Hume and the History of England," in Anne Jaap Jacobson (ed.), *Feminist Interpretations of David Hume* (University Park: Pennsylvania State University Press, 2000), p. 265.

16 In fact, I suspect that this elitist and traditional Bolingbroke is somewhat of a red herring where Scott is concerned; her preface to *Sir George Ellison*, cited below, indicates that she was more sympathetic to his emphasis on reading history that was directly useful to one's own social, political, and professional duties, exemplifying the universal causes and effects of human action through a focus on epochs and subjects relevant to the reader's national, professional, and social position. Compare Devoney Looser's discussion of the influence of ideas like Bolingbroke's and Voltaire's on Charlotte Lennox in *British Women Writers and the Writing of History, 1670–1820* (Baltimore: Johns Hopkins University Press, 2000), pp. 105, 113–17.

17 Scott to Montagu, May 21 [1758], mo5275. The specific reference here is likely to the *Works*, which were newly published, but the *Letters* formed a part of the collected works, and Scott's comments on Bolingbroke are consistently positive.

18 Bate and Strauss (eds.), *Rambler* 60, vol. III, pp. 318–23.

19 Phillips, *Society and Sentiment*, pp. xii, 10, 16–17.

20 Woolf, "A Feminist Past?" pp. 656–76; Looser, *British Women Writers*, pp. 16–21; Phillips, *Society and Sentiment*, pp. 60–62, 103–105. I find Phillips's notion of mid- to late eighteenth-century history as encompassing a broad range of genres and subject matters, as well as both analytical and sentimental styles, and inviting a combination of impartial and sympathetic reading more convincing than those arguments which have seen female historians as producing a "feminist" historiography unique in its blurring of genres, its attention to domestic subject matter, and its appeal to reader sensibility. For an example of the latter approach, see Greg Kucich, "'This Horrid Theatre of Human Sufferings': Gendering the Stages of History in Catharine Macaulay and Percy Bysshe Shelley," in Thomas Pfau and Robert F. Gleckner (eds.), *Lessons of Romanticism: A Critical Companion* (Durham: Duke University Press, 1998), pp. 448–65; Kucich sees in Macaulay a feminist historiography that I would argue is more accurately a feminized one, widespread in the second half of the eighteenth century.

21 David Hume, *Essays Moral, Political, and Literary* (Oxford: Oxford University Press, 1963), pp. 560–61, 558–59; Bolingbroke, *Letters*, pp. 151–55.

22 Phillips, *Society and Sentiment*, p. 44.

23 Stauffer, *Art of Biography*, p. 244. Stauffer later quotes extensively from Scott's preface to *Gustavus Ericson* as his example of the period's "impatience with the simple rationalizations [of motive] of courtly biographers and official historians" (pp. 339–40).

24 Scott to Montagu, April 29 [1767], mo5341. My account of Macaulay's career is indebted to Bridget Hill's *The Republican Virago: The Life and Times of Catharine Macaulay, Historian* (Oxford: Clarendon, 1992). Hill laments the fact of Macaulay's isolation as a woman writer: "There were no other English female historians in her field – or indeed outside it – with whom she could discuss history" (p. 131). It is intriguing to speculate whether Macaulay was aware of Scott's publications and to what extent the

visit was based on this knowledge; the latter's status as author of *Millenium Hall* was earlier known informally to "many" in her social sphere (Scott to Montagu, [November 1762], mo5299). At any rate, Scott's comments indicate a determination to avoid a relationship based on mutual authorship, and she participated, in the aftermath of Macaulay's second marriage (1778), in the severe condemnation of it (see my final chapter).

25 The eight volumes of Macaulay's *History of England from the Accession of James I to that of the Brunswick Line* were published between 1763 and 1783.

26 Scott to Montagu, November 30 [1763], mo5307.

27 *Horace Walpole's Correspondence*, 39 vols., ed. W. S. Lewis and A. Dayle Wallace (New Haven: Yale University Press, 1965), vol. XXIII, p. 92.

28 *Letters from Mrs. Elizabeth Carter to Mrs. Montagu*, 3 vols., ed. Montagu Pennington (London, 1817), vol. III, pp. 98–99.

29 Hill's biography traces Macaulay's very public persona in detail, and Kucich comments on the "theatricality of Macaulay's gender negotiation" (p. 452). These descriptions bear interesting parallels to Bonnie G. Smith's discussion, in *The Gender of History: Men, Women, and Historical Practice* (Cambridge, MA: Harvard University Press, 1998), of Germaine de Staël's historical writing as "staged and embodied" (p. 32), and thereby representative of history writing in a preprofessional age. According to Smith's model, Scott would seem to represent a precocious and unfeminine allegiance to the ideal of history-writing as scholarly, rational, and professionalized in the modern age of the book (pp. 23, 30).

30 Woolf, "A Feminine Past?," p. 647.

31 This comparative judgment must be qualified, though, by a recognition of its rhetorical context and function: the sisters engage in a kind of oppositional self-characterization which is to some extent part of the collaborative compositional process of their correspondence – thus Elizabeth will write self-deprecatingly that she is in London reading the "mushrooms of the day" while Sarah in Bath reads the first volume of Hume's history; see *The Letters of Mrs. Elizabeth Montagu*, 4 vols., ed. Matthew Montagu [London, 1813], vol. III, p. 291.

32 Scott to Montagu, [January 1755], mo5248.

33 See Elizabeth's "Is it not strange that our Historians shd have been ignorant of this circumstance?" (December 8 [1788], mo6177), and Sarah's reply, "The wonderful delicacy of Historians concerning Henry ye 6th always appear'd to me strange, for when I first read the English History it seem'd to me evident what was the Nature of his malady, which the insanity of his Mothers Father Charles ye 6th of France render'd the more credible" (December 13 [1788], mo5454).

34 Montagu to Scott, [1756], mo5764, and Scott to Montagu, September 2 [1756], mo5264.

35 Montagu to Scott, November 15 1790, mo6207; Scott to Montagu, November 10 [1790], mo5468.

36 Montagu to Scott, [August] 29 [1759], mo5777.

37 See especially Scott's letter to Montagu in [January] 1754 revealing the "secret" of having translated *La laideur aimable* and her plan to look out for further writing projects (mo5238).

38 Scott to Montagu, [January 31 1763], mo5300, my italics. The "Geography" referred to in this letter was apparently never published.

39 These included Voltaire's *History of Charles XII. King of Sweden* and Walter Hartes's 1759 "polished and weighty military life" of Gustavus Adolphus, Ericson's grandson (the phrase is Stauffer's, in *Art of Biography*, p. 7), but especially Vertôt's *History of the Revolution in Sweden*, the story of Sweden's Protestant revolution under Gustavus Ericson, first published in an English-language translation in 1696, republished frequently in the early decades of the eighteenth century, and reappearing again in Glasgow in 1750 and 1761 (numerous French editions were also published in Britain). The translator's preface to the "fifth edition" of this latter work shows its appeal to be at least partly in perceived parallels with English Protestantism's defeat of Jacobite threats; see *The History of the Revolution in Sweden, Occasion'd by The Change of Religion, and Alteration of the Government, in that Kingdom. Written Originally in French, By the Abbot Vertot* . . . . now done into English, By J. Mitchel, M. F. (London, 1723) – the *ESTC* dates this edition 1721). It is this edition that I cite below.

40 See Betty Rizzo, Introduction to *The History of Sir George Ellison* (Lexington: University Press of Kentucky, 1996), for an overview of this publishing chronology.

41 Scott to Montagu, October 10 [1769], mo5363.

42 The *Critical*'s reviewer Tobias Smollett found this history a valuable contribution: "This part of the work will, we imagine, prove especially grateful to the English reader; even the learned are forced to have recourse, for the annals of the northern kingdoms, to writers who have studied only to be minute, and whose greatest merit, perhaps, is their redundancy" (*CR* 10 [November 1760], p. 363).

43 Phillips, *Society and Sentiment*, p. 140.

44 Kelly has discussed the pacific strain in both *Gustavus Ericson* and *The History of Mecklenburgh*, but he interprets it as part of a feminizing rationale adopted by some women writers of Scott's time to justify their authorship (pp. 23–24).

45 In placing *Sir George Ellison* within this biographical continuum, I see it to be as much a fictional and anglicized precursor to the *Life of D'Aubigné* as a sequel to *Millenium Hall*; Rizzo also suggests that *D'Aubigné*'s "exemplary Huguenot life" can be read as "that of a Sir George Ellison with a political and religious cause" (Introduction to *Sir George Ellison*, p. xxix).

46 Scott's relative reliance on individualized and private motives and responses in structuring her narrative is illustrated by the following parallel passages from Scott and the 1721 translation of Vertôt, describing the rule of the early fifteenth-century King Eric:

> Queen Margaret's death proved very unfortunate to Eric. Equally ambitious of arbitrary power, but destitute of the authority, which her prudence and wisdome had given her, his subjects were no longer awed by a prince, who, though dreadful for his brutality, was despicable in his understanding. He fixed his residence entirely in Denmark, and sent Danish governors into Sweden, who plundered and oppressed the people, more like the cruel conquerors of a vanquished nation, than rulers over obedient subjects. Queen Margaret had left him engaged in a war with the duke of Holstein, for the duchy of Sleswick; and the Hans Towns having joined with the duke, all trade ceased in Sweden; so that while the king was robbing them of the possessions they enjoyed, he deprived them of the means of acquiring others. Eric succeeded so ill in this war, that the Germans attacked Copenhagen, and he saw no resource but flying for refuge into a monastery; when his queen Philippa, who was endowed with a more masculine courage, as well as a more engaging manner, encouraged the inhabitants so successfully, that they all took up arms, and repelled the enemy. But afterwards forming an enterprize by sea, which failed in the execution, the king was so enraged, that he beat her very severely. This insult, added to his long ill-treatment, induced her to retire into a convent at Wadstena, where she died soon after (Scott, pp. 82–84, paragraph breaks omitted).

> After her [Margaret's] Death, King *Eric* succeeded in the Three Kingdoms, but did neither inherit her Power nor her Prudence: He retir'd to *Denmark*, and sent Governors to *Sweden*, who treated the People of that Kingdome, rather as *disarm'd Enemies*, than as *free Subjects*. The Nation was overloaded with Taxes, and fill'd with Soldiers, who domineer'd over the wretched Inhabitants, and not only robb'd and plunder'd them without Controul, but added Scorn and Insolancy to their Avarice and Barbarity. The Officers conniv'd at these Disorders, and rather encourag'd than check'd the Offenders. From whence it may reasonably be concluded, that either they receiv'd a Share of the Booty, or had secret Orders to tolerate these Abuses. The Complaints of the Oppress'd did not reach the Ears of the Prince, or were rejected with Disdain; nor could they hope to see an End, or so much as an Alleviation of their Misery, without an entire Alteration of the Government. And therefore they resolved in so desperate a Case, to have Recourse to the most violent Remedies, and to free themselves from a Power that seem'd unjust at its first Establishment, and was now become tyrannical and insupportable (Vertôt translation, pp. 19–20).

47 *CR* 10 (November 1760), pp. 372–73, 373; *CR* 13 (April 1762), pp. 312–19; *CR* 33 (June 1772), p. 477.

48 *CR* 33 (June 1772), p. 477.

49 Laura L. Runge, *Gender and Language in British Literary Criticism, 1660–1790* (Cambridge: Cambridge University Press, 1997), pp. 28–30.

50 *MR* 24 (January 1761), pp. 55, 67.

51 *CR* 13 (April 1762), pp. 319, 316. Hill discusses the comparable case of the *Monthly Review*'s criticism of Macaulay for discussing the infidelity of Charles I, while praising the "delicacy becoming her sex" in her allusion to James I's sexual preferences (*Republican Virago*, pp. 136–37).

52 See, for example, Vincent Carretta, "Utopia Limited: Sarah Scott's *Millenium Hall* and *The History of Sir George Ellison*," *The Age of Johnson* 5 (1992), pp. 303–25, and Nanette Morton, "'A Most Sensible Oeconomy': From Spectacle to Surveillance in Sarah Scott's *Millenium Hall*," *Eighteenth-Century Fiction* 11 (1999), pp. 185–204.

53 Judith Dorn, "Reading Women Reading History: The Philosophy of Periodical Form in Charlotte Lennox's *The Lady's Museum*," *Historical Reflections/Réflexions Historiques* 18.3 (1992), pp. 26–27.

54 Guest, *Small Change*, p. 116.

55 Wilson, "Citizenship, Empire, and Modernity," p. 74; my italics.

56 Scott to Montagu, [September 12 1774], mo5374.

57 Hill, *Republican Virago*, p. 132.

58 *CR* 21 (April 1766), p. 288.

59 James Boswell, *Boswell for the Defence, 1769–1774*, ed. William K. Wimsatt, Jr., and Frederick A. Pottle (Melbourne, London, Toronto: William Heinemann [Yale University Press], 1960), p. 132. I am grateful to Barbara Brandon Schnorrenburg for this reference, and for allowing me to consult her unpublished essay "Who Was George Lewis Scott?"

60 *Gentleman's Magazine* 44 [August 1774], p. 376.

61 Clara Reeve, *The Progress of Romance through Times, Countries, and Manners*, 2 vols. (Colchester and London, 1785; facs. rpt. Garland, 1970), vol. II, pp. 34, 39. See chapter 7 for a fuller discussion of this text's portrayal of women writers.

THE (FEMALE) LITERARY CAREERS OF SARAH FIELDING AND CHARLOTTE LENNOX

1 Lady Mary Wortley Montagu, *The Complete Letters of Lady Mary Wortley Montagu*, 3 vols., ed. Robert Halsband (Oxford: Clarendon, 1967), vol. III, pp. 66–67.

2 Scott to Montagu, [June 20?, 1760], mo5281.

3 Christensen, *Practicing Enlightenment*, 7–11, 18, 11, 25; Donoghue, *The Fame Machine*, pp. 3–4.

4 Donoghue, *The Fame Machine*, 161.

5 Lennox to the Duchess of Newcastle, quoted in Small, *Charlotte Ramsay Lennox*, p. 28. I discuss this statement further below. Small is Lennox's principal biographer, and biographical details in this chapter are primarily based on her work, supplemented and corrected by that of Philippe Séjourné, *The Mystery of Charlotte Lennox, First Novelist of Colonial America (1727–1804)*, (Aix-en-Provence: Publications des Annales de la Faculté des Lettres [Éditions Ophrys], 1967). Where I quote from Lennox manuscript correspondence included in Small, I cite by page numbers in Small only.

6 For example, Linda Bree notes that Fielding's earnings of £110 for *David Simple* and even 60 guineas for *The Countess of Dellwyn* exceeded Scott's mere 30 guineas for *Millenium Hall* in 1762, despite the latter writer's being established as "an experienced novelist, historian, and translator" (*Sarah Fielding* [New York: Twayne, 1996], p. 25).

7 Sabor (ed.), *David Simple*, p. 345. Both Sarah Fielding's "Advertisement" and Henry's "Preface" are now also available in Sarah Fielding, *The Adventures of David Simple* and *The Adventures of David Simple, Volume the Last*, ed. Linda Bree (London: Penguin, 2002).

8 Donoghue, *The Fame Machine*, p. 163; Robert S. Hunting, "Fielding's Revisions of *David Simple*," *Boston University Studies in English* 3 (1957), p.121. For an illuminating reading of Sarah's "Advertisement" as every bit "as much assertion as apology," see Bree, *Sarah Fielding*, p. 9.

9 Gallagher, *Nobody's Story*, pp. 200, 195, 202. Part of the problem here, I suspect, is that Gallagher relies on Duncan Isles's 1970 designation of Lennox as "a relatively obscure person," (p. 201) a designation that is inaccurate for Lennox's reputation in the mid-eighteenth century.

10 Gallagher herself notes the "diffuseness of authorship in the period" (ibid., p. 202).

11 A second generally accepted contribution is the fictional autobiography of Anne Boleyn, included in the *Journey from this World to the Next*, part of Henry's 1743 *Miscellanies.*

12 Janine Barchas, "Sarah Fielding's Dashing Style and Eighteenth-Century Print Culture," *ELH* 63 (1996), pp. 646–49.

13 See, for example, *Felicia to Charlotte*, Frances Sheridan's 1767 continuation of *Miss Sidney Bidulph*, and Sarah Scott's *Sir George Ellison* as sequel to *Millenium Hall.*

14 Sarah Fielding, *The Lives of Cleopatra and Octavia*, ed. Christopher D. Johnson (Lewisburg: Bucknell University Press, 1994), p. 54. See also Johnson's introduction, pp. 20–24, for an account of Fielding's use of sources.

15 Recently it has become known that Fielding published at least one, and possibly more, anonymous pamphlets in the early 1750s, and it is very possible that she also attempted a stage play in the spring of 1754; see Donald Burrows and Rosemary Dunhill, *Music and Theatre in Handel's World: The Family Papers of James Harris 1732–80* (Oxford: Oxford University Press, 2002), p. 267, and Battestin and Probyn (eds.), *Correspondence of Henry and Sarah Fielding*, pp. 126–28.

16 Lady Mary Wortley Montagu, for example, finds Fielding's neologisms in *The Cry* "intolerable" (Halsband [ed.], *Letters of Lady Mary Wortley Montagu*, vol. III, p. 88), and it is presumably this feature, as well as the structuring of narrative according to moral system, that leads Catherine Talbot to complain about Fielding's tendency to "refinement *a perte de vue*" (Pennington [ed.], *Letters between Mrs. Elizabeth Carter and Miss Catherine Talbot*, vol. II, p. 131). Bree has discussed the significance and boundaries of

The Cry's neologisms (*Sarah Fielding*, pp. 102–3), and one of the earliest feminist recoveries of Fielding was a 1973 unpublished dissertation by Ann Marilyn Parrish focusing on her generic innovations ("Eight Experiments in Fiction: A Critical Analysis of the Works of Sarah Fielding" [Boston: Boston University Graduate School]).

17 Battestin and Probyn (eds.), *Correspondence of Henry and Sarah Fielding*, p. xxvii.

18 Lady Mary attributed *An Essay on the Art of Ingeniously Tormenting* (by Jane Collier), *The Female Quixote*, and *Sir Charles Goodville and His Family* (author unidentified) to Sarah Fielding (Halsband [ed.], *Letters of Lady Mary Wortley Montagu*, vol. III, p. 67). Henry Fielding complained, of course, that *David Simple* was falsely attributed to him, thereby inciting him to write the preface to the second edition in order to clear his name.

19 G. E. Bentley, Jr., "Copyright Documents in the George Robinson Archive: William Godwin and Others 1713–1820," *Studies in Bibliography* 35 (1982), pp. 73–76.

20 Battestin and Probyn (eds.), *Correspondence of Henry and Sarah Fielding*, pp. 148–49. Fielding negotiated 60 guineas for *The Countess of Dellwyn*, with 40 guineas more if the novel went into a second edition. I am not suggesting by these marks of achievement that Fielding's writing produced a comfortable income; Bree has concluded, after careful analysis of her career earnings, that Fielding might have netted £1,200 in nearly twenty years – a sum, Bree notes, which would have produced the £60 per annum in investment income that Elizabeth Montagu thought Fielding needed to make her comfortable in addition to her meager resources from inheritances and irregular payments from family members, had she been free enough financially to invest these earnings ("'No Situation so Deplorable': Sarah Fielding, Fiction, and Female Employment," p. 7). I am grateful to Linda Bree for allowing me to read this paper in manuscript.

21 Bree, *Sarah Fielding*, p. 56; Sabor (ed.), Introduction to *David Simple*, p. xxxiii n17.

22 *MR* 39 (July 1757), p. 39; Sabor, Introduction to *David Simple*, p. xxiii; Battestin and Probyn (eds.), *Correspondence of Henry and Sarah Fielding*, p. 175. *The Lives of Cleopatra and Octavia* is the first work upon which Fielding's name appears, in the form of "S. Fielding," as signature to the dedication.

23 The former term is Betty Rizzo's, in *Companions without Vows*, where she describes Fielding as "the theorist" of a group of Bath women attempting to model a conservative socialist community (p. 307); the latter aspersion is made by Elizabeth Montagu in a 1766 letter to Elizabeth Carter: "So you went to dine with Mrs. Fielding, a very pretty fancy! you might as well have dined with Duke Humphrey. Did she luxuriously feast you with a chapter of Epictetus? I hope her maid Sarah considered the grosser appetite of hunger, or you might come ill off, for I dare say poor Fielding never thinks of dinner till it is time to eat it" (*Mrs. Montagu, "Queen of the Blues": Her Letters and*

Friendships from 1762 to 1800, 2 vols., ed. Reginald Blunt [Boston: Houghton Mifflin, n.d.], vol. II, p. 144).

24 Battestin and Probyn (eds.), *Correspondence of Henry and Sarah Fielding*, p. 153.

25 Turner, *Living by the Pen*, p. 134; Mary Scott, *The Female Advocate: A Poem.* 1774. Rpt. with Introduction by Gae Hollady (Augustan Reprint Society, Los Angeles: William Andrews Clark Memorial Library, 1984), lines 257–58, 271–78; Hester Lynch Thrale Piozzi, *Thraliana: The Diary of Mrs. Hester Lynch Thrale (Later Mrs. Piozzi), 1776–1809*, 2nd ed., 2 vols., ed. Katherine C. Balderston (Oxford: Clarendon, 1951), vol. I, pp. 328–29; Reeve, *Progress of Romance*, vol. I, pp. 142–43; vol. II, pp. 6–7.

26 *MR* 14 (June 1756), p. 561.

27 See Small, *Charlotte Ramsay Lennox*, pp. 56–7; James Raven and Antonia Forster identify this novel as having been written by Elizabeth and Jane Purbeck (*The English Novel 1770–1829*, Volume I, 1797, pp. 726–27).

28 Small, *Charlotte Ramsay Lennox*, pp. 85–88.

29 Isles quotes this phrase from the unpublished letter, dated February 3, 1752, noting that it suggests Lennox's shift to translation was her choice, rather than an imposition of the booksellers ("Lennox Collection," 19, pp. 433, 435).

30 *CR* 9 (February 1760), pp. 116–17. For a discussion of the *Brumoy* project, see James Gray, "Dr. Johnson, Charlotte Lennox, and the Englishing of Father Brumoy," *Modern Philology* 83 (1985), pp. 142–50.

31 Isles (ed.), "Lennox Collection," 19, p. 41; George Harding in a letter to an unidentified friend, quoted in John Bowyer Nichols, *Illustrations of the Literary History of the Eighteenth Century*, 8 vols. (London: Nichols, 1817–58), vol. III, p. 19n. Laura Runge argues for the significance of both Lennox and Fielding as critics (*Gender and Language*, pp. 137–55).

32 Small, *Charlotte Ramsay Lennox*, pp. 15–17.

33 Scott, with respect to the low price she obtained for her *Millenium Hall* copy, and Fielding, in the case of the botched plan to publish her and Harris's essay on Henry Fielding as a preface to the posthumous edition of the latter's works.

34 See correspondence with Johnson and Richardson in Isles (ed.), "Lennox Collection," 18, pp. 334–42; 19, pp. 432–33.

35 Quoted in Small, *Charlotte Ramsay Lennox*, p. 50; see also "Lennox Collection," 19, pp. 177–78 for a Johnson letter apparently related to this affair.

36 Isles (ed.), "Lennox Collection," 18, p. 341; 19, pp. 45–46; quoted in Small, *Charlotte Ramsay Lennox*, p. 53, and dated by her as soon after the 1775 proposals for the edition. This particular negotiation appears to have fallen through, and the edition in question never appeared.

37 The young Charlotte Ramsay's marriage in 1747 to Alexander Lennox, who apparently proved financially unsuccessful and personally incompatible with her, and from whom she ultimately separated, deserves special mention here.

Despite the undoubtedly negative effect of her marriage on Charlotte's ultimate happiness and financial status, Lennox appears also at key points to have been useful to her, as this chapter indicates. There is no evidence that Lennox ever tried to cheat his wife out of the proceeds of her writing when they lived apart, though he appears not to have supported her either. At any rate, as Cheryl Turner points out, whatever might happen to the profits of women's publications, which might legally be claimed by an estranged husband, for example, literary property in its intellectual or artistic sense was "treated by publishers, the public, and by the authors as their own, to dispose of as profitably as they could and to acknowledge if they chose" (*Living by the Pen*, p. 100). Thus we never find Alexander Lennox credited in any way with his wife's achievements; that credit has much more likely been awarded to Samuel Johnson, especially in the case of the penultimate chapter of *The Female Quixote.*

38 Griffin, *Literary Patronage*, pp. 206–7.

39 I am deliberately avoiding here the suggestion that Lennox's apparent irascibility (and, perhaps, social awkwardness) is one explanation for her particular career pattern, especially her failure in subscription appeals. While I do not wish to discount the role of behavioral traits, they are not helpful to this comparison, since Fielding also is described in private correspondence as a loner and an impractical and rather cheerless companion.

40 Bree suggests that Fielding resided in Bath from 1739 to the early 1740s, and perhaps made her first anonymous contributions to Henry's works from there. This plausible hypothesis does not change the fact that following this, a London base would have been useful to Fielding during the first years of her own publication projects, beginning with *David Simple* in 1744. Certainly Sarah was in London from late 1744 to 1753. Martin and Ruthe Battestin note the productivity of the Henry Fielding-Sarah Fielding-Samuel Richardson triangle of this period, "in which all three authors, jealously interacting, spurred each other on to their best work" (*Henry Fielding: A Life* [London: Routledge, 1989], p. 379). Hugh Amory, in "Virtual Readers: The Subscribers to Fielding's *Miscellanies*," *Studies in Bibliography* 48 (1995), pp. 94–112, has detailed a significant degree of overlap between the subscriber lists of the *Miscellanies* and the *Familiar Letters*, including forms of names and titles, which suggests the siblings were working together to procure subscriptions.

41 Quoted in Small, *Charlotte Ramsay Lennox*, pp. 27–28.

42 David S. Kaufer and Kathleen M. Carley, *Communication at a Distance: The Influence of Print on Sociological Organization and Change* (Hillsdale, NJ: Lawrence Erlbaum, 1993), pp. 253–96.

43 The correspondence reveals her, for example, setting Johnson and Richardson to work finding translation projects, begging Richardson to intervene with prospective publisher Millar in combating the prejudicial effects of a casual conversation about her manuscript of *The Female Quixote*, and asking Johnson to feature materials from the *Memoirs of Sully* in an

upcoming issue of the *Literary Magazine* he was editing; see Isles (ed.), "Lennox Collection," 18, pp. 342–44; 18, pp. 336–40; 19, pp. 50–52; 19, p. 46.

44 Quoted in Small, *Charlotte Ramsay Lennox*, pp. 25, 51–52.

45 Quoted in ibid., pp. 27–28.

46 I base the latter speculation on Séjourné's observation that Newcastle had the power of gubernatorial appointments to the colonies; if so, this may have been the only instance where Lennox's American sojourn served her socially in England. In most cases, Lennox's use of the traditional patronage system, rather than the modified subscription form of it, made her more vulnerable than Fielding to political shifts, such as that which removed Newcastle from power in 1762 (and for good in 1766, after a brief return), apparently making it difficult for her to obtain permission to dedicate her play *The Sister* (1769) to an unidentified "great personage" (James Murray to Lennox, February 8, 1769 and notes, "Lennox Collection," 19, pp. 57–61).

47 That the possibility of pursuing a publishing career from the provinces was a real one in mid-century forms a contrast to the difficult turn-of-the-century situation Margaret Ezell illustrates in her chapter on "Getting into Print: Literary Life outside London" (*Social Authorship*). Nevertheless, social authorship as Ezell describes it, with its foundation in manuscript exchange and social networks, still strongly flavors authorial experience in the provinces, as my discussion of Fielding in Bath illustrates.

48 On the "urban renaissance," see Peter Borsay, *The English Urban Renaissance: Culture and Society in the Provincial Town, 1660–1770* (Oxford: Clarendon, 1989). Elizabeth Child's insights into the professionalizing opportunities provided by towns such as Bath in "'To Sing the Town'" have influenced my thinking in this chapter, although I see Fielding's particular use of her Bath location as somewhat more dependent on a traditional pattern of friendship networks than does Child. For this reason I find John Brewer's treatment of culture in the English provinces in "Part 6: Province and Nation" of *The Pleasures of the Imagination: English Culture in the Eighteenth Century* (Chicago: University of Chicago Press, 1997), emphasizing its conservative, traditional, amateur, and egalitarian flavor, a helpful corrective.

49 Child, "'To Sing the Town,'" pp. 163–65. Fielding's success in straddling this line is suggested by her enlisting the loyal support of James Harris, himself of a professional family whose social connections and wealth had enabled them to raise themselves to the landowning class, but who was clearly adverse to any association with booksellers and to publishing for profit himself; see Battestin and Probyn (eds.), *Correspondence of Henry and Sarah Fielding*, pp. 142–43, 156–57, 158–59, and also Probyn's biography of Harris, *The Sociable Humanist: The Life and Works of James Harris 1709–1780; Provincial and Metropolitan Culture in Eighteenth-century England* (Oxford: Clarendon, 1991). It is suggestive to note, in the light of this chapter's comparison of Fielding's and Lennox's careers, that Probyn

juxtaposes the two women's arguably most important intellectual mentors as follows: "Harris and Johnson were frequently in each other's company, but in some important ways each inhabited competing, and eventually divergent, intellectual worlds. The former has been placed, if at all, in the vanguard of cultural resistance to the new, the latter, indisputably, is seen as one of the great makers of his age's character" (p. 4).

50 Esther Lewis's "A Letter to a Lady in London," excerpted in Roger Lonsdale (ed.), *Eighteenth-Century Women Poets* (Oxford: Oxford University Press, 1989), pp. 233–34, is addressed to Sarah Fielding and celebrates their mutual enjoyment of conversation and snuff-taking.

51 Lefanu, *Memoirs*, pp. 95–96.

52 See, for example, Montagu to Scott, November 1, 1765, mo5832; [August?] 17, 1767, mo5856. Allen left Fielding £100, but Montagu believed he should rather have continued the annuity.

53 See, for example, Fielding's thanks to Samuel Richardson for "the Ten books I so kindly received through your hands I did not know how to word it be so Kind to put it in for me, and put Hon[ble] to M[rs] Spencer if it is right," with reference to *The Lives of Cleopatra and Octavia* (Battestin and Probyn [eds.], *Correspondence of Henry and Sarah Fielding*, p. 136) and to James Harris for his success and prospects in obtaining prestigious subscribers for the Xenophon project, quoted below.

54 Sabor (ed.), Introduction to *David Simple*, p. xviii.

55 Barbauld (ed.), *Correspondence of Richardson*, vol. VI, p. 102; Montagu enthusiastically promoted subscriptions for Fielding's *The Lives of Cleopatra and Octavia* while privately mocking the possibility of "a virtuous maiden who has lived in single blessedness . . . guess[ing] at all the arts of a Wanton Cleopatra" and admitting that "the whole is better than I expected" (Montagu to Scott, [1757], mo5765).

56 Alexander Lennox is thought to have been his wife's original point of contact with such key figures as William Strahan, Samuel Johnson, and Guiseppe Baretti (who taught her Italian).

57 In 1752, with proposals for a new edition of her poems, in 1775 for her collected works, in 1793 for *Shakespear Illustrated*, and the hitherto-unidentified project referred to in her above-quoted 1759 note to Thomas Birch.

58 Isles (ed.), "Lennox Collection," 19, pp. 174–75.

59 Ibid., 19, p. 184; Battestin and Probyn (eds.), *Correspondence of Henry and Sarah Fielding*, p. 167.

60 Griffin makes a similar argument, noting that the 1775 proposals written by Johnson emphasize the author's economic motives, rather than using the traditional appeal to protection and approbation (*Literary Patronage*, p. 209).

61 Janssen, "The Empirical Study of Careers," pp. 323–57. The need for professional rituals is certainly demonstrated by the all-night celebration of *Harriot Stuart*'s publication, organized by Johnson and recorded by Sir John Hawkins in *The Life of Samuel Johnson, L.L.D.*, 2nd ed. (London, 1787; rpt. New York: Garland, 1974), pp. 285–87.

62 On January 8, 1749, Fielding sent Richardson a copy of the pamphlet, calling it "this daring attempt of mentioning Clarissa . . . Often have I reflected on my own vanity in daring but to touch the hem of her garment" (Battestin and Probyn [eds.], *Correspondence of Henry and Sarah Fielding*, p. 123). Sabor notes Richardson's later claim to a third party that he had not seen the pamphlet before its publication; see his Introduction to Sarah Fielding, *Remarks on "Clarissa," Addressed to the Author*, ed. Peter Sabor London: Robinson, 1749; rpt. Augustan Reprint Society 231–32, 1985), p. v. References are to this edition.

63 Keymer refers repeatedly to Sarah Fielding as one of the earliest insightful readers of the novel's process of active interpretation – implying, indeed, in contrast to various twentieth-century critics, that she is one of the most sophisticated Richardson readers of all time (*Richardson's "Clarissa,"* pp. 57, 67, 126, 194–95).

64 Marshall, "Writing Masters," pp. 132–33.

65 Italics in original. See also my discussion of this novel's conversational model of interpretation in *The Conversational Circle*, chapter 2.

66 Probyn, *The Sociable Humanist*, p. 82.

67 Perry, "Clarissa's Daughters," p. 122.

68 Bree, *Sarah Fielding*, p. 74.

69 Beasley, "*Clarissa*," pp. 81, 79. Bree also discusses elements of the *Remarks* which represent Fielding's "own gloss on the novel" (*Sarah Fielding*, pp. 74–76).

70 Michaelson, *Speaking Volumes*, pp. 155–56; for a fuller discussion of the model in relation to the elocutionary movement (in which Sheridan's husband Thomas was a leading figure) and to the contrasting model of the solitary woman reader, see Michaelson's entire chapter, entitled "Reading and Domesticity Among the Burneys and Other Families."

71 Barbauld (ed.), *Correspondence of Richardson*, vol. III, p. 246. In turning to examples from Richardson's correspondence with very young female admirers, however, we need to stop short of assuming that they represent his view of fellow professionals, as is the case in early arguments such as Spencer's, when she reads the same letter to Westcomb as a portrait of the ideal woman writer (*Rise of the Woman Novelist*), pp. 80–81. That Richardson did not communicate with writers such as Fielding, Lennox, and Sheridan in the same avuncular, condescending manner is made clear not only in his own letters, but also in the confidence expressed by Fielding in writing to Richardson: "You cannot imagine the pleasure Miss Collier and I enjoyed at the receipt of your kind epistles. We were at dinner with a *hic, haec, hoc* man, who said, well, I do wonder Mr. Richardson will be troubled with such *silly women*; on which we thought to ourselves (though we did not care to say it) if Mr. Richardson will bear us, and not think us impertinent in pursuing the pleasure of his correspondence, we don't care in how many languages you fancy you despise us"(Battestin and Probyn [eds.], *Correspondence of Henry and Sarah Fielding*, p. 123).

72 Langbauer, *Women and Romance*, pp. 83–89. See also Patricia Meyer Spacks's chapter on "The Subtle Sophistry of Desire: *The Female Quixote*," in *Desire and Truth: Functions of Plot in Eighteenth-Century English Novels* (Chicago: University of Chicago Press, 1990).

73 In this I agree with Gallagher's argument that Arabella is not being taught the lesson of distinguishing between the fictional (represented by romance as a fantasy of power) and the real as such (*Nobody's Story*, pp. 175–95). However, my argument in this chapter parts ways with Gallagher's generalization of Lennox's project as representative of that of the mid-century novel – i.e. the instruction of women in imaginative transformations of identity to prepare them for their social role in the transfer of property (*Nobody's Story*, pp. 193–95).

74 Charlotte Lennox, *The Female Quixote*, ed. Margaret Dalziel, with Introduction by Margaret Anne Doody, Chronology and Appendix by Duncan Isles (Oxford: Oxford University Press, 1989), pp. 252–53. References are to this edition.

75 Kate Levin, "'The Cure of Arabella's Mind': Charlotte Lennox and the Disciplining of the Female Reader," *Women's Writing* 2 (1995), p. 277; Wyett, "Reading Women," p. 58. Although Arabella embarrasses the Doctor into an apology for using terms that impolitely cast aspersions on her own "Judgment" and "Virtue," he apologizes only for the ill-judged warmth of his expression, not for his characterization of these "senseless Fictions" (p. 374).

76 Marshall, "Writing Masters," pp. 120–25; Levin, "'The Cure,'" p. 277. Levin has noted furthermore that Arabella's positive characterization throughout is very much based on the contemporary view of an ideal wife (p. 276).

77 Langbauer, *Women and Romance*, p. 66; Marshall, "Writing Masters," pp. 132–33; Langbauer, *Women and Romance*, p. 87; Levin, "'The Cure,'" p. 279.

78 Levin posits, indeed, that the motive resulted from a blurring of the professional and the personal, that Lennox needed in the *The Female Quixote* to correct an impression of personal impropriety created by her 1747 volume of poems, particularly "The Art of Coquetry," and by her 1750 *The Life of Harriot Stuart.* Thus the 1752 novel "represents Lennox's moral and literary about-face, her own as well as Arabella's imprisonment in morality" ("'The Cure,'" p. 275). While this may have been Lennox's motive as part of a strategy to broaden her reader support, it clearly did not overcome the more fundamental problem of a limited social network, strengthening her professional reputation without apparently improving her social standing.

79 Donoghue, *The Fame Machine*, p. 6.

HARMLESS MEDIOCRITY: EDWARD KIMBER AND THE MINIFIE SISTERS

1 Pennington (ed.), *Letters between Carter and Talbot*, vol. III, p. 93.

2 Reeve, *Progress of Romance*, vol. II, p. 46.

3 Susan Staves, "Women's Originality," paper read at the British Society for Eighteenth-Century Studies meeting, Oxford, January 2003. As the paper

title indicates, Staves suggests that innovation is one widely recognized criterion of value that might be used in making such judgments; my analysis of contemporary commentary confirms that this criterion was valued by mid-eighteenth-century reviewers as well as in our own time.

4 Antonia Forster, "'A considerable rank in the world of *Belles Lettres*': Women, Fiction, and Literary History in the Last Quarter of the Eighteenth Century," in Katherine Binhammer and Jeanne Wood (eds.), *Women and Literary History: "For There She Was"* (Newark: University of Delaware Press, 2003), p. 115. Forster's essay provides a useful background to the specific cases I discuss, since she analyzes the reviewers' responses to all novels known or thought to be written by women in the last three decades of the century.

5 Spencer, *Rise of the Female Novelist*, chapter 3.

6 In his prefatory memoir to his father's sermons, Edward describes Charles Ackers as Isaac's "main support" from the 1730s onward (*Sermons on the Most Interesting Religious, Moral, and Practical Subjects. By the late Reverend and Learned Mr. Isaac Kimber* [London: Ackers, 1756], p. xv). My biographical account is based on Sidney A. Kimber, "The 'Relation of a late Expedition to St. Augustine,' with Biographical and Bibliographical Notes on Isaac and Edward Kimber," *The Papers of the Bibliographical Society of America* 28.2 (1934), pp. 81–96, and Frank Gees Black, "Edward Kimber: Anonymous Novelist of the Mid-Eighteenth Century," *Harvard Studies and Notes in Philology and Literature* 17 (1935), pp. 27–42. In correlating the subscription list with the Kimbers' trade connections I have also consulted D. F. McKenzie and J. C. Ross's Introduction to their edition of *A Ledger of Charles Ackers, Printer of the "London Magazine"* (Oxford: Oxford University Press, 1968, for the Oxford Bibliographical Society), pp. 1–36.

7 Kevin J. Hayes, Introduction to *Itinerant Observations in America*, by Edward Kimber (Newark and London: University of Delaware Press, 1998), p. 19; Black, "Edward Kimber," p. 28; Richard Johnson, Preface to *The Baronetage of England*, 3 vols., by E. Kimber and R. Johnson (London, 1771), vol. III, p. viii.

8 *MR* 29 (August 1763), p. 160.

9 In this I follow Virginia Blain, Isobel Grundy, and Patricia Clements (eds.), *The Feminist Companion to Literature in English.* (New Haven: Yale University Press, 1990), pp. 469 and 744, though some sources attribute the 1768–1783 novels to Susannah rather than Margaret; the matter turns on the authorship of the 1768 *Barford Abbey*, after which two of the subsequent novels are presented as by the author of that work. I do not include the 1764 *Family Pictures* in my tally, though the British Library (followed by the *Feminist Companion*) attributes it to Susannah, because there is no link on the novel's title page or in its editor's preface to the sisters' debut novel, unlike their practice for their other novels, and in particular for the 1766 *The Picture*, which positively flaunts the connection

with their first work's success, and refers to this as their second effort. Furthermore, *Family Pictures* concerns generally middling characters – a schoolmaster-clergyman, an officer in the East-India Company, a country gentleman, and their families – unlike the penchant of the other novels for scenes of high life.

10 Pennington (ed.), *Letters between Carter and Talbot*, vol. III, pp. 93, 48–49, 183, 165–66.

11 Pennington (ed.), *Letters between Carter and Talbot*, vol. II, pp. 46, 63, 131; vol. III, pp. 48–49; vol. II, pp. 108–9. For a fuller comparison of Talbot's and Carter's references to Fielding and Lennox, see my concluding chapter.

12 Todd, *Sign of Angellica*, p. 191.

13 *MR* 10 (April 1754), pp. 280, 282; Henry Fielding, *The Covent-Garden Journal* 24 (March 24, 1752), *The Covent-Garden Journal and a Plan of the Universal Register-Office*, ed. Bertrand A. Goldgar (Oxford: Clarendon, 1988), pp. 158–61; *CR* 5 (February 1758), p. 130; *Critical Remarks on Sir Charles Grandison, Clarissa and Pamela* (London: Dowse, 1754; rpt. The Augustan Reprint Society, Los Angeles: William Andrews Clark Memorial Library, 1950), p. 19.

14 *CR* 7 (April 1759), pp. 377–78.

15 *MR* 27 (July 1762), pp. 73–74.

16 *CR* 6 (September 1758), p. 261; *MR* 12 (February 1755), pp. 144–45; *CR* 18 (October 1764), p. 313; *MR* 40 (June 1769), p. 519.

17 See, for example, Black, "Edward Kimber," pp. 36–37. Tobias Smollett, future editor of the *Critical Review*, himself puts Kimber in the ranks of popular, very recent, but ephemeral fiction, when in the 1753 *Adventures of Ferdinand Count Fathom*, his own third novel in five years, a denizen of the gaol Fathom finds himself in courteously offers access to his "small collection of books," including "any of our modern authors that are worth reading, such as the adventures of Loveill, Lady Frail, George Edwards, Joe Thompson, Bampfylde More Carew, Young Scarron, and Miss Betsy Thoughtless" – all published between 1749 and 1752; see *The Adventures of Ferdinand Count Fathom*, ed. Damian Grant (Oxford: Oxford University Press, 1971), p. 185 and n. The known authors of these books, besides Kimber, are John Hill (*Lady Frail* and *George Edwards*), Robert Goadby (*Bampfyld-Moore Carew*), Thomas Mozeen (*Young Scarron*, a satire of the theater), and Eliza Haywood (*Betsy Thoughtless*). Specific Haywood-like plot devices include having a woman serve in disguise as her lover's page and defend him from bandits on the road (in *Joe Thompson*, echoing *Love in Excess*), and the handling of the recognition-of-love scene in *Maria* by means of a lover discovering his beloved gazing at a miniature (paralleling the dénouement in *Betsy Thoughtless*).

18 *MR* 3 (September 1750), pp. 366–67; *CR* 19 (June 1765), p. 466; *MR* 19 (December 1758), p. 580; *CR* 60 (November 1785), p. 394.

19 *MR* 29 (August 1763), p. 160, my italics; *CR* 16 (August 1763), p. 117; *CR* 18 (August 1764), p. 158.

20 Kimber also incorporates several abductions of virtuous young women into *Maria*.

21 Todd notes the Minifies' increasing use of gothic coloring (*Sign of Angellica*, p. 184). These examples illustrate also the oversimplification of the label "Richardsonian," for the 1780 *Count de Poland*'s combination of sentimental characters and cynical narrator might be traced more directly to Brooke's 1778 *Excursion*, or the foolishly married heroine to the title character of Fielding's 1759 *Countess of Dellwyn*.

22 *CR* 16 (August 1763), p. 108; see also the selection of pathetic and humorous passages quoted in the *Critical*'s review of *The Count de Poland* (*CR* 50 [September 1780], pp. 168–73).

23 *CR* 6 (September 1758), p. 261; *CR* 7 (February 1759), pp. 174–75; *CR* 7 (February 1759), p. 174; *MR* 10 (February 1754), p. 147; *MR* 30 (March 1764), p. 243; *CR* 19 (June 1765), p. 467.

24 See Sidney A. Kimber, "The 'Relation,'" pp. 81–95, for an account and reproduction of Kimber's notebook entries.

25 In contrast to this delayed and limited public "author function," much of Kimber's work arguably contains coded indications of authorship, suggesting the unexpected existence of a kind of coterie system even among these urban professionals. Black has listed numerous of Kimber's *London Magazine* contributions that are "surprisingly personal in their choice of subject" ("Edward Kimber," p. 40); Kimber similarly incorporates his own previously published poetry and travel experience into his fiction, and he displays the same Addison passage prominently as the epigraph to two of his novels, *Mr. Anderson* and *The Happy Orphans*, and as a quotation in *David Ranger*. As Black notes, the Bodleian Library copy of the *Monthly Review*'s account of *Maria* carries a handwritten note that its author is "Kimber, author of Joe Thomson," the posthumous edition of *Joe Thompson* in Harrison's *The Novelist's Magazine* (1783) carries his name, and, as I have already mentioned, one reviewer almost two decades after his death remembers a lesser Kimber novel well enough to assess a plagiarism of it. To those who knew Kimber, then, his shifting modes of fiction were unlikely to detract from the construction of a professional reputation as a skilled producer of a broad range of materials, a reputation that continued for some time after his death, as these examples illustrate.

26 Ezell, "'By a Lady,'" p. 64.

27 James Raven, "The Anonymous Novel in England and Ireland, 1750–1830," *The Faces of Anonymity*, p. 145.

28 *MR* 40 (June 1769), p. 519.

29 Turner, *Living by the Pen*, p. 134.

30 Lewis and Wallace (eds.), *Walpole's Correspondence*, vol. XI, pp. 196–200.

31 After her 1791 pamphlet defending herself and her daughter, *A Letter to His Grace, the Duke of Argyll*, Gunning published in quick succession *Virginius and Virginia; A Poem, in Six Parts. From the Roman History. By Mrs. Gunning. Dedicated to Supreme Fashion; but not by permission* (1791),

Anecdotes of the Delborough Family. A Novel. In Five Volumes. By Mrs. Gunning (1792), and *Memoirs of Mary: A Novel* (1793), all read in their time as containing allusions to her recent difficulties, and characterized by a combined sentimental elevation of their heroines and cynicism regarding the scandalmongering and false friendship of the fashionable world. Todd offers an interesting discussion of the fictional masks Gunning uses in representing her personal experiences in these texts (*Sign of Angellica*, pp. 186–90).

32 Indeed, the anonymous writer of the pamphlet *A Narrative of the Incidents which form the mystery, in the family of General Gunning* (London: Taylor, 1791), chastises Susannah Gunning at some length for appearing to repudiate her earlier profession as novelist, when "the confession would have done her no discredit" (p. 42).

33 *CR* 24 (December 1767), p. 430. Examples of generally damning reviews that nevertheless note effective characterizations are the *Monthly*'s reviews of *Barford Abbey* (*MR* 38 [April 1768], p. 335) and of *Coombe Wood* (*MR* 68 [May 1783], pp. 456–67).

34 *Dictionary of National Biography*, vol. XXIII, p. 350.

35 *CR* 19 (June 1765), p. 467.

36 For a recent argument to this effect, see Carole Elaine Percy, "'Easy Women': Defining and Confining the 'Feminine' in Eighteenth-Century Print Culture," *Language Sciences* 22 (2000), pp. 315–37. Although Percy makes very clear the ambiguity of uses of the term "easy," she focuses on its associations with artlessness, triviality, vulgarity, and grammatical faults, and does not address its coupling, even in some of the examples she cites, with the quality of "elegance."

37 *MR* 34 (May 1766), p. 406; *CR* 21 (April 1766), p. 288; *MR* 40 (June 1769), p. 519.

38 *MR* 19 (September 1758), p. 311; *MR* 30 (March 1764), p. 243. Regarding the Minifies' excessive use of quotations, see the *Critical Review* on *Lady Frances S——— and Lady Caroline S———* (*CR* 16 [August 1763], p. 117).

39 *MR* 20 (April 1759), p. 381, regarding *The Countess of Dellwyn*. The *Monthly*'s negative review of Fielding's *The History of Ophelia* does use the language of commerce, saying sarcastically that the story is not "a more lumping pennyworth" because the account of its having been found in an old bureau "happened to be thrown into the bargain" (*MR* 22 [April 1760], p. 328), but the metaphor seems to have more to do with the review's questioning whether the novel was worth publishing at all than with a suggestion about publishing motives.

40 *CR* 2 (November 1756), p. 379.

41 See Margaret and Susannah Minifie, *The Histories of Lady Frances S——— and Lady Caroline S———*, 4 vols. (London: Dodsley, 1763), vol. IV, p. 203; vol. I, pp. 50–52.

42 Minifie, *Lady Frances S——— and Lady Caroline S———*, vol. II, pp. 234, 131–71; Margaret and Susannah Minifie, *Barford Abbey*, 2 vols. (London: Cadell and Payne, 1768), vol. I, p. 50; vol. II, p. 17; vol. I, p. 103.

43 Minifie, *Lady Frances S ——— and Lady Caroline S ———*, vol. IV, p. 167; Margaret and Susannah Minifie, *The Count de Poland*, 4 vols. (London: Dodsley and Baldwin; Bath: Pratt and Clinch, 1780), vol. IV, p. 135; Minifie, *Lady Frances S ——— and Lady Caroline S ———*, vol. IV, p. 61.

44 Minifie, *Barford Abbey*, vol. I, p. 70. One suspects the Miss Minifies were oblivious to the irony of having one young lady repudiate the dark houses of the great in favor of living out of doors and in the sun like a milkmaid, only to describe next a planned picnic under a tent, with an accompanying band of musicians, and "a large yacht of his lordship's, finely ornamented" to carry her to it (Minifie, *Lady Frances S ——— and Lady Caroline S ———*, vol. III, p. 154). In the work of the 1780s, the city–country dichotomy is used much more effectively to offer interesting narrative perspectives and increased character depth; see, for example, Lady Ann Fostess's sneering description of good country people in *The Count de Poland*, vol. I, pp. 128–29.

45 Reeve, *Progress of Romance*, vol. I, pp. 109–11.

46 Reeve, *Progress of Romance*, vol. I, pp. 136, 141, 139, 142; vol. II, pp. 25, 35; vol. I, p. 132.

47 Reeve, *Progress of Romance*, vol. II, pp. 38–39, 46.

48 Burney's 1778 preface to *Evelina*, for example, invokes Johnson, Rousseau, Richardson, Fielding, and Smollett, with Brooke's 1785 preface to the second edition of *The Excursion* naming Richardson, Johnson, Mackenzie, and Goldsmith (see chapter 7).

49 Thus Austin Dobson, in his 1896 *Eighteenth-Century Vignettes*, names "Joe Thompson" as apparently Kimber's "solitary effort in fiction" (quoted in Black, "Edward Kimber," p. 27).

50 Black, "Edward Kimber," p. 28.

51 Todd, *Sign of Angellica*, pp. 176–77.

52 Spencer does, indeed, note that "What was happening, in fact, was that the properly 'feminine' and the properly 'literary' were both being re-defined along the same lines" (*Rise of the Woman Novelist*, p. 77).

FROM PROPENSITY TO PROFESSION IN THE EARLY CAREER OF FRANCES BURNEY

1 Frances Burney, *The Wanderer; or, Female Difficulties*, ed. Margaret Anne Doody, Robert L. Mack, and Peter Sabor (Oxford: Oxford University Press, 1991), p. 8.

2 Frances Burney, *The Early Journals and Letters of Fanny Burney*, 4 vols., *Vol. III: The Streatham Years, Part 1 (1778 – 1779)* ed. Lars E. Troide and Stewart J. Cooke, (Montreal and Kingston: McGill-Queen's University Press, 1994), p. 352. Further references to Burney's journals and letters of 1778 to 1779 are to this edition, and will be indicated by the abbreviation *EJL*. The journals and letters make frequent use of emphases; italics in quotations therefore follow the original unless otherwise indicated.

3 Madame D'Arblay *Diary and Letters of Madame D'Arblay*, 6 vols., ed. Charlotte Barrett, Preface and Notes by Austin Dobson (London:

Macmillan, 1904), vol. II, p. 93. Further references to Burney's journals and letters of 1782 to 1784 are to this edition, and will be indicated by the abbreviation *DL*.

4 Kristina Straub, *Divided Fictions: Fanny Burney and Feminine Strategy* (Lexington: University of Kentucky Press, 1987); Margaret Anne Doody, *Frances Burney: The Life in the Works* (New Brunswick, NJ: Rutgers University Press, 1988); Julia Epstein, *The Iron Pen: Frances Burney and the Politics of Women's Writing* (Madison: University of Wisconsin Press, 1989). For a brief overview of Burney's biographical and critical fortunes from Joyce Hemlow's 1958 *History of Fanny Burney*, see Betty Rizzo's review article "Yes, Miss Burney," *Tulsa Studies in Women's Literature* 22 (2003), pp. 193–201.

5 Mary Poovey, *The Proper Lady and the Woman Writer: Ideology as Style in the Works of Mary Wollstonecraft, Mary Shelley, and Jane Austen* (Chicago: University of Chicago Press, 1984). That this model is an accurate description of Burney's experience as a woman of the later eighteenth-century is the starting assumption of studies such as Straub's (*Divided Fictions*, pp. 6–8) and Epstein's (*Iron Pen*, pp. 7, 198–201).

6 See Julia Epstein, "Burney Criticism: Family Romance, Psychobiography, and Social History," and Margaret Anne Doody, "Beyond *Evelina*: The Individual Novel and the Community of Literature," *Eighteenth-Century Fiction* 3 (1991), pp. 277–82 and pp. 359–71, respectively.

7 Straub, *Divided Fictions*, pp. 3–7. However, Straub's model of an irreconcilable conflict between these two imperatives leads her to portray the former as repeatedly and inevitably overpowered by the latter.

8 Helen Thompson, "Evelina's Two Publics," *The Eighteenth Century: Theory and Interpretation* 39 (1998), pp. 147–67; Sandra Sherman, "'Does Your Ladyship Mean an Extempore?': Wit, Leisure, and the Mode of Production in Frances Burney's *The Witlings*," *The Centennial Review* 40 (1996), p. 401; Gallagher, *Nobody's Story*, pp. 216–17.

9 Janice Farrar Thaddeus, *Frances Burney: A Literary Life* (London and New York: Macmillan and St. Martin's, 2000), pp. 3, 6.

10 Doody and Straub do, indeed, address the disjunction between author and heroines through their attention to male doubles who inhabit Burney's early texts. Doody suggests that Burney creates a "male counterpart" to her early heroines in *Evelina*'s Macartney, *The Witlings*' Dabler, and *Cecilia*'s Belfield (*Frances Burney*, p. 62), while Straub discusses the "displacement and doubling" of Cecilia's quest for a satisfactory course of life in the form of Belfield's search for an appropriate social and economic place in the world (*Divided Fictions*, pp. 142–49). Yet the import of this transgendered approach has regularly been absorbed into the proper woman writer argument. Doody, for one, ultimately opts for an alignment of even the unsympathetic Lady Smatter in *The Witlings* with Burney because both, as females, must fear all forms of publicity (*Frances Burney*, pp. 89–90), and Straub suggests that for a novel like *Cecilia*, the heroine's romance plot

ultimately "edges out any other possibilities for Cecilia's empowerment" (*Divided Fictions*, p. 131).

11 George L. Justice, "Suppression and Censorship in Late Manuscript Culture: Frances Burney's Unperformed *The Witlings, Women's Writing and the Circulation of Ideas*, ed. George L. Justice and Nathan Tinker (Cambridge: Cambridge University Press, 2002), pp. 211–12. Justice's argument is similar to mine in maintaining that Burney developed clearly demarcated, rather than pathologically conflicting, public professional and private spheres of female life, and that she structured her professionalism in dichotomous relation to the amateur model of the manuscript-circulating coterie. He also focuses on *The Witlings* as a crux in this development, but reads Burney's experience of its suppression as the crucial moment in turning from coterie to print publication; the coterie in this case is her family circle of readers. I rather argue that Burney is well on the way to adopting a professional public identity by this point, and that she is in part rejecting the inevitable gender and class restrictions that a late eighteenth-century coterie such as the bluestocking circle would place upon her.

12 Scott, *The Female Advocate*, pp. vi-vii; More's epilogue is discussed in Patricia Demers, *The World of Hannah More* (Lexington: University Press of Kentucky, 1996), p. 28. Doody suggests that "by the 1770s women seemed about to come into their own as dramatists" (*Frances Burney*, p. 75), though Peter Sabor, following Ellen Donkin, discusses this as "a particularly inauspicious time"; see General Introduction to Burney's comedies, vol. I of *The Complete Plays of Frances Burney*, 2 vols., ed. Peter Sabor (London: Pickering, 1995), pp. xxv-xxvi.

13 Anna Laetitia Aikin (Barbauld), *The Works of Anna Laetitia Barbauld*, 2 vols. (London: Routledge, 1996), vol. II, p. 23; *The Gentleman's Magazine* 55 (1785), p. 535; for the Hoole and Holcroft namings, see *DL*, vol. II, pp. 216–18, and Sylvia Haverstock Myers, *The Bluestocking Circle: Women, Friendship, and the Life of the Mind in Eighteenth-Century England* (Oxford: Clarendon, 1990), p. 284.

14 These portrayals of Burney can be found on the title page of *Cecilia*; in a 1778 pamphlet entitled *Warley: A Satire* (see *EJL*, vol. III, pp. 192–94) as well as anonymous verses in the *Morning Herald* for March 12, 1782, apparently written by Charles Burney (see *DL*, vol. II, pp. 76–78); and a newspaper article (quoted in *DL*, vol. I, p. 492), respectively.

15 William McCarthy, *Hester Thrale Piozzi: Portrait of a Literary Woman* (Chapel Hill: University of North Carolina Press, 1985), pp. 24–25 (my italics).

16 Boswell, *Life of Johnson*, vol. IV, p. 275. Since Elizabeth Carter and Hannah More were closely aligned with Montagu, Johnson's basis for sorting them here is, as he indicates, not social affiliation, but the binary of professional authorship versus conversation.

17 See Rose, *Authors and Owners*, especially pp. 85–91.

18 Ibid., pp. 6–8.

19 Frances Burney, *The Early Journals and Letters of Fanny Burney*, 4 vols., *Vol. IV: The Streatham Years, Part 2 (1780–1781)*, ed. Betty Rizzo (Montreal and Kingston: McGill–Queen's University Press, 2003), p. 209. Further references to Burney's journals and letters of 1780 to 1781 are to this edition and will be indictated by the abbreviation *EJL*. The journals and letters make frequent use of emphases; italics in quotations follow the original unless otherwise indicated.

20 Ezell, *Social Authorship*, especially pp. 1–44.

21 McCarthy, *Hester Thrale Piozzi*, pp. 23, 46.

22 The running tension between Burney's records of the ascendancy of authors and encouragement of publication in this group and Hester Thrale's accounts (in *Thraliana*) of her irritation at the socially inferior Burney's proud resistance to well-intentioned patronage underscore my argument that Burney is constructing an enabling professional identity through her private writings.

23 Burney's tendency to shape her comments about Montagu and the bluestockings in a pattern of contrast to Thrale and the dynamics of the Streatham literary conversations is a particularized version of Gallagher's helpful contrast between the "Somebodies" the Burneys sought to please as patrons and the "Nobodies" whom Frances Burney imagined as the audience of *Evelina* (*Nobody's Story*, pp. 215 – 30). In the end, however, I do not agree with Gallagher's equation of Thrale and Montagu as patronesses upon whom Burney's career depended to a great extent (*Nobody's Story*, pp. 227–30). In this I am influenced by Betty Rizzo's thorough analysis of the friendship between Thrale and Burney, in *Companions without Vows*, pp. 88–96.

24 See Piozzi, *Thraliana*, vol. I, p. 368, and *DL*, vol. I, pp. 405–6, 477.

25 See *EJL*, vol. III, pp. 157–59, 162 n10. Burney's own descriptions of Mrs. Montagu insistently associate her wit with her sex in a manner that seems to delimit the superiority of that wit; see, for example, "Mrs. Thrale ranks her as the *first of Women*, in the Literary way" (*EJL*, vol. III, p. 151), and, quoting Thrale, "she fears you [Johnson] indeed, but that, you know, is nothing uncommon: & dearly I love to hear your *disquisitions*, – for certainly she is the first woman, for Literary knowledge, in England." It is Johnson who pushes at the boundaries of the gender category here in his reply: "she diffuses more knowledge in her Conversation than any Woman I know, – or, indeed, *almost* any Man" (*EJL*, vol. III, p. 152).

26 Ultimately, Burney viewed the literary-professional claim to status as alternate and equal to the social, describing Miss Monckton's "conversaziones" as "mix[ing] the rank and the literature, and exclud[ing] all beside" (*DL*, vol. II, p. 123).

27 Peter Sabor has noted that *The Witlings* is a satire of "would-be intellectuals" of both sexes, rather than of a specifically female bluestocking group (General Introduction to *Complete Plays*, vol. I, p. xx).

28 Barbara Darby, *Frances Burney, Dramatist: Gender, Performance, and the Late-Eighteenth-Century Stage* (Lexington: University Press of Kentucky, 1997), p. 27; Thaddeus, *Frances Burney*, p. 55.

29 Frances Burney, *The Witlings*, ed. Peter Sabor (London: Pickering, 1995), 1.53–58. All references are to this edition.

30 Dryden might be added to this list, though not referred to by Censor, because his condemnation by Dabler suggests he would be admired by any truly discriminating reader.

31 Doody elaborates on parallels between Dabler's and Burney's authorial behaviors (in his use of observations of others as the basis of his compositions, for example); while I agree that this disparaging portrait may well contain elements of self-mockery, I believe that Censor's stronger affirmation of the potency of authorship in a print culture should not be overlooked (in this my argument diverges from Justice's as well; see his discussion of "Suppression and Censorship," pp. 210–13). In fact, Doody's shift from paralleling Dabler and Burney to noting similarities between this character and Charles Burney, with his habit of scribbling flattering little poems to please highly placed friends, suggests that Frances may be distinguishing her work as a competent and professional imaginative writer from her father's ephemeral, amateurish productions in the specialized field of occasional poetry (*Frances Burney*, pp. 82–84).

32 Darby, *Frances Burney, Dramatist*, pp. 12, 8, 15–16. While misogyny is one facet of Censor's character, this is subsumed in the general misanthropy of the satiric moralist. Censor's gift of £5,000 to Cecilia as a marriage portion is an indication of Burney's conception of him as removed from heterosexual social norms; Crisp's objection to this aspect of the plot ("anything is preferable to Censor's interfering in the business by his unaccountable generosity" [*DL*, vol. I, p. 322]) is hardly surprising, and it seems unlikely that Burney would have included such a gift to her virtuous heroine if she had conceived of Censor as of the same gender category as Beaufort, Jack, and Dabler.

33 Edward Young, *Conjectures on Original Composition* (London: Millar and Dodsley, 1759; facs. rpt. Scolar Press, 1966), p. 17.

34 Kaufer and Carley, *Communication at a Distance*, pp. 66–67.

35 Clayton J. Delery, (ed.), Introduction to *The Witlings* (East Lansing, MI: Colleagues, 1995), p. 51n; Burney, *The Wanderer*, p. 8.

36 Doody, *Frances Burney*, p. 131.

37 Frances Burney, *Cecilia, or Memoirs of an Heiress*, ed. Margaret Anne Doody and Peter Sabor (Oxford: Oxford University Press, 1988), p. 734. References are to this edition.

38 Siskin, *Work of Writing*, p. 106; see also pp. 29–38. Siskin, however, locates this mutual development in "Romantic writing such as Wordsworth's" (p. 106).

39 Straub, *Divided Fictions*, pp. 143, 147. In this entire chapter on "Love and Work" in *Cecilia*, Straub parallels in detail the romance plot and what she calls the nongendered "course-of-life" plot in *Cecilia*, concluding that by its very nature as a novelistic romance plot, the story of Cecilia's relationship with Mortimer Delvile "inexorably" decenters the story of her attempts to pursue a morally and socially responsible course of life. The latter is thus

displaced onto Belfield. Straub's reading is very compatible with my own, with the qualification I note here.

40 Straub, *Divided Fictions*, p. 147.

41 In fact, Crisp shows himself very aware, at other points, of the economic potential of Burney's work, as indicated earlier in this chapter, and also when he urges her, in the language of the *Cecilia* miser Briggs, to keep writing for profit after the publication of her second novel:

> If you come here, come to work, – work hard – stick to it . . . "Touch the yellow boys," as Briggs says, – "grow warm"; make the booksellers come down handsomely – count the ready – the chink. Do but secure this one point while it is in your power, and all things else shall be added unto thee (*DL*, vol. II, pp. 98–99).

42 Thrale, *Thraliana*, vol. I, p. 443.

43 Compare Doody, *Frances Burney*, pp. 107–8, and Rizzo, *Companions without Vows*, pp. 87–94.

44 Rizzo, *Companions without Vows*, p. 348 n21.

45 Siskin, *Work of Writing*, p. 218.

46 Thaddeus, *Frances Burney*, p. 37.

47 Rizzo, *Companions without Vows*, pp. 87–88; Thaddeus, *Frances Burney*, pp. 25–26. Thaddeus also argues that Burney was more adept at "intellectual resistance" to her father than has often been claimed (p. 39).

48 *MR* 67 (July 1782), p. 453.

WOMEN WRITERS AND "THE GREAT FORGETTING"

1 Jane Austen, *Northanger Abbey*, 2nd ed., ed. Claire Grogan (Peterborough, ON: Broadview, 2002), pp. 58–60. Maria Edgeworth, as author of *Belinda*, is of course the target here together with Burney.

2 Looser, *British Women Writers*, p. 194.

3 Ezell, *Writing Women's Literary History*, p. 89; McDowell, "Consuming Women," pp. 222, 242–43. See my fuller discussion of Ezell's and McDowell's work in my introduction to this book.

4 Siskin, *The Work of Writing*, Part Four: "Gender: The Great Forgetting."

5 Siskin, *The Work of Writing*, p. 195. The phrase "the hands of women" is quoted from Felix Schelling's 1913 study *The English Lyric*.

6 Siskin, *The Work of Writing*, pp. 265 n8, 224, 207.

7 Austen refers explicitly to most of these texts, but also alludes, in her heroine's assumption that her world operates by the conventions of gothic fiction, to *The Female Quixote*, and in her mockery of the public stir caused by a socially inexperienced young heroine, to *Evelina*.

8 See my discussions of Lennox and Burney in chapters 4 and 6, respectively. Kate Levin has argued, indeed, that Lennox's *The Female Quixote* works to create a new history of the novel genre with *Clarissa* as the founding text ("'The Cure,'" p. 279).

9 Looser, *British Women Writers*, pp. 194, 191, 194, 201.
10 Donoghue, *The Fame Machine*, pp. 3–4.
11 Note that this argument is necessarily dependent on the silently edited published letters, whose editor, Carter's nephew, acknowledges in his preface that "a good deal has been left out of trifling chit-chat and confidential communications" (Pennington [ed.], *Letters between Carter and Talbot*, vol. I, p. v). Whatever may be missing, however, Pennington has retained references to reading across a wide range of genres.
12 Scott, *The Female Advocate*, pp. 22, 24. Scott's footnote summaries of the two women's careers are also equally weighted. For Fielding, she notes, "Mrs. *Fielding*, sister to the late *Henry Fielding* Esquire, and author of 'The Adventures of *David Simple*;' 'The *Governess*, or, the *Female Academy*;' 'The Lives of *Cleopatra* and *Octavia*' and 'of a translation, from the Greek, of Xenophon's Memorabilia of Socrates,'" and for Lennox, she supplies: "Mrs. *Charlotte Lenox*, author of 'Shakespear illustrated, with critical Remarks;' of 'The *Sister*, a Comedy;' and of, 'The *Female Quixote*.' She has also translated (from the French) *Brumoy's* Greek Theatre." Oddly, the poem "The Art of Coquetry" poem, which seems to be the basis of Scott's praise of Lennox's delineation of human nature, is not named as one of her works.
13 Pennington (ed.), *Letters between Carter and Talbot*, vol. I, p. 33; Henry Fielding claims ignorance of the narrative's source, adding "I have only to remark, that this Chapter is in the Original writ in a Woman's Hand: And tho' the Observations in it are, I think, as excellent as any in the whole Volume, there seems to be a difference in Style between this and the preceeding Chapters; and as it is the Character of a Woman which is related, I am inclined to fancy it was really written by one of that Sex" (*Miscellanies by Henry Fielding, Esq; Volume Two*, ed. Hugh Amory, Introduction and Commentary by Bertrand A. Goldgar, vol. II of *The Wesleyan Edition of the Works of Henry Fielding* [Oxford: Clarendon, 1972], p. 111 n).
14 Pennington (ed.), *Letters between Carter and Talbot*, vol. I, pp. 61, 64–65, 131. The grammatical structure of the full passage couples the Fielding work discussed here with Mme Sevigné's letters, suggesting that it is the epistolary *Familiar Letters*, as does the concluding comment that "I scarce know a greater pleasure than reading over a book one is fond of with persons of taste and candour, to whom it is entirely new"; the reference to the pride and vanity theme could, however, apply to the newly published *Volume the Last* as well.
15 Pennington (ed.), *Letters between Carter and Talbot*, vol. II, pp. 183, 188, 252–53, 356, 303.
16 Pennington (ed.), *Letters between Carter and Talbot*, vol. I, p. 367; vol. II, pp. 146, 260, 68–69, 76, 271.
17 Pennington (ed.), *Letters between Carter and Tabot*, vol. II, pp. 68-69, 76. It should be noted that Talbot and Carter thought well, in varying degrees,

of *Tom Jones* and *Amelia*, and felt free to criticize aspects of *Clarissa* and *Sir Charles Grandison*; these were no mindless Richardson acolytes. Indeed, Talbot's comment on the vanity of boasting of one's suitors, noted above, arises from a critique of Harriet Byron, the heroine of *Grandison.*

18 Of note as well is Talbot's value for good translations; see Pennington (ed.), *Letters between Carter and Talbot*, vol. I, pp. 44–45, 191. Talbot writes regularly in 1751 about reading Sully's memoirs, describing herself as "still bewitched" by them on August 16, 1751, for example (vol. II, p. 47), but these appear to be the French version, the interest in which gave rise to Lennox's translation. In June 1757, however, she is reading Sully again (vol. II, p. 253); even if this is once more in the French, her interest may have been revived by the translation, which had just gone into its second edition.

19 For example, they know, assist, and attempt to advise Johnson as author-editor of the *Rambler* papers and discuss the processes behind the compiling of Dodsley's miscellanies and the *Gentleman's Magazine*, to which Carter was an early contributor (Pennington [ed.], *Letters between Carter and Talbot*, vol. I, pp. 349–50, 357–58, 371–72; vol. II, pp. 13, 16, 18–19, 33, 200–03).

20 Levin, "'The Cure,'" p. 275.

21 November 30, [1763], mo5307; [November 27, 1778], mo5391. Scott continues, "for Dr Grahams [i.e. her new brother-in-law's] experiments have shewn that fire has a very contrary effect on her; being a Salamander it is the element truly congenial to her." This suggests a certain facetiousness, but Scott's next sentence returns to the more consistent tone of the account: "Were she flesh & blood one coud not forgive her, but being only skin & bone she deserves no mercy"; Scott sees the marriage as "a dishonour to the Sex."

22 Kelly, Introduction to *Millenium Hall*, p. 18.

23 Thaddeus, *Frances Burney*, p. 37.

24 Jane Spencer, *Aphra Behn's Afterlife* (Oxford: Oxford University Press, 2000), pp. 104, 119.

25 Barrett (ed.), *Diary and Letters*, vol. II, p. 65.

26 Spencer, *Aphra Behn's Afterlife*, p. 117.

27 Troide (ed.), *Early Journals and Letters*, vol. II, pp. 4–5.

28 Troide and Cook (eds.), *Early Journals and Letters*, vol. III, pp. 105–6.

29 Barrett (ed.), *Diary and Letters*, vol. IV, p. 476.

30 Guest, *Small Change*, pp. 115–16.

31 See, for example, Jane Spencer's *Rise of the Woman Novelist*, p. 76, and *Aphra Behn's Afterlife*, pp. 97–99, as well as Runge's *Gender and Language*, pp. 156–60.

32 Reeve, *Progress of Romance*, vol. I, pp. 118–22.

33 See also the work's conclusion, where Euphrasia refuses to discuss novels published after 1770, insisting that "The public will do them justice, and time will shew, whether they owed their success to intrinsic merit, or to the

caprice of fashion. I will not be drawn in to say any thing more of them." She then throws herself, "without asking the aid of puffing, or the influence of the tide of fashion" on the judgment of "an impartial and discerning public" (vol. II, p. 100).

34 Reeve, *Progress of Romance*, vol. I, pp. 121–22.

35 Reeve, *Progress of Romance*, vol. II, pp. 21, 30. In this reading I differ from Runge, who sees Reeve's reliance on Hortensius to speak about *Tristram Shandy* and her refusal "to even offer a title" of a Manley work as manifestations of an "inability" to speak, a "lacuna in the critical language available" that leads her to "[cast] the improper female writers into the void: silenced, veiled, in oblivion" (*Gender and Language*, pp. 159, 163). By overlooking Hortensius as one of the voices through which Reeve speaks, Runge at once denies Reeve agency in her acts of oblivion, overlooks their ambiguity, and reenacts the silencing of Reeve herself. While I differ from some of Runge's conclusions, I agree with her view of Reeve's treatise as a "serious argument in favour of female critical authority" (*Gender and Language*, p. 159), as I indicate below.

36 Reeve, *Progress of Romance*, vol. I, p. 142; vol. II, pp. 34, 39.

37 Reeve, *Progress of Romance*, vol. I, pp. xi–xii; vol. II, p. 98.

38 Runge, *Gender and Language*, p. 163.

39 Raven and Forster (eds.), *The English Novel*, vol. I, pp. 45–49. Raven and Forster's data show that, despite the claims of reviewers as early as 1773 that "this branch of the literary *trade* appears, now, to be almost entirely engrossed by the Ladies" (*MR* 48 [1773], p. 154), identified female novelists were in a minority of identified novelists until this point.

40 Brooke, *The Excursion*, pp. 1–2. Brooke does insert a French novelist, Mme Élie de Beaumont, but only in a footnote quoting her praise of Richardson.

41 Troide (ed.), *Early Letters and Journals*, vol. I, pp. 4–5.

42 Montagu, (ed.), *Letters of Mrs. Elizabeth Montagu*, vol. I, p. 8. As early as 1763, Scott writes to her sister, "I have sent your letters. the Coppier has blunderd sadly, the long time he was about them, & then my unwillingness to send them till I had corrected them defered the sending the Box. the two last letters he omitted because they were not finished so they are added in a better hand. The Man is abominably dear into the bargain" (mo5308; see also mo5825 and mo5827). Although the purpose for copying these letters is not here made clear, Matthew's insistence that Elizabeth made no effort at all to prepare her letters for publication (*Letters of Mrs. Elizabeth Montagu*, vol. II, p. 312) is suspect, especially since he simultaneously describes this publication as a "duty . . . frequently enjoined by Mrs. Montagu herself in consequence of the reiterated request of many of her correspondents, upon whose taste and judgment she had every reason to rely" (*Letters of Mrs. Elizabeth Montagu*, vol. II, p. 313).

43 Kelly, Introduction to *Millenium Hall*, p. 18.

44 Ezell, *Writing Women's Literary History*, p. 87.

CODA

1 Isles (ed.), "Lennox Collection," 18, p. 341.
2 Paula R. Backscheider, "Doubt Everything? Women Writers and Familiar Answers," paper read at the American Society for Eighteenth-Century Studies annual meeting in Notre Dame, April 1998.
3 While the existing full-length literary biographies of Sarah Fielding, Charlotte Lennox, Frances Brooke, and Frances Burney have been invaluable resources for this study, those of Lennox and Brooke are seriously outdated, and all, as literary biographies, are somewhat limited in their treatment of theoretical and critical questions.

Bibliography

This bibliography lists only works cited; it is not a full bibliography of published works for the primary authors discussed in this book. The eighteenth-century review journals cited throughout this study – *The Critical Review, The European Magazine, The Gentleman's Magazine, The Monthly Review*, and *Town and Country Magazine* – have not been included in the bibliography.

Ackers, Charles, *A Ledger of Charles Ackers, Printer of the "London Magazine."* Oxford: Oxford University Press, 1968, for the Oxford Bibliographical Society.

Aikin (Barbauld), Anna Laetitia, *The Works of Anna Laetitia Barbauld.* London: Routledge, 1996.

Amory, Hugh, "Virtual Readers: The Subscribers to Fielding's *Miscellanies.*" Studies in Bibliography 48 (1995), pp. 94–112.

Anon., *A Narrative of the Incidents which form the mystery, in the family of General Gunning.* London: Taylor, 1791.

Anon., *Critical Remarks on Sir Charles Grandison, Clarissa and Pamela.* London: Dowse, 1754; facs rpt. The Augustan Reprint Society, Los Angeles: William Andrews Clark Memorial Library, 1950.

Anderson, Benedict, *Imagined Communities: Reflections on the Origin and Spread of Nationalism*, rev. ed. London: Verso, 1991.

Austen, Jane, *Northanger Abbey*, 2nd ed. ed. Claire Grogan. Peterborough, ON: Broadview, 2002.

Ballaster, Ros, *Seductive Forms: Women's Amatory Fiction from 1684 to 1740.* Oxford: Clarendon, 1992.

Barchas, Janine, "Sarah Fielding's Dashing Style and Eighteenth-Century Print Culture." *ELH* 63 (1996), pp. 633–56.

Barker, Gerard A., *Grandison's Heirs: The Paragon's Progress in the Late Eighteenth-Century English Novel.* Newark: University of Delaware Press, 1985.

Barker-Benfield, G. J., *The Culture of Sensibility: Sex and Society in Eighteenth-Century Britain.* Chicago: University of Chicago Press, 1992.

Barrell, John and Harriet Guest, "On the Use of Contradiction: Economics and Morality in the Eighteenth-Century Long Poem." *The New Eighteenth Century: Theory, Politics, English Literature*, ed. Felicity Nussbaum and Laura Brown. New York: Methuen, 1986, pp. 121–43.

Basker, James G., *Tobias Smollett: Critic and Journalist.* Newark: University of Delaware Press, 1988.

Battestin, Martin C. and Ruth Battestin, *Henry Fielding: A Life.* London: Routledge, 1989.

Battestin, Martin C. and Clive T. Probyn (eds.), *The Correspondence of Henry and Sarah Fielding.* Oxford: Clarendon, 1993.

Beasley, Jerry C., "*Clarissa* and Early Female Fiction." *Clarissa and Her Readers: New Essays for the "Clarissa" Project*, ed. Carol Houlihan Flynn and Edward Copeland. New York: AMS, 1999, pp. 69–96.

Bentley, Jr., G. E., "Copyright Documents in the George Robinson Archive: William Godwin and Others 1713–1820." *Studies in Bibliography* 35 (1982), pp. 67–110.

Berland, K. J. H., "The True Pleasurable Philosopher: Some Influences on Frances Brooke's *History of Emily Montague.*" *Dalhousie Review* 66 (1986), pp. 286–300.

"Frances Brooke and David Garrick." *Studies in Eighteenth-Century Culture* 20 (1990), pp. 217–30.

Black, Frank Gees, "Edward Kimber: Anonymous Novelist of the Mid-Eighteenth Century." *Harvard Studies and Notes in Philology and Literature* 17 (1935), pp. 27–42.

Blain, Virginia, Isobel Grundy and Patricia Clements (eds.), *The Feminist Companion to Literature in English.* New Haven: Yale University Press, 1990.

Bolingbroke, Henry St. John, Viscount Bolingbroke, *Letters on the Study and Use of History.* London: Millar, 1752.

Borsay, Peter, *The English Urban Renaissance: Culture and Society in the Provincial Town. 1660–1770.* Oxford: Clarendon, 1989.

Boswell, James, *Boswell for the Defence, 1769–1774*, ed. William K. Wimsatt, Jr., and Frederick A. Pottle. Melbourne, London, Toronto: William Heinemann (Yale University Press), 1960.

Journal of a Tour to the Hebrides, vol. V of *Boswell's Life of Johnson*, 6 vols., ed. George Birkbeck Hill, rev. L. F. Powell. Oxford: Clarendon, 1934.

Boutelle, Ann Edwards, "Frances Brooke's *Emily Montague* (1769): Canada and Woman's Rights." *Women's Studies: An Interdisciplinary Journal* 12 (1986), pp. 7–16.

Bree, Linda, *Sarah Fielding.* New York: Twayne, 1996.

"'No Situation so Deplorable': Sarah Fielding, Fiction, and Female Employment." (Unpublished).

Brewer, John, *The Pleasures of the Imagination: English Culture in the Eighteenth Century.* Chicago: University of Chicago Press, 1997.

Brooke, Frances, *The Elements of the History of England, From the Invasion of the Romans to the Reign of George the Second. Translated from the French of Abbé Milot.* London: Dodsley, 1771.

The Excursion, ed. Paula R. Backscheider and Hope D. Cotton. Lexington: University Press of Kentucky, 1997.

The History of Emily Montague, ed. Mary Jane Edwards. Ottawa: Carleton University Press, 1991.

Lady Julia Mandeville, Introduction by E. Phillips Poole. London: Scholartis, 1930.

Marian, London: Strahan, 1800.

Memoirs of the Marquis de St. Forlaix, 2 vols. London: Dodsley, 1770.

The Old Maid, rev. ed. London: Millar, 1764.

Rosina, London: Cadell, 1783.

The Siege of Sinope: A Tragedy. London: Cadell, 1781.

Virginia, A Tragedy, with Odes, Pastorals, and Translations. London: Millar, 1756.

Brooke, Frances, to James Dodsley, British Library MS. Add. 29747.

Burke, Seán, *The Death and Return of the Author: Criticism and Subjectivity in Barthes, Foucault and Derrida.* Edinburgh: Edinburgh University Press 1998.

Burney, Frances, *Cecilia, or Memoirs of an Heiress*, ed. Margaret Anne Doody and Peter Sabor. Oxford: Oxford University Press, 1988.

The Complete Plays of Frances Burney. 2 vols., ed. Peter Sabor. London: Pickering, 1995.

Diary and Letters of Madame D'Arblay, 6 vols., ed. Charlotte Barrett, preface and notes, Austin Dobson. London: Macmillan, 1905.

The Early Journals and Letters of Fanny Burney, Vol. II. (1774–1777), ed. Lars E. Troide. Montreal and Kingston: McGill-Queen's University Press, 1990.

The Early Journals and Letters of Fanny Burney, Vol. III: The Streatham Years, Part 1 (1778–1779), ed. Lars E. Troide and Stewart J. Cooke. Montreal and Kingston: McGill-Queen's University Press, 1994.

The Early Journals and Letters of Fanny Burney, Vol. IV: The Streatham Years, Part 2 (1780–1781), ed. Betty Rizzo. Montreal and Kingston: McGill-Queen's University Press, 2003.

The Wanderer; or, Female Difficulties, ed. Margaret Anne Doody, Robert L. Mack, and Peter Sabor. Oxford: Oxford University Press, 1991.

Burrows, Donald and Rosemary Dunhill, *Music and Theatre in Handel's World: The Family Papers of James Harris 1732–80.* Oxford: Oxford University Press, 2002.

Carretta, Vincent, "Utopia Limited: Sarah Scott's *Millenium Hall* and *The History of Sir George Ellison.*" The Age of Johnson 5 (1992), pp. 303–25.

Carter, Elizabeth and Catherine Talbot, *A Series of Letters between Mrs. Elizabeth Carter and Miss Catherine Talbot*, 4 vols., ed. Matthew Pennington. London, 1809.

Letters from Mrs. Elizabeth Carter to Mrs. Montagu, 3 vols., ed. Matthew Pennington. London, 1817.

Child, Elizabeth, "'To Sing the Town': Women, Place, and Print Culture in Eighteenth-Century Bath." *Studies in Eighteenth-Century Culture* 28 (1999), pp. 155–72.

Christensen, Jerome, *Practicing Enlightenment: Hume and the Formation of a Literary Career*. Madison: University of Wisconsin Press, 1987.

Cook, Elizabeth Heckendorn, *Epistolary Bodies: Gender and Genre in the Eighteenth-Century Republic of Letters*. Stanford, CA: Stanford University Press, 1996.

Corfield, Penelope J., *Power and the Professions in Britain, 1700–1850*. London: Routledge, 1995.

Craft, Catherine A. "Reworking Male Models: Aphra Behn's *Fair Vow-Breaker*, Eliza Haywood's *Fantomina*, and Charlotte Lennox's *Female Quixote*." *Modern Language Review* 86 (1991), pp. 821–38.

Darby, Barbara, *Frances Burney, Dramatist: Gender, Performance, and the Late-Eighteenth-Century Stage*. Lexington: University Press of Kentucky, 1997.

DeBruyn, Frans, "Latidudinarianism and Its Importance as a Precursor of Sensibility." *Journal of English and Germanic Philology* 80 (1981), pp. 349–68.

Delery, Clayton J., Introduction to *The Witlings* by Frances Burney, ed. Clayton J. Delery. East Lansing, MI: Colleagues, 1995.

Demers, Patricia, *The World of Hannah More*. Lexington: University Press of Kentucky, 1996.

Dickinson, H. T., *Liberty and Property: Political Ideology in Eighteenth-Century Britain*. London: Weidenfeld and Nicolson, 1977.

Donoghue, Frank, *The Fame Machine: Book Reviewing and Eighteenth-Century Literary Careers*. Stanford: Stanford University Press, 1996.

Doody, Margaret Anne, "Frances Sheridan: Morality and Annihilated Time." *Fetter'd or Free?: British Women Novelists, 1670–1815*, ed. Mary Anne Schofield and Cecilia Macheski. Athens: Ohio University Press, 1986, pp. 324–58.

"Beyond *Evelina*: The Individual Novel and the Community of Literature." *Eighteenth-Century Fiction* 3 (1991), pp. 358–71.

Frances Burney: The Life in the Works. New Brunswick, NJ: Rutgers University Press, 1988.

Dorn, Judith, "Reading Women Reading History: The Philosophy of Periodical Form in Charlotte Lennox's *The Lady's Museum*." *Historical Reflections/Réflexions Historiques* 18.3 (1992), pp. 7–27.

Edwards, Mary Jane, "Frances Brooke's *The History of Emily Montague:* A Biographical Context." *English Studies in Canada* 7 (1981), pp. 171–82.

Eger, Elizabeth, "Representing Culture: 'The Nine Living Muses of Great Britain' (1779)." *Women, Writing and the Public Sphere, 1700–1830*, ed. Elizabeth Eger, Charlotte Grant, Cliona O Gallchoir, and Penny Warburton. Cambridge: Cambridge University Press, 2001, pp. 104–32.

Eisenstein, Elizabeth L., *The Printing Press as an Agent of Change: Communications and Cultural Transformation in Early-Modern Europe*, 2 vols. Cambridge: Cambridge University Press, 1979.

Ellison, Julie, "There and Back: Transatlantic Novels and Anglo-American Careers." *The Past as Prologue: Essays to Celebrate the Twenty-Fifth Anniversary of ASECS*, ed. Carla H. Hay and Syndy M. Conger. New York: AMS, 1995, pp. 303–23.

Epstein, Julia, *The Iron Pen: Frances Burney and the Politics of Women's Writing*. Madison: University of Wisconsin Press, 1989.

"Burney Criticism: Family Romance, Psychobiography, and Social History." *Eighteenth-Century Fiction* 3 (1991), pp. 277–82.

Ezell, Margaret J. M., *Writing Women's Literary History*. Baltimore: Johns Hopkins University Press, 1993.

Social Authorship and the Advent of Print. Baltimore: Johns Hopkins University Press, 1999.

"'By a Lady': The Mask of the Feminine in Restoration, Early Eighteenth-Century Print Culture." *The Faces of Anonymity: Anonymous and Pseudonymous Publication from the Sixteenth to the Twentieth Century*, ed. Robert J. Griffin. New York and Houndmills: Palgrave Macmillan, 2003, pp. 63–79.

Fergus, Jan and Janice Farrar Thaddeus, "Women, Publishers, and Money, 1790–1820." *Studies in Eighteenth-Century Culture* 17 (1987), pp. 191–207.

Fielding, Henry, *Miscellanies by Henry Fielding, Esq; Volume Two*, ed. Hugh Amory; introduction and commentary by Bertrand A. Goldgar, Vol. II of *The Wesleyan Edition of the Works of Henry Fielding*. Oxford: Clarendon, 1972.

The Covent-Garden Journal and a Plan of the Universal Register-Office, ed. Bertrand A. Goldgar. Vol. VIII of *The Wesleyan Edition of the Works of Henry Fielding*. Oxford: Clarendon, 1988.

Fielding, Sarah, *The Adventures of David Simple* and *Volume the Last*, ed. Peter Sabor. Lexington: University Press of Kentucky, 1998.

The Adventures of David Simple and *The Adventures of David Simple, Volume the Last*, ed. Linda Bree. London: Penguin, 2002.

The Lives of Cleopatra and Octavia, ed. Christopher D. Johnson. Lewisburg: Bucknell University Press, 1994.

Remarks on "Clarissa," Addressed to the Author, ed. Peter Sabor. London: Robinson, 1749; rpt. Augustan Reprint Society Los Angeles; William Andrews Clark Memorial Library, 1985, p. v.

Forster, Antonia, "'A considerable rank in the world of *Belles Lettres*': Women, Fiction, and Literary History in the Last Quarter of the Eighteenth Century." *Women and Literary History: "For There She Was,"* ed. Katherine Binhammer and Jeanne Wood, Newark: University of Delaware Press, 2003, pp. 106–18.

Foucault, Michel, "What Is an Author?" *Language, Counter-Memory, Practice*, ed. Donald F. Bouchard; trans. Donald F. Bouchard and Sherry Simon. Ithaca: Cornell University Press, 1977, pp. 113–38.

Gallagher, Catherine, *Nobody's Story: The Vanishing Acts of Women Writers in the Marketplace, 1670–1830*. Berkeley and Los Angeles: University of California Press, 1994.

Garrick, David, *The Letters of David Garrick*, 3 vols., ed. David M. Little and George M. Kahrl. Cambridge, MA: Belknap Press (Harvard University Press) 1963.

Grant, Charlotte, "The Choice of Hercules: The Polite Arts and 'Female Excellence' in Eighteenth-Century London." *Women, Writing and the Public Sphere, 1700–1830*, ed. Elizabeth Eger, Charlotte Grant, Cliona O Gallchoir, and Penny Warburton. Cambridge: Cambridge University Press, 2001, pp. 75–103.

Gray, James, "Dr. Johnson, Charlotte Lennox, and the Englishing of Father Brumoy." *Modern Philology* 83 (1985), pp. 142–50.

Griffin, Dustin, *Literary Patronage in England, 1650–1800*. Cambridge: Cambridge University Press, 1996.

Grundy, Isobel, "'A novel in a series of letters by a lady': Richardson and Some Richardsonian Novels." *Samuel Richardson: Tercentenary Essays*, ed. Margaret Anne Doody and Peter Sabor. Cambridge: Cambridge University Press, 1989, pp. 223–91.

"Samuel Johnson as Patron of Women." *The Age of Johnson* 1 (1987), pp. 59–77.

Guest, Harriet, *Small Change: Women, Learning, Patriotism, 1750–1810*. Chicago: University of Chicago Press, 2000.

Habermas, Jürgen, *The Structural Transformation of the Public Sphere: An Inquiry into a Category of Bourgeois Society*, trans. Thomas Burger with the assistance of Frederick Lawrence. Cambridge, MA: MIT Press, 1989.

Hawkins, Sir John, *The Life of Samuel Johnson, L.L.D.*, 2nd ed. London, 1787; rpt. New York: Garland, 1974, pp. 285–87.

Hayes, Kevin J. Introduction to *Itinerant Observations in America*, by Edward Kimber. Newark and London: University of Delaware Press, 1998.

Hill, Bridget, *The Republican Virago: The Life and Times of Catharine Macaulay, Historian*. Oxford: Clarendon, 1992.

Holmes, Geoffrey, *Augustan England: Professions, State and Society, 1680–1730*. London: Allen and Unwin, 1982.

Home, John, "Home's *Douglas*." Ed. Hubert J. Tunney. *Bulletin of the University of Kansas Humanistic Studies* 3 (1924), pp. 1–94.

Hudson, Nicholas, "Arts of Seduction and the Rhetoric of *Clarissa*." *Modern Language Quarterly* 51 (1990), pp. 25–43.

Hume, David, *Essays Moral, Political, and Literary*. Oxford: Oxford University Press, 1963.

The Philosophical Works, 4 vols, ed. Thomas Hill Green and Thomas Hodge Grose. London, 1882; rpt. Darmstadt: Scientia Verlag Aalen, 1964.

Hunting, Robert S. "Fielding's Revisions of *David Simple*." *Boston University Studies in English* 3 (1957), pp. 117–21.

Ingrassia, Catherine, *Authorship, Commerce, and Gender in Early Eighteenth-Century England: A Culture of Paper Credit.* Cambridge: Cambridge University Press, 1998.

Isles, Duncan (ed.), "The Lennox Collection." *Harvard Library Bulletin* 18 (1970), pp. 317–44; 19 (1971), pp. 36–60, 165–86, 416–35.

Janssen, Susanne, "The Empirical Study of Careers in Literature and the Arts." *The Psychology and Sociology of Literature. In Honor of Elrud Ibsch*, ed. Dick Schram and Gerard Steen. Amsterdam: John Benjamins, 2001, pp. 323–57.

Johnson, Richard, Preface to *The Baronetage of England*, 3 vols., by Edward Kimber and Richard Johnson. London, 1771, vol. III, p. viii.

Johnson, Samuel, *The Rambler*, vols. III–V of *The Yale Edition of the Works of Samuel Johnson*, ed. W. J. Bate and Albrecht B. Strauss, gen. eds. A. T. Hazen and J. H. Middendorf, 16 vols., 1958. New Haven: Yale University Press, 1969.

The Letters of Samuel Johnson, 3 vols., ed. Bruce Redford. Princeton: Princeton University Press, 1992.

Justice, George L., "Suppression and Censorship in Late Manuscript Culture: Frances Burney's Unperformed *The Witlings*." *Women's Writing and the Circulation of Ideas*, ed. George L. Justice and Nathan Tinker. Cambridge: Cambridge University Press, 2002, pp. 201–22.

Kaufer, David S. and Kathleen M. Carley, *Communication at a Distance: The Influence of Print on Sociological Organization and Change.* Hillsdale, NJ: Lawrence Erlbaum, 1993.

Kelly, Gary, "Bluestocking Feminism." *Women, Writing and the Public Sphere, 1700–1830*, ed. Elizabeth Eger, Charlotte Grant, Cliona O Gallchoir, and Penny Warburton. Cambridge: Cambridge University Press, 2001, pp. 163–80.

Kernan, Alvin B., *Printing Technology, Letters, and Samuel Johnson.* Princeton: Princeton University Press, 1987.

Keymer, Tom, *Richardson's "Clarissa" and the Eighteenth-Century Reader.* Cambridge: Cambridge University Press, 1992.

Kimber, Edward, *Itinerant Observations in America*, ed. Kevin J. Hayes. Newark and London: University of Delaware and Associated University Press, 1988.

Kimber, Isaac, *Sermons on the Most Interesting Religious, Moral, and Practical Subjects.* London: Ackers, 1756.

Kimber, Sidney A., "The 'Relation of a late Expedition to St. Augustine,' with Biographical and Bibliographical Notes on Isaac and Edward Kimber." *The Papers of the Bibliographical Society of America* 28.2 (1934), pp. 81–96.

King, Kathryn R., *Jane Barker, Exile: A Literary Career, 1675–1725.* Oxford: Clarendon, 2000.

Klein, Lawrence E., "Gender and the Public/Private Distinction in the Eighteenth Century: Some Questions About Evidence and Analytic Procedure." *Eighteenth-Century Studies* 29 (1995), pp. 97–109.

Kraft, Elizabeth, *Character and Consciousness in Eighteenth-Century Comic Fiction.* Athens: University of Georgia Press, 1992.

Kucich, Greg, "'This Horrid Theatre of Human Sufferings': Gendering the Stages of History in Catharine Macaulay and Percy Bysshe Shelley." *Lessons of Romanticism: A Critical Companion*, ed. Thomas Pfau and Robert F. Gleckner. Durham: Duke University Press, 1998, pp. 448–65.

Langbauer, Laurie, *Women and Romance: The Consolations of Gender in the English Novel.* Ithaca: Cornell University Press, 1990.

Larson, Edith Sedgwick, "A Measure of Power: The Personal Charity of Elizabeth Montagu." *Studies in Eighteenth-Century Culture* 16 (1986), pp. 197–210.

Larson, Magali Sarfatti, *The Rise of Professionalism: A Sociological Analysis.* Berkeley and Los Angeles: University of California Press, 1977.

Lefanu, Alicia, *Memoirs of the Life and Writings of Mrs. Frances Sheridan.* London: Whittaker, 1824.

Lennox, Charlotte, *The Female Quixote*, ed. Margaret Dalziel. Oxford: Oxford University Press, 1989.

Levin, Kate, "'The Cure of Arabella's Mind': Charlotte Lennox and the Disciplining of the Female Reader." *Women's Writing* 2 (1995), pp. 271–90.

Livy, *The Early History of Rome: Books I–V of The History of Rome from Its Foundation*, trans. with Introduction by Aubrey de Selincourt. Baltimore: Penguin, 1960.

London, April, *Women and Property in the Eighteenth-Century English Novel.* Cambridge: Cambridge University Press, 1999.

Lonsdale, Roger (ed.). *Eighteenth-Century Women Poets.* Oxford: Oxford University Press, 1989, pp. 233–34.

Looser, Devoney, *British Women Writers and the Writing of History, 1670–1820.* Baltimore: Johns Hopkins University Press, 2000.

Lovell, Terry, "Subjective Powers? Consumption, the Reading Public, and the Early Eighteenth-Century Domestic Woman." *The Consumption of Culture 1600–1800: Image, Object, Text*, ed. Ann Bermingham and John Brewer, London and New York: Routledge, 1997, pp. 23–41.

Marshall, David, "Writing Masters and 'Masculine Exercises' in *The Female Quixote*." *Eighteenth-Century Fiction* 5 (1993), pp. 105–35.

Maseres, Francis, *The Maseres Letters 1766–68*, ed. W. Steward Wallace. Toronto: University of Toronto Press, 1919.

McCarthy, William, *Hester Thrale Piozzi: Portrait of a Literary Woman.* Chapel Hill: University of North Carolina Press, 1985.

McDowell, Paula, "Consuming Women: The Life of the 'Literary Lady' as Popular Culture in Eighteenth-Century England." *Genre* 26 (1993), pp. 219–52.

The Women of Grub Street: Press, Politics and Gender in the London Literary Marketplace 1678–1730. Oxford: Clarendon, 1998.

McMullen, Lorraine, *An Odd Attempt in a Woman: The Literary Life of Frances Brooke.* Vancouver: University of British Columbia Press, 1983.

Merrett, Robert, "The Politics of Romance in *The History of Emily Montague.*" *Canadian Literature* 133 (1992), pp. 92–108.

Michaelson, Patricia Howell, *Speaking Volumes: Reading and Speech in the Age of Johnson.* Stanford: Stanford University Press, 2002.

Minifie, Margaret and Susannah Minifie, *Barford Abbey*, 2 vols. London: Cadell and Payne, 1768.

The Count de Poland, 4 vols. London: Dodsley and Baldwin; Bath: Pratt and Clinch, 1780.

The Histories of Lady Frances S ——— and Lady Caroline S ———, 4 vols. London: Dodsley, 1763.

Montagu, Elizabeth, *The Letters of Mrs. Elizabeth Montagu*, 4 vols., ed. Matthew Montagu. London, 1813.

Mrs. Montagu, "Queen of the Blues": Her Letters and Friendships from 1762 to 1800, 2 vols., ed. Reginald Blunt. Boston: Houghton Mifflin, 1923.

Montagu, Elizabeth and Sarah Scott, Correspondence in the Montagu Collection. Henry E. Huntington Library.

Montagu, Lady Mary Wortley, *The Complete Letters of Lady Mary Wortley Montagu*, 3 vols., ed. Robert Halsband. Oxford: Clarendon, 1967.

Morton, Nanette, "'A Most Sensible Oeconomy': From Spectacle to Surveillance in Sarah Scott's *Millenium Hall.*" *Eighteenth-Century Fiction* 11 (1999), pp. 185–204.

Mosner, Ernest Campbell, *Forgotten Hume: "Le bon David."* New York: Columbia University Press, 1943; rpt. New York: AMS, 1967.

Myers, Sylvia Haverstock, *The Bluestocking Circle: Women, Friendship, and the Life of the Mind in Eighteenth-Century England.* Oxford: Clarendon, 1990.

Needham, Gwendolyn B. "Mrs. Frances Brooke: Dramatic Critic." *Theatre Notebook* 15 (1960–61), pp. 47–52.

New, W. H., "*The Old Maid*: Frances Brooke's Apprentice Feminism." *Journal of Canadian Fiction* 2 (1973), pp. 9–12.

Nichols, John Bowyer, *Illustrations of the Literary History of the Eighteenth Century*, 8 vols. London: Nichols, 1817–1858.

Parrish, Ann Marilyn, "Eight Experiments in Fiction: A Critical Analysis of the Works of Sarah Fielding." Unpublished dissertation. Boston: Boston University Graduate School, 1973.

Pearson, Jacqueline, *Women's Reading in Britain, 1750–1835: A Dangerous Recreation.* Cambridge: Cambridge University Press, 1999.

Percy, Carole Elaine, "'Easy Women': Defining and Confining the 'Feminine' in Eighteenth-Century Print Culture." *Language Sciences* 22 (2000), pp. 315–37.

Perry, Ruth, "Clarissa's Daughters: Or, The History of Innocence Betrayed." *Clarissa and Her Readers: New Essays for the "Clarissa" Project*, ed. Carol Houlihan Flynn and Edward Copeland. New York: AMS, 1999, pp. 119–41.

Phillips, Mark Salber, *Society and Sentiment: Genres of Historical Writing in Britain, 1740–1820*. Princeton: Princeton University Press, 2000.

Piozzi, Hester Lynch Thrale, *Thraliana: The Diary of Mrs. Hester Lynch Thrale (Later Mrs. Piozzi), 1776–1809*, 2nd ed. 2 vols., ed. Katherine C. Balderston. Oxford: Clarendon, 1951.

Pohl, Nicole and Betty A. Schellenberg (eds.), *Reconsidering the Bluestockings*. San Marino, CA: The Huntington Library, 2003.

Poovey, Mary, *The Proper Lady and the Woman Writer: Ideology as Style in the Works of Mary Wollstonecraft, Mary Shelley, and Jane Austen*. Chicago: University of Chicago Press, 1984.

Probyn, Clive T, *The Sociable Humanist: The Life and Works of James Harris 1709–1780; Provincial and Metropolitan Culture in Eighteenth-century England*. Oxford: Clarendon, 1991.

Raven, James, "The Anonymous Novel in Britain and Ireland, 1750–1830." *The Faces of Anonymity: Anonymous and Pseudonymous Publication from the Sixteenth to the Twentieth Century*, ed. Robert J. Griffin, New York and Houndmills: Palgrave Macmillan, 2003, pp. 141–66.

British Fiction 1750–1770: A Chronological Check-List of Prose Fiction Printed in Britain and Ireland. Cranbury, NJ: Associated University Press, 1987.

Raven, James and Antonia Forster, with Stephen Bending (eds.), *The English Novel, 1770–1829: A Bibliographical Survey of Prose Fiction Published in the British Isles, Volume I: 1770–1799*. Oxford: Oxford University Press, 2000.

Reeve, Clara, *The Progress of Romance through Times, Countries, and Manners*, 2 vols. Colchester and London, 1785; facs. rpt. Garland, 1970.

Richardson, Samuel, *Clarissa*, ed. Angus Ross. Harmondsworth: Penguin, 1985.

The Correspondence of Samuel Richardson, 6 vols., ed. Anna Laetitia Barbauld. London, 1804.

Rizzo, Betty, *Companions without Vows: Relationships among Eighteenth-Century British Women*. Athens: University of Georgia Press, 1994.

"Yes, Miss Burney." *Tulsa Studies in Women's Literature* 22 (2003), pp. 193–201.

Rose, Mark, *Authors and Owners: The Invention of Copyright*. Cambridge, MA: Harvard University Press, 1993.

Runge, Laura L. *Gender and Language in British Literary Criticism 1660–1790*. Cambridge: Cambridge University Press, 1997.

Saxton, Kirsten T. and Rebecca P. Bocchicchio, (eds.), *The Passionate Fictions of Eliza Haywood: Essays on Her Life and Work*. Lexington: University Press of Kentucky, 2000.

Schellenberg, Betty, *The Conversational Circle: Rereading the English Novel, 1740–1775*. Lexington: University Press of Kentucky, 1996.

Scott, Mary, *The Female Advocate: A Poem*, with Introduction by Gae Holladay. 1774; rpt. Augustan Reprint Society, Los Angeles: William Andrews Clark Memorial Library, 1984.

Scott, Sarah, *A Description of Millenium Hall*, ed. Gary Kelly. Peterborough, ON: Broadview, 1995.

The History of Gustavus Ericson, King of Sweden. With An Introductory History of Sweden, from the Middle of the Twelfth Century. London: Millar, 1761.
The History of Mecklenburgh, from the First Settlement of the Vandals in that Country, to the Present Time; Including a Period of about Three Thousand Years, 2nd ed. London: Newbery, 1762.
The Life of Theodore Agrippa D'Aubigné, containing A Succinct Account of the Most Remarkable Occurrences during the Civil Wars of France in the Reigns of Charles IX. Henry III. Henry IV. and in the Minority of Lewis XIII. London: Dilly, 1772.
Séjourné, Philippe, *The Mystery of Charlotte Lennox, First Novelist of Colonial America (1927?–1804).* Aix-en-Provence: Publications des Annales de la Faculté des Lettres (Editions Ophrys), 1967.
Sellwood, Jane, "'A Little Acid Is Absolutely Necessary': Narrative as Coquette in Frances Brooke's 'The History of Emily Montague.'" *Canadian Literature* 136 (1993), pp. 60–79.
Seward, Anna, *Letters of Anna Seward: Written between the Years 1784 and 1807*, 6 vols. Edinburgh, 1811.
Sheldon, Esther K., *Thomas Sheridan of Smock-Alley.* Princeton: Princeton University Press, 1967.
Sher, Richard B., "'The favourite of the favourite': John Home, Bute and the Politics of Patriotic Poetry." *Lord Bute: Essays in Re-interpretation*, ed. K. W. Schweizer. Leicester: Leicester University Press, 1988, pp. 181–212.
Sheridan, Frances, *Conclusion of the Memoirs of Miss Sidney Bidulph.* London: Dodsley, 1767.
Memoirs of Miss Sidney Bidulph, ed. Patricia Koster and Jean Coates Cleary. Oxford: Oxford University Press, 1995.
The Plays of Frances Sheridan, ed. Robert Hogan and Jerry C. Beasley. Newark: University of Delaware Press, 1984.
Sherman, Sandra, "'Does Your Ladyship Mean an Extempore?': Wit, Leisure, and the Mode of Production in Frances Burney's *The Witlings.*" *The Centennial Review* 40 (1996), pp. 401–28.
Shevelow, Kathryn, *Women and Print Culture: The Construction of Femininity in the Early Periodical.* London: Routledge, 1989.
Siskin, Clifford, *The Work of Writing: Literature and Social Change in Britain, 1700–1830.* Baltimore: Johns Hopkins University Press, 1998.
Small, Miriam Rossiter, *Charlotte Ramsay Lennox: An Eighteenth Century Lady of Letters.* New Haven: Yale University Press, 1935; rpt. Archon Books, 1969.
Smollett, Tobias, *The Adventures of Ferdinand Count Fathom*, ed. Damian Grant. Oxford: Oxford University Press, 1971.
Smith, Bonnie G., *The Gender of History: Men, Women, and Historical Practice.* Cambridge, MA: Harvard University Press, 1998.
Spacks, Patricia Meyer, *Desire and Truth: Functions of Plot in Eighteenth-Century English Novels.* Chicago: University of Chicago Press, 1990.

Review of Todd, *The Sign of Angellica, Eighteenth-Century Fiction* 2 (1990), pp. 364–65.

Spector, Robert Donald, *English Literary Periodicals and the Climate of Opinion During the Seven Years' War*. The Hague: Mouton, 1966.

Spencer, Jane, *The Rise of the Woman Novelist: From Aphra Behn to Jane Austen*. Oxford: Blackwell, 1986.

Aphra Behn's Afterlife. Oxford: Oxford University Press, 2000.

"Women Writers and the Eighteenth-Century Novel." *The Cambridge Companion to the Eighteenth-Century Novel*, ed. John Richetti, Cambridge: Cambridge University Press, 1996, pp. 212–35.

Stanton, Judith Phillips, "Statistical Profile of Women Writing in English from 1660 to 1800." *Eighteenth-Century Women and the Arts*, ed. Frederick M. Keener and Susan E. Lorsch. New York: Greenwood, 1988, pp. 247–61.

Stauffer, Donald A., *The Art of Biography in Eighteenth Century England*. Princeton: Princeton University Press, 1941; facs rpt. University Microfilms, 1967.

Staves, Susan, "Douglas's Mother." *Brandeis Essays in Literature*, ed. John Hazel Smith, Waltham, MA: Brandeis University Press, 1983, pp. 51–67.

"Women's Originality." Paper read at the British Society for Eighteenth-Century Studies meeting, Oxford, January 2003.

Straub, Kristina, *Divided Fictions: Fanny Burney and Feminine Strategy*. Lexington: University of Kentucky Press, 1987.

Temple, Kathryn, "'Manly Composition': Hume and the History of England." *Feminist Interpretations of David Hume*, ed. Anne Jaap Jacobson, University Park: Pennsylvania State University Press, 2000, pp. 263–82.

Thaddeus, Janice Farrar, *Frances Burney: A Literary Life*. London and New York: Macmillan and St. Martin's, 2000.

Thompson, Helen, "Evelina's Two Publics." *The Eighteenth Century: Theory and Interpretation* 39 (1998), pp. 147–67.

Todd, Janet, *The Sign of Angellica: Women, Writing and Fiction, 1660–1800*. New York: Columbia University Press, 1989.

Aphra Behn Studies, ed. Janet Todd. Cambridge: Cambridge University Press, 1996.

Tomaselli, Sylvana, "The Enlightenment Debate on Women." *History Workshop Journal* 20 (1985), pp. 101–24.

Turner, Cheryl, *Living by the Pen: Women Writers in the Eighteenth Century*. London and New York: Routledge, 1992.

Utter, Robert Palfrey and Gwendolyn Bridges Needham, *Pamela's Daughters*. New York: Russell and Russell, 1972.

Vertôt, Abbé René Aubert de, *The History of the Revolution in Sweden, Occasion'd by The Change of Religion, and Alteration of the Government, in that Kingdom*, trans. J. Mitchel, M. F. London, 1723.

Vickery, Amanda, "Golden Age to Separate Spheres? A Review of the Categories and Chronology of English Women's History." *The Historical Journal* 36 (1993), pp. 383–414.

The Gentleman's Daughter: Women's Lives in Georgian England. New Haven: Yale University Press, 1998.

Walpole, Horace, *Horace Walpole's Correspondence*, 39 vols., ed. W. S. Lewis and A. Dayle Wallace, vols. XI, XXIII. New Haven: Yale University Press, 1944.

Wheeler, David, "The Pathetic and the Sublime: The Tragic Formula of John Home's *Douglas.*" *Man, God, and Nature in the Enlightenment*, ed. Donald C. Mell, Jr., Theodore E. D. Braun, and Lucia M. Palmer. East Lansing, MI: Colleagues, 1988, pp. 173–82.

Whyte, Samuel, *Miscellanea Nova*, 2nd ed. Dublin, 1800; facs. rpt. Garland, 1974.

Wild, Min, "'Prodigious Wisdom': Civic Humanism in Frances Brooke's *Old Maid.*" *Women's Writing* 5 (1998), pp. 421–35.

Wilson, Kathleen, "Citizenship, Empire, and Modernity in the English Provinces, c. 1720–1790." *Eighteenth-Century Studies* 29 (1995), pp. 69–96.

Wiseman, Susan, "Catharine Macaulay: History, Republicanism and the Public Sphere." *Women, Writing and the Public Sphere, 1700–1830*, ed. Elizabeth Eger, Charlotte Grant, Cliona O Gallchoir, and Penny Warburton. Cambridge: Cambridge University Press, 2001, pp. 25–45.

Wollstonecraft, Mary, *Political Writings.* Oxford: Oxford University Press, 1994.

Woodmansee, Martha, "Genius and Copyright." *The Author, Art, and the Market: Rereading the History of Aesthetics.* New York: Columbia University Press, 1994, pp. 35–55.

Woolf, D. R., "A Feminine Past? Gender, Genre, and Historical Knowledge in England, 1500–1800." *American Historical Review* 102 (1997), pp. 645–79.

Wyett, Jodi L., "Reading Women: Female Novelists, Female Readers, 1751–1818." Unpublished dissertation. Detroit, MI: Wayne State University Press, 1999.

Young, Edward, *Conjectures on Original Composition.* London: Millar and Dodsley, 1759; facs. rpt. Scolar Press, 1966.

Index